GW00702129

Praise for *Write Way to Stop Smoking*

'Of everyone alive today, some 500 million will eventually be killed by tobacco. One person dies every 10 seconds due to smoking-related diseases. These facts have been documented in the World Health Organisation's *Tobacco Atlas*. Joe Armstrong's book *Write Way to Stop Smoking* is attuned with the smoking cessation model advocated by the World Health Organisation, moving smokers from pre-contemplation to successful quitting. I commend the Irish Government's move to ban smoking in the workplace and commend this book to any smoker seeking to break free from their addiction. The synergy that will occur between increased public-place smoking bans and support to smokers to quit through this publication will ensure the long-term sustainability and success of tobacco control in Ireland.'
— *Dr Derek Yach, Representative of the Director General, World Health Organisation, Geneva.*

'When Joe Armstrong began his research for *Write Way to Stop Smoking*, he consulted the Health Promotion Department at the Irish Cancer Society. At the Society, Joe was introduced to the

authoritative 'stages of change' model of smoking cessation which we employ in our established and long-running smoking cessation programmes. We are delighted that his book uses that highly recognised model as its basis and structure. Having advised on the book at its conception, the Society is pleased that the book is finally seeing the light of day.'
—— *Norma Cronin, Smoking Cessation Specialist, Irish Cancer Society*

'This book does not puritanically tell you to give up smoking. Instead it nicely leads you to that conclusion for yourself. I wish I had the benefit of this book when I stopped smoking nearly 20 years ago. (I will keep a copy handy in case I ever relapse.) A wonderfully simple and practical guide and aid that when used as intended can only serve to add years to life and life to years.'
—— *Sylvester Cronin, Vice-Chairman of the Health and Safety Authority and Safety and Health Advisor, SIPTU (Services Industrial Professional Technical Union)*

'This is a comprehensive and deeply challenging programme on many levels but it comes with great support and carefully planned strategies and after five weeks of the 12-week programme I have stopped smoking the pipe after 45 years.'
—— *Frank Marshall, writer and playwright*

'I smoked for 35 years. Writing the daily morning journal made me focused and grounded and enabled me to stop smoking. Garner all the help and support you can and with this book you too can become a non-smoker.'
—— *A.B.*

'Joe Armstrong's *Write Way to Stop Smoking* wisely encourages smokers to talk to their doctors about nicotine replacement therapy and medication. Of course nicotine replacement products or medication alone are less likely to succeed without the changes to thinking and lifestyle advocated in this book. Combined with the thinking and behavioural changes explained here, readers at least double their chances of stopping smoking.'
—— *Dr Fenton Howell, Dean of the Faculty of Public Health Medicine, former Chairperson of ASH Ireland and Past President of the Irish Medical Organisation.*

'This book goes far beyond merely trying to get a smoker to stop smoking. Its clearly stated aim is to enjoy 'freedom, fullness and good fortune' in life rather than just quitting 'the weed'. It shows readers how to stop the thinking that underlies addictive behaviour and how

to live their lives to the full without smoking or other addictions. Joe consulted me early in his research and impressed me with the clarity of this approach. His book comes out at a very appropriate time when as a society we are moving towards a healthier lifestyle. I recommend this book as a practical manual and a source of encouragement to all those making such a change.'
— Dr. Elizabeth Dunne, Dept. of Applied Psychology, University College Cork.

'This is a comprehensive, engaging approach to smoking cessation. A well-researched programme, it gives smokers every opportunity to think about, plan and most importantly achieve a smokefree life. A very timely book given the Minister of Health's commendable ban on smoking in the workplace.'
— Dr Owen Metcalfe, Associate Director, Institute of Public Health in Ireland

Write Way to Stop Smoking

How to Get Your Life Unstuck

Joe Armstrong

GLEBE

Write Way to Stop Smoking

Published by GLEBE
Cortown Glebe, Cortown, Kells,
County Meath, Republic of Ireland.
Website: www.writeway2stopsmoking.com

Origination by DTP Workshop, Dublin.
Cover artwork by Ruth Armstrong, Kathryn Murtagh and Patricia Weldon
Cover design by Fergus O'Keeffe, okgraphics@eircom.net
Printed in Ireland by Colourbooks Ltd. Dublin.

ISBN: 0-9546610-0-1

Dedication

To Ruth, John and Sarah, with all my love.

And to all smokers who find this book an instrument for their freedom, fulfilment and good fortune.

Acknowledgements

Gratitude is an integral part of this programme and yet I fear leaving anyone out! Necessarily, I cannot mention everyone as hundreds of people have been instrumental in the creation of this book. So please forgive me if you are not mentioned by name here. I thank you from the bottom of my heart. In particular, I thank the Minister for Health and Children, Mr Micheál Martin, T.D. for agreeing to launch this book and for his support for smoking cessation and tobacco control to protect Irish workers. I thank the Irish Cancer Society, especially smoking cessation specialist Norma Cronin for her great assistance from the start; Valerie Coghlan of ASH Ireland; Dr Elizabeth Dunne of the Department of Applied Psychology, UCC, Madeleine O'Callaghan and Phyllis Howing for their brilliant feedback on early drafts. I thank Dr Prannie Rhatigan for her inestimable encouragement and support. I thank Chris Tomasino for her friendship, invaluable advice and for being there for me at crucial times. Thanks too to Morgan Llywelyn, for her support along the way. I thank Dr Derek Yach of the World Health Organisation; Sylvester Cronin, Vice-Chairman of the Health and Safety Authority; Dr Fenton Howell, Dean of the Faculty of Public Health Medicine; and Dr Owen Metcalfe, Assistant Director of the Institute of Public Health in Ireland. I am grateful for Ann Breen, Frank Marshall, Judy Davoren, Patricia Weldon, Sharon O'Farrell and Niall Mulligan.

I am deeply indebted to the smokers who have worked this programme and for the time and effort they gave to doing so. I thank them for their feedback and suggestions and, not least, for encouraging me to have this book published and published soon! I thank them for their faith in the programme, for their belief in the non-addicted part of them that wanted to gain or regain freedom, fullness and good fortune.

I want to thank my dear wife Ruth for her love, for believing in me and for her rare common sense. This book could never have seen the light of day without her. I am profoundly blessed by God in Ruth. I also thank my two children John and Sarah for making me a far richer human than money could buy.

I want to thank you, gentle reader, for choosing this book either for yourself or for someone you love or care for. I pray that it may help smokers to stop smoking for good and to live their lives to the full. If the copy you hold saves a life, or helps someone to live more authentically and do what he or she was sent to do, that is all that can be hoped for. Finally, I thank God for inspiring this book and guiding me to write it to completion.

Contents

Preface

This is the thinking person's guide to quitting smoking. Many people can succeed without help but if you feel that you need some support in the form of an exciting adventure then this book is for you.

Like most smokers you probably love the cigarette but hate the habit. This ambivalence is well recognised. If you have just picked up this book and are toying with the idea of quitting remember that it will take a lot of strength and resolve to break free of this addiction. Tobacco is a substance more addictive than heroin and quitting smoking has been described by a group of ex-smokers as "Finding the strength to kill your best friend".

Joe makes this whole traumatic business of quitting seem like fun. He sets out the plan in a clear, concise and practical way. You will have plenty of time to examine issues which are important to you – you are not forced into quitting – the decision must come from you. The research has shown that those who spend time exploring options and preparing to quit are more likely to remain non-smokers once they do quit.

I should tell you that when I read the draft of this book it was the only occasion in my life when I regretted the fact that I wasn't a smoker. I wanted to be able to engage in the exercises, take the challenges, reap the rewards of success and enjoy all the little treats along the way. I wanted to be part of this exciting concept and journey that was unfolding before me.

Quitting smoking is a really big life task but this book allows you to do it in a creative, supportive way. It allows you to get inside your own skin and to be comfortable with the change rather than having it imposed upon you. You follow a path that leads you through thoughtful exercises, searching missions, exploring issues and building ammunition to ultimately face down the fear associated with making this big change. While all the time taking care of the whole person and preparing at all levels to develop new healthy habits to replace the old one.

You make the decisions that will work for you. What I particularly like about this book is that if you do make the decision to quit in Week Five you are very well supported afterwards. The support for the new behaviour is stalwart right to the end, enabling you to create new ways to adapt to and cement the role of non-smoker. By Week Seven you are being skilfully guided through the early recovery stage and at Week Nine you celebrate the one-month smokefree watershed and get further armour to deal with challenges at this time.

This clearly laid out plan of action will allow you to make the transition from being a smoker to being a non-smoker while making many exciting discoveries along the way. You will grow in ways that you may not have thought possible.

Not, as Joe points out, that all problems will suddenly disappear once you stop smoking but this book puts lots of little gems your way which may allow you to look at life's ups and downs in a different light, without having to resort to smoking.

If you are considering quitting smoking, as a medical doctor I must give you a word of encouragement – tobacco is the only product which kills people when used *as intended* and quitting smoking is the single most important thing that you can do for your health – ever.

Good luck with your decision.

Dr Prannie Rhatigan
Former director of the smoking cessation programme of the Irish College of General Practitioners / Smoking Target Action Group.

November 2003

Introduction

You do *not* need to stop smoking before you choose this book. In fact, it is recommended that you *continue smoking* until the start of *Week Five* of this programme. You do *not* need to feel confident that you *can* stop smoking. You do *not* even need to feel sure that you *want* to quit. It is enough that you are *thinking* about quitting. Maybe a part of you wants to quit, while another part of you wants to smoke. You see advantages to quitting and to smoking.

Perhaps you have decided to quit and feel determined to succeed. You may already be off cigarettes for some time and want to stay stopped. Or maybe you relapsed and you are thinking of trying again. So long as you are *thinking* about stopping, or staying stopped, regardless of where you are on your path, *Write Way to Stop Smoking* (*WW2SS*) is for you.

Your Personal Mission

You want to live *your* life to the full – becoming yourself, using your unique talents, charting your own course, creating things with your personal imprint. You want to be healthy, enjoying your body, mind, emotions, relationships, good habits and spiritual life. You want to be the person you alone were born to be and do the things only you were born to do. You want to follow your bliss, be fully alive and fulfil yourself.

The primary aim of this book is to assist you to live your life and its distinctive purpose to the full. That is our starting point before tackling any addictions. It is my belief that addictions come into play when we are not doing what we were born to do. So, in Week One, you will be asked to say what your personal mission at this time in your life is, as you understand it. Of course one's mission changes from time to time. At times we may be single or celibate, at other times married or in a relationship. We might be studying, at other times we may have a family, career, business, hobby or other passion.

I do not believe it is ever part of anyone's personal mission to be addicted to anything. An addiction is a block. It is a way in which we are stuck in some way in our life. However, if you believed that smoking were part of your personal mission, you should continue to smoke! Indeed, if you did not smoke, you would be untrue to yourself. But if smoking is not part of your personal mission, your higher self (that part of you that isn't and never was addicted) will ask you to stop smoking because it is holding you back from becoming your best self.

Secondary goal: quitting smoking

If you decide that smoking (or any other addictive substance or process such as alcohol, gambling, drugs, caffeine, compulsive sex, compulsive shopping, excessive work etc.) is holding you back from living your life to the full, giving up tobacco (or other addictions) will nevertheless remain a secondary goal. Your first aim will be to become who you were born to be and to fulfil your potential.

Your Decision

Only *you* can decide what is best for you. If you decide that smoking is not part of your personal mission, that decision is for you alone to make. Your reasons, or reason, for quitting will be unique to you, and will be strongest if linked to your personal mission. You will examine this in Weeks One and Two and decide whether or not you really want to quit smoking. Or, to be more precise, whether you want to stop smoking *more* than you want to *keep* smoking.

Quit Date

If you decide to quit smoking, you will do so on Day One of Week Five. Do *not* be tempted to quit before then (unless, of course, you have already quit and you are taking this programme to strengthen and embolden you). You have work to do first. If you decide to run a marathon, you do not simply put on your trainers and jog for 26 miles. You need to analyse what you want and plan how to get there. Or if you want to build a house, you do not turn up on day one with bricks and mortar, tiles and windows. You first need to *analyse* what you want. What do you want to happen in each room of your house? What will you do in each room? What features do you want? Once you've analysed what you want, you still do not rush in and start building. Before that, you need to *plan*. You need to get professional drawings done of the home you want to live in. You need to plan before you *do*. Only then – after analysis and planning – do you implement your plan. Which is why, in this programme, you do not attempt to quit until Day One of Week Five. You spend the first two weeks analysing what you do and don't want and Weeks Three and Four planning how you will quit.

Moreover, given the long-term perspective of this programme, you do not want to achieve 'mere abstinence' from nicotine and other addictions, however commendable an achievement that will be. Your higher aim is to live your life to the full *without wanting* to resort to any addictions, compulsions or bad habits.

It is important now to take a calendar and pick a Quit Date no sooner than four full weeks from now. Choose a day you expect to be calm, with no extra stresses in your life. So avoid times like moving home, changing jobs or a painful anniversary. Once you decide on your Quit Date, that will become Day One of Week Five. Only then can you calculate backwards to Day One of Week One, and thereby know your Start Date for the programme. It is important to get your Quit Date, and hence your Start Date, right. Even if that means postponing this programme for some time yet. On the other hand, you don't want to push your Start Date too far away into the future. Some people who have taken this programme at first decide not to start for several months but then decide to go for it sooner rather than later. One woman who moved forward her start date is, as I write, more than nine weeks off cigarettes after 35 years' smoking. She feels understandably delighted with her achievement.

Sponsor

You might like to consider having a sponsor to support you. Alcoholics Anonymous and Nicotine Anonymous programmes confirm the importance of a sponsor. Your sponsor could be a friend who used to smoke. There is no big deal to asking someone to be a sponsor. It might simply mean meeting, phoning or emailing each other once a week to discuss how you're getting on. You do not need to have a sponsor, but it is better if you do. There are lots of ex-smokers around and whoever you ask will probably be honoured to be asked to help.

Self-help, Group or Personal Guided Support

You can use *WW2SS* alone as a self-help manual or with a group, depending on which you find most helpful. Support groups can dip into it as a resource or use it as a structure for some or all of their meetings. Since the 12-week programme is longer than many support groups such as the excellent smoking cessation programmes run by the Irish Cancer Society or by health boards, *WW2SS* can provide added support for members during and/or after a group has ended.

Personal guided telephone and/or email support through the 12 weeks of the *WW2SS* programme is offered for a nominal fee, subject to terms, conditions and availability. For details, check out our website www.writeway2stopsmoking.com or email info@writeway2stopsmoking.com.

The Irish Department of Health and Children has set up the National Smokers' Quitline telephone 1850 201 203 offering free confidential advice on quitting. It can connect people by telephone to the Irish Cancer Society's experienced smoking cessation counsellors (see Appendix E).

In Britain, the charity QUIT offers free telephone support when you dial 0800 00 22 00. QUIT also offers email support where counsellors personally respond to smokers' emails, a service particularly popular among women. For free one-to-one professional support, send an email to stopsmoking@quit.org.uk. QUIT also offer confidential support to groups of up to 12 teenagers in school settings as well as offering support to the corporate sector. Check out their website www.quit.org.uk.

Your Path

In Week One you will explore whether your best self or higher self is inviting you to quit smoking. We'll look at why you want to quit. In Week Two you get in touch with the part of you that doesn't want to quit. At the end of Week Two, you reach a turning point – whether to proceed with the programme and to plan for your Quit Date or to continue smoking for the foreseeable future. If you choose to proceed, in Week Three you explore self-belief and observe your smoking patterns, while in Week Four you plan how you'll manage without smoking and prepare for Quit Day – the first day of Week Five. Before your Quit Day, ideally *early* in Week Three, you will have consulted your doctor to receive advice on nicotine replacement therapy or other treatment options best suited to you.

One Day One of Week Five you quit smoking. You will be guided through the challenges of that week, especially the first three days. In Week Six you grow in self-acceptance and acceptance of others and you grow in the belief that everything is happening as it should. In Week Seven, you see the big picture and grow more in responsibility (the ability to respond), wisdom and love. You explore relapse in Week Eight, discovering that it can be part of the learning process and merely a sign that you had something else to learn before exiting addictive behaviour for good. By Week Nine, you increasingly realise that stopping acting out of compulsions is not an ego trip but a spiritual quest. You grow in compassion for yourself and others. In Week Ten you consider your call to service and how your experience can enrich others. You recognise the need for constant vigilance in Week Eleven, while Week Twelve looks at lifestyle balance, interdependence and the full embrace of life.

Your Birthright

If smoking is not part of your personal mission, it follows that it is your birthright to quit. You *can* do it by getting in touch with the part of you that isn't, and never was, addicted.

Core Beliefs

Here are some basic principles of *WW2SS*:

- I was born *free*. Dependency on cigarettes (or any other substances or activities) has diminished my freedom but *I can become free again*.

- Although cigarettes (and possibly other compulsions) have damaged my personal control, *I can regain control*.

- I can *enjoy my life to the full without smoking.*

- Freedom is my *birthright.*

- I have *nothing to fear* in quitting smoking or any other addictions.

- Each time I decide not to smoke, I become *more myself.* I come closer to doing what I was *born to do.*

- My higher self wants me to stop smoking and to be free of all addictions.

- When I refuse to abstain from a cigarette, *I deny my best self.*

- Each time I take a step in the direction of quitting smoking, I grow as a person.

- I am responsible for my dependency on nicotine.

- I am willing to look at the *uncontrolled use* of alcohol, drugs, work, sex, food, gambling, stealing, shopping or any other compulsions in my life.

- My desire to quit smoking and other addictions is good.

How to Use *Write Way to Stop Smoking*

Read a chapter each week, if possible taking a chapter in one sitting and doing a few of the set activities there and then. You can do more of the activities over the rest of the week. Do not feel that you have to do every activity. If you work from Monday to Friday, you might like to read the chapter and do some of the activities on Saturday or Sunday when you may have some free time. Have a 'healthy selfishness' – make time for the programme. By doing so, you will have more to give to others.

Early to Bed

Sleep is very important for your health. It restores you in mind, body and spirit. Some people say they are willing to do anything to quit smoking but if you ask them to go to bed earlier they say they cannot. They would not sleep. Or they enjoy watching television or reading at night. Or it is the only time they see their spouse or partner.

Choosing to go to bed 30 minutes earlier at night is one practical way you can gain control over your lifestyle. If you are too busy to go to bed earlier, you are too busy. If you remain too busy for too long, you will become ill. You may need to negotiate with your partner about sharing more household tasks or with you employer about having too much work to do.

Early to Rise

If you found the suggestion to get to bed earlier challenging, you might think that getting up 30 minutes earlier is unrealistic. It's just not practical, you might think. I have children screaming around me first thing in the morning or work to get to – no way am I getting up before I need to!

Going to bed earlier and rising earlier is a practical way you can change your lifestyle. Treat it as a test run for the greater challenge of quitting smoking. By retiring and rising earlier, you make space each morning to write your journal, which, as you are about to see, is a core activity of this programme (and the main reason for retiring and rising earlier).

Morning Journal
Write what you think

Your morning journal is your opportunity to express yourself. There is no wrong way to write it. Show it to nobody else. It is completely private. You write whatever comes into your head and keep writing until you fill three pages. You might choose a hardback A4-sized (210 by 297-millimetre) lined writing book as your journal. When I propose this to groups there are usually gasps of incredulity. Me? Write three pages! Every morning! If you reject the activity, consider that if you keep on doing what you've always done, you'll keep on getting the same results.

You do not need to think about what to write – simply write down what you are thinking. If you think 'What on earth will I write?' write that down. And keep writing everything you are thinking until you have done three pages. Our brains are constantly bombarded with thoughts, so you'll have no shortage of what to write. In fact, one of the great things about the journal is that it slows down your rampaging brain. It settles you. You express your thoughts, emotions, things you have to do, dreams you've dreamt, experiences you've had.

Since nobody is reading what you write, you can express yourself freely. Spellings, grammar, handwriting and style do not matter. You can say what you like about anybody. Express your thoughts, feelings, fantasies and ambitions. Your hopes and fears, aims and plans emerge on the page. However you're feeling, let it all out. Consider the journal an emotional poultice, a friend who accepts you fully, including all dark places in your consciousness.

Do not censure what you write. Things that you might not like to admit thinking can lose their control over you once you write them down. The journal grounds you; it is a way to get to know yourself. Take risks with what you write. If you lose interest in keeping your journal, you might be holding back from writing down thoughts, feelings or describing behaviours you find 'unacceptable'. Trust yourself and your higher self to embrace the whole of you, hidden shadows and all.

The truth will out in the journal. You think you bear no ill will to anyone but in your journal a feeling of resentment recurs. You see that you need to deal with it. Or you are writing fairly ordinary stuff when as if from nowhere an insight dawns on you. Your journal will revitalise you. It will reveal, and remind you of, your personal mission and values.

Underline actions

If, while writing your journal, you record things you need to do that day or in the week ahead, underline key words so that you can easily spot them while planning your day or week. From time to time, you might write a list of things to do on some home or work project. You can stick a Post It sticky label on such pages to earmark them so you'll easily find them. Apart from that, there is no need to re-read what you write in your journal. Simply express yourself on the page and leave it there. Trust in the process.

Thoughts and Feelings

Your thoughts and feelings will emerge on the page, clarifying where you stand and how you feel about things. If you need to discuss something with someone, you will be more confident of your position. You will know how you think or feel and already have come up with the words.

New Ritual

Start to think of your journal as an essential part of your morning. If you cannot think of starting the day without washing, cleaning your teeth or dressing, consider your journal to be equally indispensable. It is getting in touch with who you are, with what is going on inside you. It is listening in a simple but profound way.

Your Voice

The journal can help you to listen to the part of you that is independent of nicotine – the part of you that never became dependent on tobacco. Even if you have become highly addicted to nicotine or anything else, a part of you remains free inside. Your journal will give your higher self (the free, non-addicted part of you) the chance to speak.

In your journal, you test your belief in your personal mission. You hear the part of you that believes in you, thinks big on your behalf and sustains hope and faith in you when you feel crushed. In the journal, you can see your future self, freed from dependencies and doing what you were born to do, as surely as the designer 'sees' the completed house while still looking at the empty field.

You could come to regard your morning journal as morning prayer – regardless of whether or not you believe in God. On the page, you face self-doubt. You test your inner call. You are challenged to believe in the power of the non-addicted part of you to regain your personal power and freedom. You are invited to believe in your best self, your capacity to fulfil your personal mission in life and to overcome obstacles, including all bad habits, compulsions and addictions.

90 Mornings

Dependency on nicotine is a tough nut to crack. Going on from there to fulfil your personal mission and potential is not for the faint-hearted. People starting out on a Twelve-Step programme such as Alcoholics Anonymous and Nicotine Anonymous are advised to attend 90 meetings in 90 days.

You are being asked to commit to writing your journal every morning. Some people ask 'Could I not write it in the evenings?' Yes you could. But it is far better doing it in the mornings. You are fresher from your sleep. The day is about to begin – not ending. You are grounding yourself for the day ahead. So many things can happen in the course of the day that by deferring your journal until later, there is a greater likelihood that you will not do it, despite your best intentions. The addicted part of you would much prefer you not to write in your journal or to postpone it until the evening. Ask yourself if any resistance you feel to setting aside time for your personal growth and freedom each morning might not be the addicted part of you resisting change.

Three pages

Write three pages. Often, key insights can arise simply by plodding on thinking with your pen until you get to the bottom of the third page. Your commitment is to quantity, not quality. So long as you're writing what is actually going on in your head, you will be surprised at how fast you will write. As you are constantly thinking, there is no shortage of what to write. It's like eavesdropping on your brain and feelings.

Fear

In your journal, you can recognise what you are afraid of and decide not to live out of fear. You can gain the strength to try something you would never otherwise have dreamed of doing. You can gain confidence in developing a new project.

Unexpected things can happen. You may find that not only do you want to quit smoking, you wish to curtail or stop your use of alcohol too. You might decide to work less and spend more time with your family or friends. You might unexpectedly plan a holiday, the idea for which arose while writing your journal. You might write a book, start a new business, or propose to your boyfriend or girlfriend prompted by working your morning journal.

Poultice

The journal can act as a poultice for difficult emotions, like jealousy, anger and loneliness, drawing out how you feel so you can deal with it. In your journal, you express all of youself, the good and the bad. It can help you to accept and love yourself. You can gain compassion for yourself and grow in self-knowledge, trust and a healthy inner confidence. Your truth will emerge on the page and you will discover that you are a far more interesting, resourceful and powerful person than you realised.

Safe Place

Having a safe place for your journal is important. You need to be confident that what you write will be seen only by you. You do not show it even to your spouse or sponsor. Depending on your personal circumstances, you might like to discuss with you spouse or partner or anyone you might live with that you are writing a journal and devise a strategy or procedures to keep it away from prying eyes. If you are unlucky enough not to have a partner you can trust, you might explore that lack of trust in your journal! Or discuss it with a trusted friend, doctor, counsellor or social worker.

Abstinence versus 'Sobriety' from Nicotine

The Greek word *metanoia* means change of mind. It suggests turning away from a current way of thinking, feeling and behaviour and choosing a new direction. Stopping smoking involves becoming aware of and changing unhelpful habitual or addictive thoughts, feelings and behaviours. Merely abstaining from nicotine without also changing how you think about your compulsions will leave you vulnerable to relapse. A person who drinks too much alcohol learns that their first objective is abstinence. But the greater aim beyond 'mere' abstinence (itself no mean achievement!) is sobriety – a life lived to the full without alcohol.

'Sobriety' is yours when you enjoy a balanced, healthy lifestyle without even thinking of smoking or other drugs. Your body no longer craves nicotine. Your mind no longer feels deprived by not smoking. You no longer need cigarettes to enjoy yourself socially, and you feel good about yourself as you are. You have turned from being at the mercy of the addicted part of you and live under the domain of your higher self (the non-addicted part of you), living a mentally, physically, emotionally and spiritually fulfilling life.

While you actually quit smoking on Day One of Week Five of this programme, the greater goal (and one of the reasons why we keep going until Week Twelve) is to attain 'sobriety' over nicotine and any other compulsive thinking, substances or processes. You can be abstinent without attaining 'sobriety' (that is, you have stopped smoking but still think as you used to) but you cannot become 'sober' (re-gaining your freedom from all addictions) without first becoming abstinent.

Congé

Congé is the French word for holiday. You are invited in this programme to set aside two hours each week just for you. You take nobody with you. It is a time to explore joy and play in your life. It is a weekly mini-holiday where you get yourself off the hook of duty, obligations and work.

No sooner have you heard the suggestion than reasons flood into your head as to why you cannot do it. You are too busy. You do not have two hours to set aside per week. It sounds selfish. What will my spouse or partner think! It's too vague – what on earth would I do? All of these are, of course, excuses to avoid exploring authentic joy and pleasure in your life.

Even though you will not quit smoking until Week Five, choose not to smoke during your congé from Week One and avoid places where people smoke. If you find it hard to have coffee or alcohol without a cigarette, abstain from them too during your congé. If you think it could be difficult to abstain from smoking on your congé, think of all the times you already go for more than two hours without cigarettes. For instance, you do not smoke while you are asleep or in no-smoking areas such as on public transport, in hospitals or schools, cinemas, concert halls or the homes of non-smoking friends. And, of course, increasingly in the workplace.

Your mission is to enjoy yourself. Use this weekly time to explore new joys or to reactivate former joys. It need not cost money. The best things in life really are free. You could go for a walk or a bike ride. Explore local places that tourists visit. Window-shop, possibly buying a CD or a book. Walk by the sea, through a field or climb a hill. Watch a movie, go to the theatre or walk barefoot in the grass. Public leisure centres tend to be inexpensive – enjoy a swim, a sauna or a Jacuzzi. Consider a workout in a local gym or avail of a free lunchtime concert. Or treat yourself to a massage.

As a smoker, you possibly look to cigarettes for relaxation and a mental break. The congé will help you choose many more ways to enjoy yourself, relax and have fun. The part of you that does not need to smoke knows lots of ways that you can enjoy yourself. If you are too busy to take your congé, you are too busy; and that might be part of the reason why you're smoking. There are 168 hours in the week. Do your best to set aside two of them to explore joy and play in your life. It is not selfish: you will have much more to give to people if you do it. You may need to ask someone to help with the children or to share chores so you can take your congé. For some of us, practising asserting our needs and asking for help, and being willing to help the other person in return, is itself a benefit of the congé, a practical step from dependency on nicotine to interdependency with others.

At the beginning of each week decide when you will take your congé. Be precise. Instead of saying 'I'll do something maybe on Friday' be specific. For instance, schedule a trip to your local leisure centre for a swim and sauna next Friday from 4 p.m. to 6 p.m.

As you begin to integrate a congé into your weekly schedule, you may be tempted to incorporate some errands to make it somehow productive. But joy is its own end. A congé spent posting letters, checking bank balances or doing the weekly shopping is not a congé at all. To develop your relationship with that part of you that can thrive and enjoy life to the full without cigarettes, cigars or the pipe, keep your congé for enjoyment only – not for work.

The part of you that is dependent on cigarettes will not like the notion of you enjoying yourself without nicotine. If you feel cynical or sceptical about the value or feasibility of a weekly congé, ask yourself who is talking. Is it the addicted part of you who does not want your higher self to reveal to you that you can enjoy life without addictive substances? Or you might feel addicted to work or to helping others and feel you could not possibly take two hours out of 168 per week to explore joy in your life. Such lack of lifestyle balance could be part of the reason why you smoke and why you really need to make time for your weekly congé.

Look forward to it. Let your congé become as essential a part of your week as eating, sleeping, working or family responsibilities. It's time for *you*. Your whole life could take a different shape because of your congé. Just do it!

Trust Yourself

To make progress towards abstinence and 'sobriety' from nicotine, follow the plan. At all stages, you retain absolute freedom as to whether or not to take the next step. You are not asked to commit yourself to not smoking. Rather, you are being asked to commit yourself to following the plan and trusting yourself.

At its most basic, that means choosing to go to bed a half an hour earlier than you might feel like doing. It means rising earlier than you might want to. It means writing your morning journal, taking your weekly congé, talking to your sponsor. This programme is a voyage of self-discovery and empowerment. The tools are simple, the rewards immense.

Practical Steps

- Buy yourself a journal. Find a safe place for it. Discuss it – its privacy and why you are keeping it – with your partner if appropriate.

- Decide which room and chair you will use for journal writing. Make sure you will be warm, comfortable and have sufficient light. You might have facilities for making a hot drink nearby or prepare a flask the night before.

- If necessary, buy a new alarm clock. If you find it hard to get up in the mornings, buy a second noisier alarm clock and leave it out of reach so you have to get out of bed to turn it off. If you share a room with someone else, the threat of that second alarm going off can motivate you to get out of bed before it disturbs the other person. Moreover, once you go to bed earlier and get sufficient sleep, rising will not prove so difficult. Lastly, when you have a higher reason for rising – namely you commitment to yourself in this programme – getting up becomes an integral part of the adventure.

- Decide on a time by which you will be in bed with the lights out at night. Try your best to keep to it. For a while, you may have difficulty in getting to sleep at this hour, but so long as you rise at the earlier time, no matter how well you have slept, your body's natural rhythms will soon adjust to your new routine.

- Persevering with the new earlier-to-bed, earlier-to-rise routine is a practical way for you to change a personal habit and cultivate a new one. Of itself, it is a significant lifestyle change. Treat it as a test run for the more difficult habit of quitting smoking. You can write in your journal about how you find the new sleeping pattern, saying how you think and feel about it. Write too about any other changes it brings about, such as not working so late at night, adjustments to your social life, reduced or earlier alcohol consumption or less time spent watching television.

- Visualise yourself going to bed at the earlier time. Imagine where you will be when you need to put into practice what you decided to do. Who, if anyone, will you be with? How will you handle it if someone suggests that you stay up later? How will you handle other temptations to stay up later, such as if there is something interesting on television? By imagining how you will manage these situations, you are practising the skill of visualisation which you will use later in planning how to avoid smoking.

- By choosing to retire earlier at night, you strengthen your inner power and control. You are less at the mercy of passing sensations that can seize your attention and you become more attuned to your higher purpose. You are already well on your way to proactively living your personal mission and stopping smoking.

- Changing to an earlier-to-bed earlier-to-rise routine can take time. Be gentle with yourself. Don't nag yourself if you find yourself staying up later than you decided to or if you miss getting up despite your decision to rise earlier. Like abstinence from smoking, retiring and rising earlier is a new habit, and new habits take time and effort to establish. Just as the nicotine-dependent part of you does not want you to change, a part of you (possibly the same addictive part of you) will protest at the new sleeping routine. Take it a day at a time and try your best.

- If others are awake or making noise in the house when you go to bed, you might try earplugs. A blindfold, such as the kind you get on long haul flights, can keep you undisturbed if someone is putting on the light in your room later on.

- Decide now when you will take your congé next week. What will you do? Where will you go?

You Can Do It

You are about to begin a 12-week personal journey which could make your life significantly more enjoyable and fulfilling. Do not worry about reaching the summit of the mountain. Rather, choose to take the next step today. Commit to doing what already lies within your control.

There is no magic involved. You do the work. *WW2SS* shows the path, based, as it is, on authoritative research of the process of leaving behind addictive behaviour. At all times you are free to continue towards 'sobriety' from nicotine or to stay as you are. You choose. You will become increasingly aware of the part of you that does not need to smoke. You will learn practical, specific, measurable tasks to break the habit, if that is what you choose to do. You might like to think of the powerful non-addicted part of you inviting you to embark on this journey.

When you are ready to proceed with the programme (having chosen your Quit Date as outlined above and counted backwards to your Start Date), it is advisable to make a commitment to yourself. Be aware that the nicotine-dependent part of you will resist this journey and discourage your commitment. Only make this commitment if you are willing to try your best, with the aid of your higher self (the part of you that isn't addicted), to put into practice the practical tools of this programme. Return to this commitment over the course of the 12-week programme, especially if your self-belief is low or falters or if the addicted part of you appears to gain the upper hand. (In this regard, believe that your higher self is stronger than your addicted self, even if that might be hard for you to accept at times.) Copy the words below into your journal or onto a piece of paper where you will see it every day. If you prefer, use your own words to make a similar commitment.

Commitment

I want to become more myself. I want to know myself. I want to love and accept myself as I am. I want to become all that I was born to be. I want to do what I was sent to do. I want to fulfil my potential and live my life to the full.

Realising that I may need to quit smoking and any other addictions for good to accomplish this, I am willing, with the help of my higher self, to stop smoking and to stop acting out of any other addictions.

I commit myself to taking this 12-week journey. I commit to retiring and rising early to write three pages in my journal every morning, taking a weekly congé, finding a sponsor, reading a chapter of WW2SS each week and doing some of the set activities.

I commit to self-nourishment, to looking after myself. I shall get enough sleep, eat properly, take regular exercise and live, to the best of my ability, a balanced lifestyle for the next 12 weeks.

Signed:

Date:

WEEK

1

Your Call

We focus this week on why you want to stop smoking and acting out any other addiction. Next week, we explore why you don't want to quit. There is nothing wrong with wanting and, at the same time, not wanting to stop addictions. In fact, exploring your ambivalence is the central goal of the first two weeks of this programme. (You may still be exploring it for the rest of your life!) This book is about facilitating you to become free from being trapped in your ambivalence. Its aim is to help you to get unstuck. But, surprisingly perhaps, we don't start with why you want to stop smoking or acting out any other addictions. Rather, we start with what you would love to be doing with your life. Let's call it your personal mission.

Personal Mission

You were born with a purpose. You have a personal mission in life. Do you know what it is? If you have figured out or written your personal mission, when did you last revise it? Companies and organisations spend time, money and effort writing their core mission statements so that they know who they are and what they are about. You too will benefit from knowing or updating your personal mission in life.

Mission Statement

Having a sense of your personal mission is one thing but writing it down is better still. There is nothing mysterious about it. It is simply a short statement saying who you are and stating your aims, objectives and values. Aims are core things like 'I want to be healthy, live a balanced lifestyle and live my life to the full', or 'initiate, sustain and grow a loving relationship with my spouse or partner'. If you have young children, your core aims might include something like 'I want to be the best parent I can be for my children, helping them to be happy and to become self-confident, contributing members of society'.

Objectives are specific markers along the way moving you closer to achieving your aims. For example, objectives might include 'Get fit', 'Stop smoking' or 'Get a job more attuned to my core personal mission'. Objectives flow from you aims. If you wrote as an aim that you want to be the best parent you can be for your children, a natural objective flowing from that might be 'Stop drinking' if you are an alcoholic. Or 'Stop Smoking' because, by smoking, your children are much more likely to smoke too, to the detriment of their physical, mental, psychological and spiritual health, even if they aren't exposed to your second-hand smoke.

Mission statements should be short – just a few sentences or short paragraphs. And perhaps three to five objectives, each of about a sentence, is probably as much as any human can be getting on with at any one time! If you can come up with some key words, all the better. For instance, an excellent school I once taught in, Saint Bonaventure's, Forest Gate, in London's East End, came up with its mission statement. For me, the key word from that statement was 'growth'. In all our dealings with pupils, the central idea became how, in this situation, could I help this pupil to grow? Whether teaching an academic subject, engaged in a pastoral activity or managing an incidence of poor behaviour, the central tenet became 'growth'. In choosing how I behaved in relation to pupils, the recollection of that one word 'growth' guided me in how best to manage situations. Likewise, your mission statement can guide you in making decisions that confront you in your life. You could find, for instance, that a course of action you intended taking is not in keeping with your mission statement. For example, if in your mission statement you wrote 'Authenticity is more important to me than money' and yet you were thinking of chucking in a personal development programme because it clashed with a new job, you might decide not to take the new job after all.

You start this programme by writing your mission statement. It puts your desire to quit smoking into its proper context. You want to fulfil your mission. You are choosing to take steps to become your best self, to fulfil your potential, to be who you were born to be. Hence, from the outset you avoid 'deprivation thinking'. The focus isn't on 'giving up' smoking or anything else you might be addicted to. The focus is on the marvellous adventure of becoming who you were born to be. It's a positive choice. You are not choosing not to smoke. You are choosing to have the energy and rewards that come with choosing your authentic path.

Blocks to Fulfilment

Any dependency can block you from fulfilling your potential and getting on with your life's work. This is true even if you have already made substantial progress in fulfilling your personal mission. If you are not going forward to achieve your next personal goal, you are moving backwards.

For instance, a musician might have considerable achievements behind her but instead of continuing to create wonderful music, she becomes hooked on drugs and loses ten years from her career. Or a film star, part of whose mission is to love his wife and remain faithful to her, separates from her because he is surrounded by many beautiful women and feels he will be unfaithful. But he never truly loves another partner and lives the rest of his life alone. Or the comic writer who, despite international success, comes to the crazy belief that he cannot write without alcohol.

Smoking can be a manifestation of your fear of success or failure. Perhaps you are an accountant or shop assistant, but you would really have liked to be a painter and you choke your personal calling to paint with every cigarette inhaled. You might cite family or financial obligations as your excuse for not proceeding with your calling. Or you might be a teacher who would really much prefer to earn your living as a writer. But your fear of the unknown or some initial obstacles see you clinging to your permanent, pensionable 'secure' job. In fact, if you were to follow your personal calling and set out to achieve your personal mission, you would discover that your security lies within yourself.

Cigarettes, alcohol, caffeine, work, sex, gambling, drugs, shopping, dependent relationships – anything that we use to change our mood or energy – can all-too-easily become addictive. When we become addicted, we become self-forgetful. We set aside our core life aims and objectives, stumbling along cul-de-sacs of compulsiveness and self-depletion. A cigarette, drink or bet is a poor substitute for taking calculated risks towards pursuing what you were put on this planet to do.

Your next practical step in moving towards quitting smoking and other addictions for good, if that is what you choose to do, is to write, or revise, your personal mission statement. When you know your personal mission, you can make an adult choice whether or not to be guided by it. Implementing your mission can motivate you to overcome obstacles like compulsive sex, overeating or not eating enough, leaving a dissatisfying job or, of course, quitting smoking.

Your Personal Mission Statement: An Exercise

Your personal mission is as distinctive as you are. There is nobody else the same as you on this planet and there never will be. You were born to do something that only you can do in your particular way. No matter how old or young you are, your higher self (the non-addicted, free part of you) is appealing to you even now as you read this to pursue your mission. It is never too late or too early to set out or begin anew. The right time is now. Nobody else has been, or can be, given your personal mission. If you do not fulfil it, you and the world will be a lesser place.

Since your personal mission in life is unique to you, no two mission statements are the same. Do not shy away from your uniqueness, your distinctiveness, your singularity. You are unrepeatable. As the psalmist in the Judaeo-Christian scriptures prays: "For the wonder of myself I thank you." (Psalm 139).

Do you accept and love your distinctive self? Or would you prefer to bury your distinctiveness and blend in with everyone else? For some people, being accepted within a group is one reason for smoking. The herd instinct can also lead people to stay stuck in their addictions, comforted by fellow addicts. But your higher self wants you to know and celebrate who you are and to enjoy your never-to-be-repeated singularity. This programme will help you to get to know yourself more. It will help you to express yourself, first to yourself and then to others. It starts now with your expression of your personal mission. Do not think that this is complicated. It is simple. I have found that everyone from the highly educated to the most disadvantaged of our society can, with relative ease, articulate their core mission. For instance, I have recently been invigorated and humbled by the rugged honesty and authenticity that emerged when a group of homeless men I worked with wrote down and read out their personal mission statements.

You have a truth to speak to the world. Your mission statement seeks to encapsulate your truth in a very short space — what you're about, what you feel called to do. It's not fixed in stone. It will change and develop with you. But it starts off with the best few words you can string together on your aims, objectives and values.

Enough talk. It's time for you to have a go at writing your mission statement, or revising one your wrote before. Keep it short and simple. In six months time you will probably want to tweak it. A year or a decade from now it will be different again. You might say something about your relationship with yourself (for instance that you want to know yourself better and break free of addictions). And you'll probably include something about your aims for key relationships in your life (for example, finding, loving, growing together with a 'significant other' or your aims for your children). Probably too it'll say something about your work, be it paid, voluntary or homework. Your mission statement might not need to refer to your current job (if you're employed), which could be a transitional job or one to which you don't feel called, but it will almost certainly say something about the work you want to do or feel called to doing.

The shorter your mission statement, the more effective it will be as a tool to help you make decisions. If it is so short that you can memorise it, or key words in it, all the better, just as I've shown the key word "growth" helped me on occasion in managing situations where I used to teach.

If you decide that smoking or other addictions are not in keeping with your mission statement, then your motivation to abstain from addictive behaviour (and live life to the full without it) will be all the stronger. In the moment of temptation, rather than choosing negatively ('not to smoke') you will choose positively. You will know that by choosing not to smoke (or indulge in other addictive behaviour) you will gain more energy towards fulfilling your personal mission. Choosing not to smoke becomes an act of self-belief in who you are and the work you've been sent to do. You will know that by choosing your higher path rather than yielding to compulsive behaviour you will directly impact in a very tangible way on fulfilling your personal mission. For instance, you will have more energy in your relationship with your children, your spouse and have more of you to offer in your work. Indeed, there is a direct and measurable correlation between your personal effectiveness and your decision to abstain.

To write or update your mission statement, you could write the words Self, Others, and Work on the left side of a sheet in your journal, as shown below. (If you prefer, you may, of course, write in this workbook, for this and all subsequent exercises.) To the right of each word, write down your aims for that aspect of your life. When you have written your core general aims, you could then write down specific objectives to help fulfil your aims. You are encouraged to stop reading now and to write your personal mission.

Personal Mission Statement

Self	
Others	
Work	
Objectives	* * * * *
Values	

© Joe Armstrong 2004 www.writeway2stopsmoking.com

Now that you've written your mission statement, you have a map to guide your decision-making. For instance, if you have written down in the "Work" row that you want to earn your living as a writer working from home but currently you are a full-time office-worker, you now know where you want to get to. If you have written down that you will accept only well paid work but you are currently working for less than you are worth, naming that discrepancy will itself help motivate you to change it. You can gain confidence from your mission statement to turn down poorly paid work. If you have written down in the 'Others' row that you want to enjoy a great relationship with your partner but you spend little time together, you can take steps to rectify this.

With your personal mission statement composed, copy it out on a card and place it in a prominent place where you will see it every day. How do you feel about putting your personal mission statement on display where family or friends may see it? Would you prefer to keep it secret? If so, why? If you feel uncomfortable about letting others know what your greatest aims and objectives are, you might explore that reticence in your journal or talk to your sponsor about it. Wherever you put your statement, make sure that you at least see it daily.

Some people can benefit from professional help in discovering their personal or professional mission. For instance, if you are not sure what your life's work is, consider consulting a career analyst. Good career analysis involves exploring your interests, personality, skills, education, and family background and generally includes competency tests for things like words, numbers or mechanical reasoning. It is often combined with an interview and written report. You could emerge from career analysis, possibly conducted over a weekend, with a very clear sense of your life's work.

Fulfilling My Mission: An Exercise

Take three minutes now to play with the following questions in your journal: What is holding me back from knowing or fulfilling my personal mission? What can I do about it today? (When we're stuck, we usually know what we need to do.)

Call to Quit Smoking

Where does smoking or quitting smoking feature in your mission statement? Is smoking at variance with any aspect of your call to live your life to the full? If it contradicts any aspect of your mission statement, you might see this as a call from your higher self, the free part of you that isn't addicted to anything, to give up the weed.

Your call to quit smoking is unique to you. It is an inner call and an outer call. Your higher self nudges you towards quitting all dependencies, bad habits, and addictions, so you can celebrate life to the full. Perhaps your higher self is suggesting that it is time to *move on* from the smoking part of your life, to leave compulsive behaviour behind you. Perhaps you no longer feel at ease about depending on cigarettes or other addictions. Or maybe your doctor, a crisis, or some other event in your life has acted as a catalyst for change.

Catalyst

You are hearing a call (whether from within yourself or from an external source) to consider a change or you would not be reading this book. Something has happened that has opened up the possibility of your quitting smoking. Possibly some happening (again it could be something within yourself or originating outside yourself), an apparent coincidence or a twist of fate has prompted you to consider life beyond smoking or other addictions. You find yourself contemplating a radically different, unexpected life of coping, managing and enjoying life without compulsive behaviour. And being motivated to do so to fulfil a newly discovered, or long forgotten, higher aim in life.

Your familiar world of smoking begins to feel stifling. You have a hunch that you need to move on to develop further as a person and commit or recommit to doing what you were born to do. You are outgrowing your dependency on cigarettes and other dependencies. You want to be able to manage your thoughts, feelings, and moods, and deal with difficult people or situations, without the crutch of nicotine or other compulsions. A threshold similar to that which you experienced when you were ready to leave your mother's womb is at hand.

Your Call to Quit: An Exercise

In your journal, write down what is prompting you to quit smoking. Do not write what you think you ought to say. Write what you feel. For instance, logic might suggest that quitting smoking for health reasons is a good idea. But that might not be a motivating factor for you. Try to discover the link between what is prompting you to consider quitting and your personal mission. For instance, if you want to be the best parent you can be, you might find that smoking leaves you with less spiritual energy (your human spirit is depleted or self-absorbed) to engage with your children. Or you might want to make a success of a personal or work project and you believe that abstaining from nicotine will help give you an edge in achieving your goals. Perhaps a young grandchild has told you she wants you to be alive for her wedding or you simply have the sense that smoking is holding you back from growing into a more authentic human being. There are no right answers – only the reason or reasons you personally discern. A single personal reason to move on and grow beyond the smoking phase of your life can be enough motivation to achieve your goal, even if there are hundreds of excuses to keep smoking.

Soon, it will be time to stop reading and to try to express in your journal or in this workbook your distinctive call, as you understand it, to stop smoking and any other addictions. This is an important exercise. Take as long as you need to do it. Feel free to add to it in the coming days and weeks as you think of further reasons to stop acting out compulsions. You might even like to copy whatever you come up with onto a card and put it in your purse or wallet to carry about with you. Insofar as you can, see if you can categorise your reasons into internal or external calls. Of course, some reasons to stop can be both, such as if you want to improve your health (internal motivation) while a doctor might also have suggested you quit (external motivation).

My Personal Call to Quit Smoking

My personal inner call to stop smoking	External sources of my call to quit

© Joe Armstrong 2004 www.writeway2stopsmoking.com

Below you can read a sample but remember there are no 'right' answers – only what is true for you. It might be better if you fill in your own table before you read the sample below.

My Personal Call to Quit Smoking (Sample)

My personal inner call to stop smoking	External sources of my call to quit
I feel bad at not being able to stop.	Manufacturers admit that smoking kills.
I hate acting out of any compulsion.	Financial cost of smoking.
If I can beat smoking, I can do anything.	Increasing social unacceptability of smoke.
I want to be able to cope without cigarettes.	If I can't do it, how can my children?
I admire people who have quit for good.	Smelly clothes and breath.

© Joe Armstrong 2004 www.writeway2stopsmoking.com

By doing the above exercise, you have taken another practical step towards quitting smoking. Simply writing your reason or reasons for wanting to abstain from nicotine actually increases your personal motivation. Each time you add to your list, or write a copy of it or read it silently or aloud, you deepen your motivation and increase your chances of success. That this is so is confirmed by the authoritative *Motivational Interviewing: Preparing People to Change Addictive Behaviour* by William R. Miller and Stephen Rollnick where they show that merely expressing self-motivational statements "tips the balance a little further in the direction of change".

Indeed, the goal of Week One of this programme is, in the words of Miller and Rollnick, to increase your "intrinsic motivation, so that change arises from within rather than being imposed from without".

Removing Mental Blocks

What are your mental blocks to quitting nicotine? When you think about abstaining from cigarettes, what thoughts get in the way? Do you feel it will be too hard? Do you fear that the journey will be too long? Do you fear failure and, rather than risk failure, are you tempted to stay smoking? Or have you tried to quit before and relapsed?

Change is demanding. There can be a feeling that it is safer to stay with the status quo. You do not know where giving up tobacco might take you. You might fear the unknown. Possibly you do not want to change how you think. You might fear being unable to deal with success: if you succeed at quitting smoking, what else might your higher self invite you to do? You might fear being expected to take your personal mission more seriously.

Fear teaches us. For instance, you could fear that you are setting yourself up for a fall. You might fear that if you strive to quit smoking and do not succeed, or relapse, that you will lose your confidence or lose face before others. This is where your journal is so important because you can explore such fears as you express them. Simply by writing down your fear, you gain a measure of control over it – and it loses some power over you.

Shortly in this chapter you will look at how to turn obstacles and fears to your advantage. But before turning mental blocks to your advantage, you need to know what they are. Do the following exercise in your journal or in the space provided below. Try to express your blocks to quitting tobacco.

My Blocks to Quitting Smoking

1.
2.
3.
4.
5.

© Joe Armstrong 2004 www.writeway2stopsmoking.com

Beyond Blocks

Mental blocks to quitting tobacco can include the following:

If I stop smoking…

1. I would not know what to do with my hands

2. I would feel awkward in company

3. I would put on weight

4. I would feel stressed and anxious

5. I would have to change my friends

6. I could not continue in my present job

7. I could not pass my exams

8. I could not enjoy a drink

9. I could not enjoy a coffee

10. My friends would laugh at me

11. My sexuality would be questioned

12. I might become violent

13. I fear I could lose my mind

14. It would be like losing my best friend

15. I would not know how to treat myself

16. I could relapse and feel terrible

17. I relapsed before so what's the point?

18. I could fail again and feel worse than if I hadn't tried

19. I could become addicted to something else

Now imagine if you discovered that *none* of these things came to pass. You *can* quit smoking and know what to do with your hands. You too can give up smoking and *feel at ease* in company. You can stop and *not put on weight*. You can enjoy a much more *stress-free life*. You can turn from smoking *without having to change your friends* (indeed many people are lucky in that many of their friends don't smoke). You can go smokefree and *stay in your present job* (unless of course succeeding at ditching tobacco gives you the confidence to go for and get the job of your dreams). You *can* pass your exams without the crutch of cigarettes. So long as you are not addicted to alcohol or caffeine, you can give up smoking and still enjoy these pleasures. You will *not* lose true friends by kicking the habit. You *can* quit and feel even more at ease in your sexuality. You can choose never to smoke again *without* feeling or becoming aggressive or violent. You *can* abstain and *enjoy* your mind more than ever before rather than losing it. You *can develop and deepen* great friendships, with soul friends supporting your regained freedom, improved health and more focused personal mission. You can be done with smoking and *learn how to treat yourself really well*. You *can learn* and *grow* from any experiences of relapse, strengthening you finally to stop addictive behaviour for good. And you *can* abstain from cigarettes without becoming addicted to anything else. Indeed, you can stop smoking and other addictions while finding the process insightful, empowering and a major turning point for good in your life.

Translate Your Blocks to Affirmations: An Exercise

A simple and highly effective tool to enhancing your motivation to kick the habit and believe in your considerable personal potential is to translate each mental block into a positive affirmation. You can release remarkable confidence, energy and self-belief through this exercise.

Look at your personal list of mental blocks which you wrote for the *My blocks to quitting smoking* exercise above. Soon you will translate each of them into a personal affirmation. An affirmation is another form of self-motivational statement, which, as we've seen above in referring to Miller and Rollnick's important work, is a highly effective way to promote change. Affirmations are the kind of self-motivational statements which are imbued with optimism about change. In the table below or your journal, rewrite each of your mental blocks as a personal affirmation.

Translating My Blocks to Stopping Smoking into Affirmations

My Mental Blocks to Quitting (see work you've already done above)	Affirmations
1.	
2.	
3.	
4.	
5.	

© Joe Armstrong 2004 www.writeway2stopsmoking.com

Try to translate your personal blocks into affirmations before looking at the example below, remembering that it is *self*-motivational statements which have the greatest power to effect change.

Translating My Blocks to Stopping Smoking into Affirmations (Sample)

My Mental Blocks to Quitting	Affirmations
1. If I quit smoking, I will get fat.	I can quit smoking and stay trim and look great.
2. If I quit smoking, I will not have much fun.	I can quit smoking and discover greater pleasures than I enjoyed while I smoked.
3. If I quit, I will lose my friends.	I can quit smoking, keep true friends and make great new friendships.
4. If I quit smoking, I will get addicted to something else.	I can quit smoking without developing other addictions and enjoy an inner freedom and self-control I could only have dreamed of before.
5. If I quit smoking I will lose the buzz of smoking, be less confident and be unable to relate with others.	I can quit smoking and become more energised, confident and capable of great empathy with others because I will know myself so well.

© Joe Armstrong 2004 www.writeway2stopsmoking.com

Your Blocks to Other Personal Goals

You have already translated your personal mental blocks to quitting smoking into affirmations. Do the same exercise now for some other personal goal. List your blocks and translate them into affirmations. For instance, if you want to travel somewhere for a holiday, what thoughts are blocking you from doing so? Or if your goal is to get married, pursue a course of study, make your fortune, develop new friendships or take the next step in your career, write down the negative beliefs that are holding you back. Choose one goal only and name your mental blocks. Now translate each into an affirmation or self-motivational statement.

Translating My Blocks to Another Goal into Affirmations

My Mental Blocks to Another Goal	Affirmations
1.	
2.	
3.	
4.	
5.	

© Joe Armstrong 2004 www.writeway2stopsmoking.com

Do you see any correlation between your blocks to quitting smoking and your blocks to pursuing the goal you chose to work with? If so, do not conclude that you are doubly blocked and a hopeless case! Rather, appreciate how by succeeding in quitting smoking you can remove obstacles elsewhere in your life too. Now that you have written your personal affirmations, you will soon see how you can use them to beat your mental blocks. First though, we take a brief look at any other areas of your life, apart from smoking, in which you might have experience of compulsive behaviour.

Other Addictions

I have found in delivering this programme to individuals and groups that people often have experience of other addictions too apart from smoking. You may be an alcoholic, a compulsive gambler, or a drug addict. Perhaps you have experience of addiction to food or caffeine, compulsive sex, compulsive shopping, dependent relationships (co-dependency), kleptomania, or being a workaholic. The compulsive self can also be given to predominant ways of thinking and behaving such as perfectionism, nostalgia, power seeking, the need to be the best, or even helpfulness, as systems such as the Enneagram have taught. The Enneagram, about which many books have been written, is primarily a motivational tool and instrument for self-knowledge and personal change, based on identifying one's predominant compulsion, with each of nine basic personality types compulsively looking at the world in a habitual way.

While there is not space here to explore other addictions in detail, with the emphasis necessarily being on smoking, most of the exercises in this book can equally be applied to other addictions. Moreover, as this programme aims to help you to get back on track to fulfilling your unique mission statement and to quit smoking and other addictions because they inhibit you doing and being what you were sent to do, it is desirable to tackle all addictions you may have simultaneously. Hence, if you are currently acting out of any other addiction, try to set Day One of Week Five as your Quit Date for these other compulsions too. Insofar as you may not currently be acting out other addictions, you can nevertheless explore all dependencies while getting to know yourself better on this programme. With this in mind, it would be good for you now to write down things you are or have been addicted to. The exercise below aims to help you name any such addictions, compulsions or dependencies.

My Other Addictions, Compulsions or Dependencies

List below anything that you have ever been, or still are, addicted to, even if you no longer act out of that compulsion or if the period of acting out of it was short-lived or long ago.	In the column below, state whether you still act out of the addiction, even from time to time. If you no longer act compulsively in this area of your life, when did you last do so and how did you stop it?
1.	
2.	
3.	
4.	
5.	

© Joe Armstrong 2004 www.writeway2stopsmoking.com

You may possibly need professional help in dealing with some of these addictions, such as alcoholism or drug addiction. Contact your doctor who should be able to put you in touch with professional counsellors or therapists, who can guide you through this special time of opportunity in your life. If you feel reluctant to do so, why not repeat the exercise above on Blocks to Stopping Smoking, this time doing the exercise for your other addiction(s). Make sure to translate each block into an affirmation or self-motivational statement!

Affirmations

How many negative thoughts have you had today – or even in the last few minutes? How many thoughts have you endured today which discouraged you from believing in your potential, in your ability to stop smoking and other addictions, or to achieve some other personal goal?

Affirmations or self-motivational thoughts are a simple and effective way of stopping negative self-talk. Your work so far has identified the thoughts that hold you back and you have come up with affirmations for each blocking thought. What do you do with the affirmations? You repeat them. You have been repeating your blocks over and over again, possibly for years. Now it is time to counteract those recurring blocks by repeating your affirmations. Repeat them in your head and in your journal.

When you say or write an affirmation, the addictive part of you smirks, jeers and mocks your fragile self-belief. As you reiterate the affirmation, it is like standing up to an inner bully. But this is not some mindless, passive, repetitive act, like children learning their arithmetic tables by rote. Rather, in repeating the affirmation, you listen for any self-mocking, disbelieving part of you. And you can, in turn, translate these into affirmations.

In his excellent book *The Enlightened Smoker's Guide to Quitting*, B. Jack Gebhardt proposes what he calls the enlightenment exercise. It is not dissimilar to translating negative blocks into affirmations. His technique is to translate every unpleasant thought into an enjoyable thought. The method is eminently suited to the journal writing method recommended in *WW2SS*. His suggestion is that every time you catch yourself thinking a negative thought – such as the dream I have my heart set on will not happen – cross out the words you don't like and re-write such negativity in a more enjoyable way. You can have fun with it. What you write doesn't need to be logical. Just so long as it's more enjoyable than your negative thought you're doing it right. And you can keep crossing out words and replacing them with more enjoyable thoughts as often as you'd like to. Or as often as you keep thinking negatively. Think of the new energy that you would tap into if you were to do this! Imagine what life would be like no longer being governed by negative thinking. However, because we usually let life go by without actively reworking negative thinking into affirmations or more enjoyable thoughts, those esteem-damaging thoughts continue to affect us, depleting us of self-belief.

Personal Affirmations: An Exercise

Pause for a moment before reading on and think of *one* negative thought you have had in the last five minutes. (For most humans, that's pretty easy to do!). If you can't think of one that you thought in the last five minutes, then choose a negative thought you had sometime within the last 24 hours. Simply play with the thought in your journal until you have re-worked it into something more pleasant, something more enjoyable to think than the original negative thought. Don't read on until you've done this exercise!

Have you done that? Isn't it much nicer thinking the more pleasant thought? And it gives you heart to go on and take whatever next step you need to take, without being encumbered by a nasty negative thought damaging your confidence. As soon as you catch yourself on thinking another negative thought, stop reading, write out *that* negative thought and rework it too to something more enjoyable.

Using affirmations, especially those you have devised having translated them from your personal negative thinking and mental blocks, gives you confidence. For instance, one client who took the *WW2SS* programme wrote: "The once impossible is merely a hurdle". Indeed, nothing is impossible to your higher self. You can see how reworking mental blocks can stimulate an inner dialogue, which shifts energy, perspective and instils confidence. For instance, when you say the affirmation 'I can quit smoking', the addicted part of you might scoff, saying you cannot. You have tried before and failed. It is too late, or too early, to quit. Now is not a good time. To each inner objection, you gently repeat the same affirmation: 'I *can* quit smoking.' And rework any counterbalancing negative thought into a new affirmation.

If you can, learn some of your personal affirmations by heart, especially those which translate from your negative beliefs. If you're finding your journal hard work some morning, you could simply write out affirmations instead, or conclude your three pages with selected affirmations, writing each out several times. You can, of course, also work with the affirmations/self-motivational statements you devised to counteract mental blocks towards other goals you hold dear.

If you think affirmations are silly, consider this: people who do not smoke or act out other addictions and who are already fulfilling their personal mission and achieving their goals habitually think the way you are training yourself to think through self-motivational affirmations. You too can learn to *think* differently, and *thinking* precedes action. Each time you catch yourself thinking a mental block, take the time to rework it into a more pleasant, self-motivational affirmation. The more often you do it, the more highly self-motivated you will become. It is not a waste of time or a distraction and it is almost certainly more important than whatever else you might be involved in at the time. Besides, you can re-think self-defeating, brow-beating addictive thinking even while doing other things, although the ideal is to write down the negative thought and rework it, having fun with it, until it actually becomes a self-motivational affirmation (as we've explored above).

Daily Journal Affirmations

Look at the affirmations below. Combined with your personal affirmations devised from your mental blocks, you now have to hand an armoury of self-motivational statements. You could conclude your journal each morning by writing out a few affirmations five or ten times, using some of your own and some from the selected ones below.

When you quit smoking from Day One of Week Five, repeating a mental affirmation will be one of the many ways in which you will be able to counter a craving for a cigarette. For instance, some people who have taken this programme discover great resilience during a bout of craving to mentally recall that "Any acute craving will pass within five minutes. I can last that long." Repeating affirmations can remind you that your higher power, your authentic self and your core personal mission are much stronger than your addicted self's demand for nicotine or other addictive substances or processes.

Some affirmations below anticipate your non-smoker status from Week Five onwards, but you can use these affirmations already. A part of you is already a non-smoker. By even now using affirmations such as 'I love being a non-smoker' you are preparing your mind for stopping smoking and other addictions. However, do not give in to any temptation to quit before Week Five. You have some more analysis and planning to do first.

Selected Affirmations

1. I can quit smoking.

2. I can stop smoking with the help of my higher power.

3. When I become an ex-smoker, I will feel great.

4. When I stop smoking and other addictions, I will grow as a person.

5. The journey is more important than arriving.

6. I do not smoke anymore.

7. Any acute craving will pass within five minutes. I can last that long.

8. I love no longer acting out addictions.

9. As I continue on my path, I am being healed.

10. My higher and authentic self wants me to stop smoking.

11. I believe in my personal mission.

12. I shall dare to be myself.

13. I listen to my authentic self being expressed in my journal.

14. I forgive myself for the damage I have done to my body.

15. I forgive others for their part in my smoking.

16. Stopping smoking and other addictions is good for me.

17. My body will reward me for my decision to quit smoking.

18. My friends will thank me for stopping smoking.

19. My children will personally benefit from my decision to quit.

20. Quitting smoking is the most important thing I can do this year.

21. I am willing to stop smoking.

22. I am willing to stop acting out other addictions.

23. I am willing to live my personal mission.

24. I am willing to ask for help in breaking free from nicotine.

25. I am open and willing to discover authentic joy in my life.

26. I discover wholesome ways to treat myself.

27. I enjoy the taste of food now that I have stopped smoking.

28. I like my improved skin now that I have quit.

29. I am willing to stand up as I am, wounded and all.

30. I cherish my freedom from dependencies.

31. I am willing to take calculated risks to do what I was sent to do.

32. I am willing to change my thoughts, feelings, judgements and behaviour.

33. I take back the power I gave to nicotine.

34. I take back the power I gave to other addictive substances or processes.

Activities for Week One

1. Buy a small notebook, small enough to fit comfortably into your handbag or pocket. You are used to carrying smoking paraphernalia: get used to carrying this as part of your daily routine. It will have many uses while you do this programme. This week, you can use it to record some favourite affirmations. When you have a few moments free during your day – perhaps while you smoke a cigarette – read or write out an affirmation a few times. And yes, you could choose 'I love being a non-smoker' even as you inhale cigarette smoke. You can also record extra reasons for why you would like to stop smoking or other addictions. It can become a mini-journal too, in which you can write down how you feel about anything.

2. Write your story of addiction in your journal, including your addiction to smoking and to any other addictive substance or process, from when you had your first cigarette to the present day. (I've often found that people struggling to write in their journal suddenly feel they could write a book when given this activity!)

3. In your journal, draw your family tree, showing who in your family and extended family smoked or were addicted to anything else.

4. Write in your journal the names of anyone from your past or present who discouraged you from believing in yourself. Write down the names of anyone who has undermined your confidence that you can stop smoking and any other addictions. Pick one of the names you have written from either list and write them a fantasy letter in your journal saying how their disbelief in you affected you.

5. Write in your journal the names of people who have encouraged you to believe in yourself, people who respect you and believe in you. Write down what they have said or done to encourage your self-belief. If you can, send one of them a thank you note or ring them up and say how you appreciate their support.

6. If your focus is only on cigarettes, ask yourself if you might be dependent or rely heavily on any other mood-altering substance or process? For instance, would you find it difficult to enjoy yourself with friends in a pub if you weren't drinking alcohol? Could you get through the day without caffeine? Have you become dependent on drugs (illegal, prescribed or over-the-counter)? Has your interest in sex become compulsive? If you start shopping, gambling, or work, can you stop? Are you addicted to physical exercise, or do you have compulsive problems concerning food? If you think any of these things might be a concern for you, write about it in your journal and consider discussing it with your spouse/partner, sponsor, doctor, counsellor or therapist.

7. Take some physical exercise this week. Consult your doctor before embarking on any new exercise routine. This is especially important if you have not taken physical exercise for some time or if you have certain medical conditions such as a heart complaint. Even a brisk 20-minute walk can do wonders for your circulatory system, enhance your mood, and help you think straight, look great and feel refreshed.

Week One Review

Comprehensive research by authorities in the field of addiction shows that one of the key predictors of successfully quitting smoking and other dependencies is whether or not you adhere to advice and keep to a systematic programme. Do this review at the end of Week One, ideally the night before you read the next chapter on Week Two. Do the review in your journal. It need not take more than ten minutes. This weekly review could form the framework for the discussion with your sponsor.

1. Did you go to bed a half an hour earlier each night? Did you rise earlier and write three pages in your journal every morning? How did you find keeping the journal — what was good and what was bad?

2. Did you take your congé? What did you do? Did you enjoy it? Did you go alone, and did you avoid smoking and smoky environments?

3. Write down a word or image that describes your experience of the week. Did you feel encouraged at any point in the last week? What encouraged you?

Refusal of Your Call

This week we look at what you like about smoking and the part of you that wants to continue smoking. We see if there might be a discrepancy between what you want to do with your life and continuing to act out any addictions, including smoking. In short, we look at your inner resistance to change. By the end of this week, you make a major decision: whether to continue along the path towards abstinence and 'sobriety' from cigarettes and other addictions or whether to remain smoking and continuing with other addictive behaviour for the foreseeable future. This is an important week. As addiction authorities William R. Miller and Stephen Rollnick say in *Motivational Interviewing: Preparing People to Change Addictive Behaviour* "unless a client is helped to resolve the 'I want to but I don't want to' dilemma, progress is likely to be slow-going and short-lived".

Refusing Your Personal Mission

You are called to live your personal mission: called to be yourself, to become who you were born to be and to do what you were sent to do. You are called to "freedom, fullness and good fortune", as Sarah

Ban Breathnach so well expressed our aims in *Simple Abundance: A Daybook of Comfort and Joy*. You are called especially to freedom from addictions; life lived to the full (as Saint Irenaeus said "The glory of God is man fully alive"); and good fortune (since 'fate favours the prepared'). But you are free to choose otherwise. Invited to fulfil your potential, you can choose not to achieve it. Called to freedom, you can languish in addiction. Invited to fullness, you can remain unfulfilled. Beckoned by Lady Luck, she can find you unprepared.

There is a comfort in staying with familiar thinking, feelings, habits and ways of behaving. The devil you know can seem less bothersome than the whole uncertain project of becoming your more authentic self. So long as you can maintain the belief that you could have done something wonderful with your life without actually having to put it to the test, you can stay stuck where you are until you die.

You can refuse your higher call almost without noticing it, just as you can keep on smoking while suppressing the part of you that wants to move on. You can decide not to believe in your personal mission or conclude that the personal cost of change would be too great. You can refuse the call in simple ways. Staying up later at night than you decided to. Skipping your morning journal, having committed to do it for three months. Doing work on your congé. Eating more, or less, than you need. Drinking more than is good for you, or any at all if you are an alcoholic.

You can deny your call. Like the born writer who buries his vocation fearing the financial unpredictability of the creative life. Or you can convince yourself that you are beyond help, resigning yourself to your addiction, persuading yourself that you are too bad a case to make a change.

You can feel called to quit smoking and other addictions as the next step to take in living your personal mission, but still choose not to respond to that call. You can feel called to leave a job but remain there, resigned to an assured income. You can procrastinate, thinking you will take up your dream when you retire. Or you can ignore it, tell it to go away or cod yourself that life beyond the status quo is a delusion. Faraway hills are green and you decide to stay put. Your present life may not be perfect, but it is tolerable. For some, life becomes intolerable. As they say in Alcoholics Anonymous, a time comes when you're sick and tired of feeling sick and tired. That can be a turning point towards authenticity, healing and growth.

Fear

Even when you know what is best to do, it can, of course, still be difficult to do it. It is all too easy to stay put instead of taking a step into the dark, seeking to overcome an obstacle that has long stood in your way.

It can be a terrible thing to believe in yourself! The responsibility is scary. Sticking your neck out. Daring to be you. Letting the inside come out. Admitting who you are is one thing (a process facilitated by your morning journal), but acting in accordance with your inner truth, in sync with your personal mission and growing self-belief can be like walking through glass – to use an image from a dream I once dreamed. You will look more closely at your self-belief in Week Three, but first you need to become aware of the things that are holding you back. What do you think is holding you back from fulfilling your personal mission, from living your life to the full, from achieving your aims and goals?

How do you believe you would cope if you achieved your personal mission? For instance, could you be rich or famous without losing your head, values or humanity? Do you fear your marriage or a significant relationship might break up? Might success go to your head? Could you handle quitting smoking and other addictions without feeling superior to others and setting yourself up for a fall?

Refusing, or accepting, the call does not have to concern bigger changes like switching jobs or career. It comes down to the present moment. In this moment you are free to choose whether to keep reading or to do something else. You are free whether to stop work on time or to keep working, possibly to the detriment of your health and relationships. You are free whether or not to take some physical exercise, and whether or not to schedule time for relaxation and reflection into your daily round.

Alcohol

During these 12 weeks, you are seeking to get to know, and live more fully, your personal mission in life. By the end of this week you will have decided whether or not to proceed towards stopping smoking and other addictions for good. By the end of these twelve weeks, your aim is to have attained 'sobriety' from nicotine – an authentic lifestyle promoting health and wellbeing for your mind, body and spirit.

One obstacle that could prevent you from attaining abstinence and 'sobriety' from nicotine, and the celebration of your personal mission, is alcohol. It is a fact that people quitting smoking find it more difficult to do so while they are drinking alcohol. Alcohol weakens the resolve and diminishes self-control. Many people trying to quit slip back into smoking or relapse while drinking alcohol. And this is true even for people who have not smoked for years.

You do not need to abstain from alcohol forever, unless you are an alcoholic, in which case you should talk to your doctor about treatment options. But even if you are not dependent on alcohol, are you open to considering abstaining from it from Day One of Week Five until the end of the programme? You do not have to and people taking this programme have, of course, succeeded in quitting smoking while continuing to drink socially. But even those who were successful conceded that they nearly relapsed on an occasion when they had had an alcoholic drink. The choice, and risk, is yours. Together with retiring earlier to bed, getting lots of sleep, writing your journal, taking your congé, reading *WW2SS*, doing suggested activities, taking regular physical exercise, consulting your doctor early next week about nicotine replacement therapy and other options, seven weeks without alcohol would significantly strengthen your chances of success.

If you feel it could be difficult to enjoy yourself socially without a drink, you might like to write about that in your journal or discuss it with your sponsor. Do not be afraid to consider the possibility that you might have some element of dependency on alcohol. Trust in your personal mission, trust in your higher power and accept yourself as you are, warts and all. If you tried quitting smoking before, but had a slip while drinking alcohol or a full relapse triggered by alcohol, you should seriously consider abstaining from alcohol even for some weeks from Day One of Week Five. You might find it easier to be in a bar while neither drinking nor smoking than drinking but not smoking. Consider reducing or eliminating your visits to places where alcohol is consumed for the first few weeks after you stop smoking. A temporary abstinence from alcohol can be a realistic recognition of your human fragility and a pragmatic demonstration of your determination, with the help of your higher power, to quit smoking.

A temporary abstinence from alcohol can help you keep to your programme of getting to bed early and rising each morning to write your journal. It can help you to keep your weight in check, because alcohol increases weight. Alcohol is a depressant, leaving you more prone to wanting the boost of a cigarette. Especially taken late at night, alcohol will diminish the quality of your sleep. You have committed yourself to self-care for these twelve weeks. Getting lots of restorative sleep is an important component of taking care of yourself.

I have found that quite a few people taking this programme can have other addictions too. It really can be advisable in this, as in many other freedom-from-addiction programmes, to abstain from all mood-altering substances, even if only for a number of weeks from your Quit Date, namely Day One of Week Five. Your journal is a godsend in exploring your moods. Instead of trying to disguise or hide your moods most of all to yourself, through mood-altering substances or processes, learn to express those moods in the safe place of your journal. Get it out on the page. Draw pictures if you like, with colours. Do not fear that some insane part of you – or a part of you that you might feel is insane – might emerge on the page. If something troubles you, discuss it with your sponsor, doctor or a counsellor or therapist. But the healing begins with your pen! If you are taking this programme in conjunction with another detox programme, feel free to share some of what you express in your journal with whoever is helping you to quit other addictions too.

The Company of Smokers

I must preface this section by saying that, generally speaking, two broad categories of people take this programme. In one group are those whose friends, in the main, smoke, while the other sector comprises those who find themselves practically the only smoker left in their circle of friends and associates. What follows below is mainly directed at those in the former category. It will be less relevant for those who tend to find themselves the sole smoker.

While some friends, members of your family or acquaintances can support you in your goals, it is a fact that many smokers fail to quit, or relapse, while interacting with their other people, particularly with friends, who smoke. A friend offers you a cigarette and, before you realise it, you are smoking it.

You will prepare practical strategies to manage these and similar encounters in Week Four. But for now be aware that someone you know, unwittingly or otherwise, could tempt you back to smoking after you have quit – possibly even months or years after you have stopped smoking. Later in this programme you will learn how to stay on guard against relapse, even for years to come.

You are in the process of leaving behind your dependency on nicotine. You need to become, and remain, aware of all potential threats to your emerging freedom, fullness and fortune. While the greatest threat lies within you – in the part of you that is dependent on nicotine – never forget the pervasive threat that can be posed by a friend's teasing or casual offer of a cigarette.

Your routine of going to bed early and, if you choose to do so, a period of abstinence from alcohol, will almost certainly reduce your exposure to any threat posed by friends to you quitting smoking. Just as a period without alcohol will be good for your body, a period of reduced exposure to friends in whose company you might be tempted to smoke can help strengthen your resolve from Week Five. If you find it helpful, you can discuss your temporary absence from them in advance. You have a few weeks to prepare the ground and explain to them that quitting smoking is important and not being around people smoking could increase your chances of success at the early stages. True friends will understand and encourage you.

A word too about unhelpful friends: your move to quit smoking and live your life to the full will threaten some people. They will feel challenged by your move to get on with your life's work and to quit smoking. It is realistic to expect that not everyone will support you and that some will oppose you. It is best if possible to avoid such people, at least for a period from the start of Week Five. If you cannot avoid them, the skills you develop in Week Four will help.

Self-doubt

While fear, alcohol and friends can hold you back from responding to your higher call, self-doubt can be an even more pervasive threat to your continued progress. Many people would love to pursue their life's work, just as many people profess that they would like to quit smoking. Often, they make little progress because they do not have a systematic programme as you do. Specifically, they do not tackle their thoughts and feelings of self-doubt, as you are already doing in translating personal blocks to affirmations. You will explore self-belief – the opposite of self-doubt – in Week Three.

Just Do It

You have written your personal mission. You have committed to doing this programme. You will decide by the end of this week whether quitting smoking is a goal you want to commit to and so proceed with your life's work. But a week or two into your programme, you can find yourself staying up late rather than going early to bed, skipping your morning journal or being lacklustre about your congé.

'Follow the plan' is the key maxim to beating attempts by the nicotine-dependent part of you (your addictive self) to de-rail your success. It does not matter whether you feel enthusiastic about going to bed or not – just follow the plan. You might feel that what you write in your journal is silly or a waste of time. Follow the plan anyway. You have envisaged what you want to create. Whether you feel enthusiastic or not, by following the plan you get nearer to fulfilling your goal. If you do not follow the plan unless you feel like it, you will not achieve anything. The architect who has created the new house mentally ensures that the contractor pours the foundations, builds the walls, erects the roof, inserts the windows, and installs piping, electric cables and sockets. If either the architect or contractor stalled progress because they didn't feel like working, the house would not get built.

Following the plan, as you saw while reviewing Week One, is one of the prime indicators of future success. You envisage your life's work, target intermediate steps such as quitting smoking and take the necessary steps to move forward, by simply taking the next step.

Focus on what lies within your control. Do not ask 'Have I quit smoking for good yet?' but rather 'Have I gone to bed on time, done my morning journal, taken my congé?' Do these things that lie within your control, and stopping smoking and doing your life's work will look after itself.

Doing what lies within your control positions you for success. Following a workable plan gets you living in the here and now, focusing on what you can do at this moment, rather than being daunted at the prospect of scaling the mountain, or considering matters that lie outside your control. As is often said, the journey of a thousand miles begins with a single step. Take your next step now.

Habit

Do not underestimate the power of habit. Smoking is a habit and an addiction. But even if it were 'only' a habit, it would be difficult to stop it. It is difficult to change any habit and it takes time to create new habits. Habits save us the bother of having to think things through from conception to action. They save time, enabling us to do things efficiently and without awareness. You do not usually need to think which socket to turn on when boiling a kettle. The kettle plug is usually in the same socket. But if you change which socket the plug is in, you can find yourself automatically going to turn on the wrong socket for weeks after the change.

When you quit smoking on Day One of Week Five, the sheer force of habit can pull you back time and again towards your smoking habit, just as a recently widowed woman might think of going in to tend to her dying husband even after he has died. In Week Four, you will learn practical tools to increase your chances of breaking the habit. You are already putting together the building blocks of new habits for the next phase of your life. Your decisions to go to bed earlier at night will shortly become a habit. Your probable inclination to go to bed later can be an instructive reminder of the powerful force of habit. By working on your new sleeping routine, you are developing new habits that will help you break the habitual aspect of smoking.

Likewise, you are putting in place the building blocks of a healthier lifestyle by your commitment and practice to take regular physical exercise. If you have neglected physical exercise before starting this programme, you will know that taking regular exercise also involves the cultivation of a new habit, which in turn necessitates changing an older, possibly ingrained, habit of sedentary living.

In all the new habits you have begun to establish, focus on the personal benefit you gain from the activity. Visualise the completed 'house' you are building. Look forward to the benefits of enjoying your new home, one designed by you and for you, tailor-made for your calling, desires and needs; co-created, if you like, with your higher self. When you love that towards which you are heading, you will accept the work required to get there, just as, if you love looking and feeling fit, you will exercise. When you focus on the benefit you will gain, change becomes easier.

Discrepancy: Personal Mission versus Behaviour

When you realise there is a gap between what you love and what you do, you can discover a powerful inner motivation. For instance, if you have children, you will probably have referred to them in your mission statement. They will almost certainly rank highly in your list of loves and values. And yet, if you are dependent on nicotine, you might find an example of a way in which, in a given moment, you might behave as if smoking were more valuable than your children. If you can think of such a moment from your own life and reflect upon it, you realise that there is a discrepancy between what you say you love and what you love in practice.

Discrepancy: An Exercise

Can you think of any specific moment in which you valued cigarettes more than one specific need of your children or another loved one? If that doesn't ring any bells, write about an incident in which your dependency on nicotine came first ahead of something else that you have expressed as a primary life purpose in your mission statement.

This exercise is *not* intended to be a guilt trip. Rather, as Miller and Rollnick put it in *Motivational Interviewing: Preparing People to Change Addictive Behaviour*: "When a behaviour is seen as conflicting with important personal goals (such as one's health, success, family happiness, or positive self-image), change is likely to occur."

Benefits of Smoking

One thing that could prevent you from quitting smoking is a denial on your part of the benefits of smoking. You are not a fool. You have been gaining apparent benefits from smoking all these years or you would not have gone on smoking. The perceived benefits you got when you started smoking might not be the same as the payoffs you enjoyed subsequently. Now that you are thinking of quitting, you will have a better chance of success by acknowledging what you seem to gain by smoking.

Benefits of Smoking: An Exercise

This is an important exercise, so do not skip it. Write about or list your perceived benefits from smoking. Keep it personal. Be as specific as possible. If you say 'I enjoy the taste', go a little further

49

and try to say specifically what you like about the taste. If you say 'It helps me feel at ease in company', give an example of a time smoking helped you to break the ice. Most importantly, do not be afraid to admit that you enjoy smoking – just be as specific as you can about what you enjoy about it.

In Week One, you saw that your call to quit smoking is personal to you: it is linked to your personal mission. When you know what your prime motivation to stop smoking is, your chances of quitting are high. We saw that your prime motivation might be to have greater spiritual energy to proceed with your life's work, which might mean being able to engage more fully with people, or being more authentic. As one smoker taking the programme said to me: "I want to stop feeling like a junkie".

If you know why you smoke and the benefits you feel you get from smoking, you will be more willing to trade that for your higher calling to stop smoking. So, without any guilt, get in touch with the pleasure, the relief, the release of stress, the sensual experience, the anticipation of joy and the afterglow of satisfaction that, at its best, you enjoy from smoking. Write a list now of the personal benefits you feel you get from smoking, either in your journal or in the table below, remembering to be as personal, explicit and specific as possible. You can include former benefits, even if you no longer enjoy them. (You can, of course, write more than five things if you wish.)

What I Enjoy about Smoking

1.
2.
3.
4.
5.

It is best to do your own joys and benefits from smoking before looking at the following sample. Try not to be influenced by it. Your own work is far superior to this because your motivation to smoke is personal to you. Therefore, necessarily, an example won't be as true for you as your own work.

What I Enjoy about Smoking (Sample)

1. I find it sexy. The oral touch of cigarette in mouth, the sense of mystique and adulthood.
2. I love the paraphernalia of smoking, the ritual. I love lighting up, the first drag.
3. It calms me. It relieves stress for five minutes.
4. It expresses the rebel in me. I smoke because I want to. It's like a forbidden pleasure.
5. I enjoy it — that is reason enough.

© Joe Armstrong 2004 www.writeway2stopsmoking.com

Weighing Your Ambivalence

Do not be disturbed if the last exercise reignited your love for smoking or seemed to undermine your resolve to kick the habit. Ambivalence, as we've seen, is a central theme of this programme, especially this week and last, just as you can also feel ambivalent about whether or not to believe in and pursue your personal mission. Ambivalence can be most keenly felt as you set out on your journey to quit smoking and other addictions.

Your ambivalence is not new to you. You knew before you started this programme that part of you wanted to quit smoking and part of you wanted to continue as you were. In light of your mission statement written or reworked in Week One, you may believe that your higher self does indeed want you to leave behind addictive behaviour and knows that you can. But even if that is the case, the part of you that enjoys smoking and does not want you to quit has not gone away.

You really are free. True, you have lost some freedom to the extent that you are or may be addicted to nicotine. You want to quit. You want to smoke. Accept that both can, and probably are, true within you in any one moment. Your choice right now is to decide whether or not to explore further your ambivalence.

Dialogue Exploring Ambivalence: An Exercise

Accept your ambivalent thoughts and feelings. Write them down in your journal. Develop the facility to discern which part of you is speaking, the part calling you to believe in your personal mission overcoming all obstacles that lie in its path or the part of you that is dependent on nicotine, or any other dependency. By expressing both parts of your ambivalence in your journal, you slow yourself down. You can stand back from the part of you that disbelieves in yourself and let your higher self respond. You can enjoy writing a creative dialogue between the two parts of you, committing to paper what each part of you is saying. If you want, you can write in the margin AD for 'addictive self' and HS for 'higher self', letting the inner dialogue flow (see 'Dialogue: An Example' in Week Seven).

Your Ambivalence Scales or Decisional Balance

Look again at what you wrote in Week One in the table 'My Personal Call to Quit Smoking', where you explored your personal inner and outer call to quit smoking. Imagine that what you wrote there, and in particular what you see as your prime motivation for giving up smoking, as weighing down one side of your personal ambivalence scales. The best addiction counsellors and therapists confirm the importance of the decisional balance, including Prochaska and DiClemente, and Miller and Rollnick. It is the approach taken by the World Health Organisation, the Irish Cancer Society, the Irish College of General Practitioners, and counsellors with Great Britain's Quitline are also trained in this approach.

Now look at what you wrote for the table 'What I Enjoy about Smoking' in this chapter. The weight of that pulls against what you wrote as your call to stop smoking and acting out other addictions. The two weights are tugging you in opposite directions. You can enjoy and love smoking but if what you wrote for your personal call to quit weighs more heavily for you, your chances of success are very good. For simplicity, it could be useful for you to graphically draw (below or in your journal) your ambivalence scales or decisional balance. Try to fill in something in all four columns. You've already done most of the work for this in previous exercises. Which side of the scales has most weight for you?

Personal Ambivalence Scales/Decisional Balance

I want to smoke & continue with other addictions		I want to stop smoking and stop acting out other addictions	
Advantages	Disadvantages	Advantages	Disadvantages

© Joe Armstrong 2004 www.writeway2stopsmoking.com

Personal Ambivalence Scales/Decisional Balance (Sample)

I want to smoke & continue with other addictions		I want to stop smoking and stop acting out other addictions	
Advantages	Disadvantages	Advantages	Disadvantages
Easiest option	Bad for my health	Re-gain control over an addiction	I might fail and feel worse
I like it	Expensive	If I can beat this, I can do anything I set my mind to	I might put on weight
I've enough on my plate now	Disgusting habit	Increased self-esteem	I'd find it difficult to drink without a fag
I love the first one in the morning	I'd like to stop	Enjoying myself without the crutch of a cigarette	I might feel left out — smoking breaks the ice
		I feel smoking and another addiction is holding me back	

© Joe Armstrong 2004 www.writeway2stopsmoking.com

Don't worry if what you write in the various columns of your Ambivalence Scales/Decisional Balance is mutually contradictory. Just get down as many reasons as you can in each column. Of course, one strong reason in one column can outweigh several weaker factors in another column, so it's not merely a question of the number of points in each column, but their quality. When you have completed it, tick off the column where most energy lies for you. Are your scales pulling down strongly towards quitting smoking or staying smoking?

Crossing Your First Threshold

You have done enough work by now to prepare you for a decision. As this week draws to an end, you need to make your decision whether to proceed on the journey to stopping smoking and other addictions or to return to your familiar world of smoking and addiction. If you choose to proceed, you will spend Weeks Three and Four planning how you will abstain from Day One of Week Five. After that, you target 'sobriety' from nicotine, a process through which you gain or regain freedom, fullness and good fortune, as you make your own luck doing what you were born to do.

One last thing about crossing this threshold: do not leave open any possibility of return. Do not think 'I will quit smoking, but I might have just one in a crisis or at a wedding, or if I suffered a bereavement, lost my job or my marriage broke up.'

Burn your bridges. Proceed with hope. In crossing this threshold, you are deciding that you will never come back.

Crossing Your First Threshold: An Exercise

You may fear crossing the threshold from smoker to non-smoker. Recall a time in your life when you stood at the brink of making a significant change that you are now glad you took. It might have involved leaving home, electing to do a course of training or study, taking or leaving a job, emigrating, joining or leaving an organisation, ending a relationship, getting married, having a child, taking out a mortgage.

In your journal, write down how you felt before you crossed that threshold. What were your fears? Say what you were afraid of. What thought, belief or feeling persuaded you to cross the threshold despite your fears? What did you gain by crossing that threshold? What would your older, experienced self, looking back, say to your younger self as you considered crossing that threshold? You might like to share the fruits of this reflection with your sponsor.

Ask for Help

You were born probably with the assistance of a doctor and/or midwife, to say nothing of the labour of your mother. You did not have to do it on your own. Look again at the 'Crossing Your First Threshold' exercise above and the example from your past that you reflected on. If you accept that the universe itself supported you when you crossed that threshold, write down ways in which you were helped.

Write in your journal any seeming coincidences or events that contributed to your crossing that threshold. Julia Cameron in *The Artist's Way* talks of 'synchronicity' or serendipity, seemingly unrelated events which conspired, as it were, to nudge you towards something important. If you believe, with Shakespeare, that a hidden destiny guides our ends, what circumstances may now be leading you or aiding you to proceed with this major life change of leaving behind addictive behaviour? Write down the names of anyone who is helping you to cross this threshold and any events, circumstances or 'coincidences' that are moving you towards stopping smoking for good and fulfilling your immense potential.

Ask for help from your higher self that you will proceed towards your potential, unencumbered by any dependencies. Ask that you will do your life's work, freed from any addictions. Ask for help from your sponsor, members of your family, select friends or, if you are doing counselling or therapy, ask for help from these supporters too.

Cry of the Heart: An Exercise

Write a 'prayer' – your cry of the heart. Ask your higher self to help you fulfil your mission and calling. Self-awareness is at the heart of personal growth. The more self-aware you are, the stronger you become. One of the good things about craving is that it is felt in the present moment – just as life can be lived only in the present. So, in composing your prayer, try to write it in the present tense. Let your prayer come from who you are, not from who you would like to be.

Activities for Week Two

1. Last week you wrote your personal mission. How does smoking or any other addiction fit into that picture of your highest aspirations and goals? Does it fit in?

2. How willing are you to change? Do you feel that you need to change? Do you have confidence that you can change your addictive behaviour, with the help of your higher self (the part of you that never became addicted) or God, if you believe in God? Do you intend, as best you can, to continue to work this programme?

3. Look again at your work on 'What I Enjoy about Smoking'. Pick one thing you wrote in that exercise. You could start with the thing you enjoy most about smoking or the greatest benefit you perceive you get from it. In your journal, write down as many ways as you can imagine to achieve a similar benefit *without* smoking. Indeed, your higher self knows far more effective ways of getting the same benefit. You might like to use the table below as a guide for your journal work. When you have filled in one such table for one perceived benefit from smoking, do a similar exercise on a second, third and fourth and so on until you have thought of better ways than smoking that you can reap such a benefit. This exercise takes some time to do, but do not skip it. By the end of it, if you have five main reasons for smoking, you could have fifty better ways of reaping a similar or better benefit – without smoking!

| **Better ways than smoking that I can ....** |
| (Write in the space above one perceived benefit you get from smoking. Below, write down alternative ways that you can achieve a similar or greater benefit.) |
| |
| |
| |
| |
| |
| |
| |
| |

© Joe Armstrong 2004 www.writeway2stopsmoking.com

The following example may help or inspire you in doing this exercise. Some people believe that smoking helps them to concentrate. The sample below suggests ten better ways to concentrate than smoking.

Sample: Better ways than smoking that I can...'CONCENTRATE'
Plan my week.
Prioritise tasks each day and start with the most important.
Ensure my posture and the design of my workstation facilitates optimum concentration.
Set specific, measurable, half-hourly goals.
Take frequent short breaks of stretching or deep breathing relaxation techniques every half-hour.
Go to bed earlier.
Take physical exercise every day.
Declutter my desk.
Remove or reduce aural distractions, e.g. turn off the radio, wear earplugs in noisy office or work where I will not be distracted.
Avoid a heavy meal or alcohol before a time when I need to concentrate.

© Joe Armstrong 2004 www.writeway2stopsmoking.com

4. You can increase your personal motivation for your personal mission and quitting smoking and other addictions simply by completing the following statements. Copy them into your journal or complete them below:

- I see smoking as a problem because...

- Smoking is more of a problem for me than I realised because...

- I'm worried that by smoking I will...

- As a smoker, I feel really concerned that...

- To do my life's work, I need to...

- To quit smoking, I need to...

- To stop acting out other addictions, I need to...

5. Write out the following affirmations in your journal or pocket notebook. Copy each five times and repeat them often.

- I am confident that I can and will stop smoking.

- I can and will live my personal mission to the full.

- I am going to beat this dependency, with the help my higher power.

6. What short and simple thing could you do today that would lead you in the direction of fulfilling your personal potential? Do it.

7. Be sure to take some physical exercise every day, or at least three to four times this week and every week. Consult your doctor first if you have a medical condition before embarking on any new physical exercise routine.

8. Check that there are no circumstances remaining in your mind under which you would consider going back to smoking after Day One of Week Five.

9. Schedule a phone call, email or short meeting with your sponsor to discuss your experience of the programme this week. In particular, tell your sponsor about your crossing of the threshold, that is, your decision to proceed towards quitting smoking and other addictions. You might like to tell your sponsor your prime motivation for proceeding to kick the habit and possibly share your work on any of the activities above.

Week Two Review

1. Did you write your morning journal every morning? Have you found it helped you become more self-aware? Did it bring up any insights for you?

2. Did you take your congé? Did you enjoy it? Describe how you felt.

3. Do you feel closer to living your personal mission? Did anything happen during the week that encouraged you to further pursue your goal of stopping smoking and any other addictions? Did any seeming coincidences happen during the week to move you closer to fulfilling your personal mission? Write down what happened and how it could help you achieve your goals.

Self-belief

This week we dare to believe in ourselves. We tap into the innate energy of our higher self, the self we are deep down, the self we can manifest more and more, the self that is not addicted to nicotine or anything else. We grow in awareness of our smoking habits. We keep smoking but note where and when we smoke, who we smoke with and how we're feeling when we reach for tobacco or other addictions. We look at simple relaxation techniques. We explore resistance and consider the support you can experience while pursuing your objective of recovering from all addictions. We see that thought precedes action, in quitting smoking as in everything else you've achieved in life.

Confidence in Your Personal Mission

Self-belief is at times an act of blind faith. You have no guarantee that you have interpreted your mission correctly. But you write your morning journal and, by doing so, your conviction deepens that you are doing what you were born to do. If you are not yet doing your life's work, you are taking steps towards doing so. You have consulted with a career analyst if needs be about what career to pursue (regardless of your age!), or with careers advisers at school or college. You have discerned, or you are in the process of discerning, a new direction for your life. Or you keep on your current path, more confident than ever that it is the right one for you, and you do so with a higher and more satisfying level of personal engagement. You are willing to take calculated risks to see your dreams come true. You know that life is short, too short to waste on anything other than daring to be you, enjoying yourself and fulfilling your life's work. You are listening as you express yourself in your journal. You dare to believe in your gut expression of your emerging self. You have written your personal mission for this stage of your life. You know what you're about and have a growing sense of your singular gift or blessing to the world.

Self-belief: An Exercise

Write in your journal a short statement beginning 'I believe in myself...' You might like to include that you believe in your skills, talents, hunches and intuition. Incorporate a current project or goal that you are working on. Read it aloud. Then copy what you have written onto a card and display it where you will see it often. Read it aloud every day.

Your Affirmations as a Bookmark: An Exercise

In Week One, you wrote your personal affirmations, having translated them from negative self-talk. Find a piece of card and copy your personal affirmations onto it. Use it as a bookmark in your journal. When your current journal is full, use this affirmations bookmark in your new journal. Continue to choose some affirmations every day and write them out a number of times at the end of your morning journal, including some of the affirmations presented in Week One to complement your own. When you have copied out your affirmations and your selection from those presented in Week One, choose the one that most appeals to you right now and write it out five times in your journal. Don't skip this! If you 'hear' any negative self-talk as you write your affirmations, translate such blocks to your personal fulfilment into new affirmations, as before.

Personal Mission and Quitting Smoking

Quitting smoking remains a challenge you face in order more fully to live your personal mission. If you focus on the purpose for which you were sent into this world, on fulfilling your life's work and becoming more fully yourself, you increase your chances of successfully moving on from acting out this, and other, addictions. Yours is a personal trail of quitting smoking. When you find the nicotine-dependent part of you reacting against the part of you that believes in your personal mission and in your call to leave addictive behaviour behind, express, as before, both parts of you in your journal. Just because you have continued with the programme and crossed the threshold at the end of Week Two and decided to give up smoking does not mean that the nicotine-dependent part of you has vanished. But you know this. And you know that the addicted part of you will continue to attempt to undermine your self-belief and your decision to kick the habit.

Meeting your Doctor

Do not feel embarrassed about meeting with your doctor to discuss your plan to stop smoking. Tell your doctor how many cigarettes you smoke a day. Ask him or her to advise you on the most appropriate smoking cessation product for your pattern of smoking and your health profile. New products are coming on the market all the time, and there are already excellent aids available such as gum, patches, tablets, inhalers and medication (see below). Be sure to follow your doctor's instructions carefully. If pride urges you to try to go 'cold turkey' – without any nicotine replacement products (NRT) or medication – know that you will thereby significantly reduce your likelihood of success. Indeed, clinical trials have shown that NRT doubles your chance of successfully quitting smoking. The woman with the broken leg needs a crutch until she is strong enough to walk unaided. It is much more difficult to break the smoking habit and addiction than for a broken leg to heal!

Treatment Options

Products currently on the market include patches, gum, inhaler, microtab, lozenges and Zyban. As with all medicines, *Always read the instructions carefully before you use any nicotine replacement product or medication.* Talk to your doctor or pharmacist about any possible side effects. Patches, gum and the inhaler are usually taken for, or up to, a 12-week period. The microtab and lozenges tend to be taken for at least 12 weeks, followed by a gradual reduction. Zyban is taken for seven to nine weeks. Unlike other products, you start taking Zyban for eight to 14 days *before* your Quit Date, hence the importance of seeing your doctor *early* this week, in case your doctor prescribes it for you. See Appendix A for a table showing the dosage, advantages and disadvantages of each product. A brief summary of each product follows below.

Patch

Used if you are moderately dependent on nicotine, the patch roughly doubles your chances of success, especially if used with *WW2SS* or similar programmes. The 24-hour patch comes in three strengths, 21 mg, 14 mg and 7 mg. The 16-hour patch is available in 15 mg, 10 mg and 5 mg. More heavily addicted smokers start off with stronger patches. They are easy to use and are designed to give the correct dose. The 24-hour patch makes early morning cravings easier to handle. If you use patches, you begin them on your Quit Day.

Gum

You are meant to 'park' the gum between your cheek and gum having chewed it for a while. Heavy smokers should use the 4mg version, while the 2mg product can help lighter smokers. You might use 10 to 15 pieces of gum a day, with each piece lasting about half an hour. It can provide emergency aid when you have an acute craving. They come in different flavours. Their absorption is hindered by acidic liquids, such as coffee, juices or soft drinks.

Inhaler

The inhaler is good for people with a moderate dependency on nicotine, that is, who smoke between 10 and 20 cigarettes per day. If you like gesticulating with your hands, the inhaler might suit you too. A cartridge lasts about 20 minutes. It's important to change it after that as it ceases to be effective, even though you will still taste the nicotine. Use between six and 12 cartridges a day.

Microtab

Ideal for heavy smokers, you can use up to two tablets per hour, which dissolve in the mouth. They provide a quick release of nicotine into the body. Heavy smokers might use 16 to 24 per day, with lighter smokers using eight to 12 per day.

Lozenge

Try to keep to a fixed schedule if using lozenges, such as taking one lozenge every one or two hours. You suck the lozenge until you notice a 'spicy' taste. Place the lozenge between the gum and the inside of the cheek so that nicotine can be absorbed. Wait until the taste fades and suck again. Place the lozenge in different parts of the cheek. As with nicotine gum, nicotine absorption is hindered by consuming acidic drinks.

Zyban (Bupropion)

Smokers take a 150mg tablet for six days. Thereafter, two tablets are taken for six to eight weeks. You start taking it a week to a fortnight before your Quit Date, hence the recommendation to see your doctor early this week in case it is prescribed for you so that you will be on schedule for your Quit Date on Day One of Week Five. Your doctor will not prescribe Zyban if you have any history of, or predisposition towards, seizures. Neither will you be prescribed it if you are pregnant or breastfeeding. Other contraindications include alcohol abuse or being on certain other drugs at the same time, such as insulin for diabetics. As with all medicines, tell your doctor if you have any adverse reactions.

Varenicline

This medication works on neurological mechanisms in the body. It fools the brain into thinking it has received nicotine and so reduces cravings. Yet, unlike smoking, it doesn't lead to craving. It is the first medication specifically designed to help smokers regain control over nicotine, given that Zyban began its life as an antidepressant.

Doctor and Depression

Nicotine is a mood-altering substance. The healthy person does not need substances to cope with their needs. Make it your goal, insofar as it lies within your power, to manage your moods maturely, without altering them artificially. If you fear that you will not be able to cope with moods of depression or sadness without cigarettes, or in the withdrawal phase from other addictions, discuss this with your doctor. Your doctor could counsel, prescribe or refer you to a therapist or addiction clinic, depending on the nature of your other addictions.

Triggers: Times, People, Places, Moods

This week, the first of two weeks of planning how you will stop smoking, you need to become aware of your 'smoking triggers'. A trigger is like a switch in your head that, once turned, usually results in your smoking a cigarette. Become aware of your triggers throughout this week by taking a few seconds each time before lighting up. In this space between reaching for tobacco and actually smoking, write down the time, where you are, who you are with, and what your mood is. Also record to what extent you are even *aware* that you are smoking. If you can, record if your mood changes after you smoke. You can do this in your pocket notebook, which is probably no bigger than a pack of cigarettes, or you can photocopy the Smoking Log template opposite and use it instead.

When you have gathered that information by the end of this week, you will be in a better position to know the specific immediate challenges you will face when you quit. You will have the information you need, so that in Week Four you can put together detailed plans for how you will handle each smoking-associated trigger. Edwin B. Fisher, in his excellent book 7 *Steps to a Smoke-Free Life*, endorsed by the American Lung Foundation, suggests that you might also record how badly you felt you needed each cigarette.

Smoking Log: An Exercise

For 24 hours from this minute, track each cigarette you smoke (or each time you reach for your pipe or cigar). Use a pocket notebook or a photocopy of the smoking log below. If you insert it into your cigarette box make sure not to discard it when the pack is empty! Copy the column headings below into your notebook, ideally working from the back page. That way it will not get in the way of anything else you want to write in your notebook. You might find it best to write the column headings across the side to give you more space to write.

In the first column write down the time you smoke each cigarette. The second column records who you are with or talking to, including on the phone, when you smoke. If nobody is with you, simply write 'Alone'. You record where you are at the time of smoking in the next column. In the fourth column, write down your mood or feelings before and after you smoke, such as 'stressed' or 'happy'. If your mood or feelings do not change, simply record 'Same' in the 'After' column. The last column records your level of self-awareness at the moment you chose to light up and while you smoked. Sometimes you might find yourself smoking without being conscious of having chosen to do so. Your low self-awareness may persist while smoking the cigarette, not really tasting or enjoying it. You may stub it out hardly realising you were smoking at all. For other cigarettes smoked you might find a high level of awareness when you decide to smoke. You might go on to really enjoy that cigarette, inhaling every breath deeply and feeling that you really needed it. Write a separate entry for each cigarette smoked and make sure to carry the notebook, card or template (and a pen!) with you for the next 24 hours.

Smoking Log

Time	People	Place	Mood/Feeling		Awareness High/Mid/ Low
			Before	After	

© Joe Armstrong 2004 www.writeway2stopsmoking.com

When you have done that exercise, repeat it for each day this week. If you think keeping the log for a week seems daunting, just take it a day at a time. By the end of this week, you will have to hand invaluable information which you will use next week to plan strategies for your Quit Day on Day One of Week Five and beyond.

Smoking Log: Analysis

Twenty-four hours from now you will have a personal record of one day's smoking. Look at the times when you smoked and the times when you did not smoke. Rather than focusing only on the times you did smoke, look also at the times you did not smoke. What did you do during these smoke-free times? Did you find any of them easy to enjoy without cigarettes, cigars or the pipe? Were there times when you did not even think about smoking? Where were your thoughts during these times? Were you were happy without cigarettes?

Notice any pattern in the 'People' column. Are there people you always or usually smoke with? Can you imagine being in their company and not smoking? Can you imagine them offering you a cigarette and you replying in a confident tone that neither needs to explain nor justify itself: 'No thanks. I've quit.' Notice the number of cigarettes you smoke alone and any cigarettes you smoke in company when others are not smoking. Become aware of any people or places you absent yourself from in order to smoke. Are there any places where you always smoke or places where you never smoke? Imagine what it would be like to be in a place where you have always smoked but where you will not smoke anymore.

Look at the 'Mood' column. Do you tend to respond to certain moods by smoking? What is, or would it be like, to experience that mood without smoking? Does smoking change certain moods? If so, what moods seem to change by smoking? Does smoking reinforce certain moods? If so, which moods?

By the end of this week you can look at your completed 'Awareness' columns and highlight with a circle the cigarettes you chose to smoke and enjoyed with high self-awareness. Out of 20 cigarettes, how many did you smoke with high awareness? How many with middle-grade awareness, and how many did you smoke with low awareness? When you stop smoking, you will find the low awareness cigarettes the easiest to cut out and the high awareness cigarettes the most challenging.

Relaxation

It is essential that you develop or enhance daily and weekly ways to relax. Just as you plan your work, you should also schedule periods for relaxation. Already, you have begun to plan for a weekly congé. During that time, you explore new, or revisit old, ways of joy and relaxation. You enjoy a necessary mental break from responsibilities, work and other people.

The chances are that you rely on cigarettes to give you mini-breaks during the day. Just because you quit smoking from Day One of Week Five does not mean you will not need to relax. On the contrary, you will appreciate your continued daily need for short and longer periods of relaxation.

One good thing about smoking is that if you inhale, you enjoy the experience of deep breathing. True, what you inhale is poisoning you. But the experience of deep breathing is one that you can go on enjoying after you quit smoking. There are many breathing techniques you can use to enjoy a three- or five-minute calming break, one of which, alternative nostril breathing, you will read about below. Just as you are used to scheduling smoking breaks, you can begin to develop the habit of planned relaxation breaks. A selection of short relaxation activities is presented below.

Alternate Nostril Breathing

This is a simple exercise that has a remarkably calming effect. You simply cover your left nostril with a finger, exhale through your right nostril, and then inhale through the right nostril. Now cover the right and exhale through the left nostril. Inhale through the left and exhale through the right, repeating the process for three to five minutes. This exercise slows down your breathing and facilitates deep abdominal breathing and the expansion of the lungs. You can do it almost anywhere inconspicuously. But even if someone does see it, it is much less ridiculous and a lot more natural, effective and healthy than smoking. Be careful if you feel a bit dizzy after it — all that deep, satisfying breathing without the acrid cocktail of smoking can surprise your brain with more oxygen than you're used to. Alternate nostril breathing has been called the natural sedative. It's an immediate and effective calming technique to use before an interview, speaking in public or to counterbalance anything likely to induce anxiety.

Body Awareness

Simply sitting comfortably and becoming aware of the feel of your feet, legs, buttocks, back, chest, shoulders, arms, hands, neck, head and face can have a remarkably calming effect. You can start by tensing and releasing the muscles in your right foot, gradually working your way around each body part. Alternatively, you can become aware of the touch of your clothing, footwear or the pull of gravity and so awaken to the feel of each body part. Ten minutes doing this simple body awareness exercise can be very relaxing.

Yoga

There are many short yoga exercises you can do almost anywhere to help you relax during a three- to five-minute break. Consider taking a yoga class to learn specific exercises for relaxation. If you find it hard to still your mind, yoga can help because the physical poses it employs complement its mental and spiritual disciplines. It is active relaxation, not unlike the activity of smoking, which you probably associate with relaxation. And, as with smoking, breathing is at the heart of its practice.

Walking or Running on the Spot

If you work alone but do not have the time or opportunity to go out for a short walk – which is itself a great way to relax, clear the head and feel better mentally and physically – you can enjoy a three- to five-minute cardiovascular workout by walking on the spot. Let it be a brisk 'walk', raising your arms and knees high; or, if your feel up to it, you can 'run' or march. This simple exercise will increase your heartbeat and intensify your breathing, and you enjoy the added benefit of working the major muscles and joints in your arms, legs and back. It can enhance your mood, warm you up on a cool day, and help you to feel invigorated and confident. You can do it in any room. You avoid the hassle of getting kit together to go out for a jog and you can do it regardless of the weather.

Calculated Risks

If you suspect that a major change will be required to achieve lifestyle balance and fulfil your personal vocation in life, do not worry about 'what you are to eat or how you are to be clothed'. If you are attuned to your personal mission, trust that you already have everything that you need. Do not be tempted to stay in a job, relationship or situation that is not in keeping with your higher calling, or who you are deep down. You may need to consider taking a calculated risk to get you to where you need to be.

Calculated Risks: An Exercise

Think of a time when you took a calculated, healthy risk. In your journal, or in the space provided, write down the risk you took. What fears did you have before taking it? How did you grow as a person by taking that risk? Can you think of five examples of calculated risks you took and name the fears you overcame? The table that follows gives a guide to help you complete this exercise, together with an example to get you going. Fill it in here or in your journal, as you prefer.

Calculated Risks Taken

Calculated Risk Taken	Fears Beforehand	My Growth by Taking Risk
Example: I wanted to see if I could earn my living as a landscape gardener and I left a permanent, pensionable job to go for it.	Financial fears. Fear of failure. Fear of the unknown.	Discovered new talents. Confirmed my vocation. Earned more than previously. Loved being my own boss. Pride in my achievements.
1.		
2.		
3.		

© Joe Armstrong 2004 www.writeway2stopsmoking.com

Self-belief: An Exercise

Write in your journal your own arguments for believing in yourself and in your ability to quit smoking for good.

Resistance

Expect to experience resistance this week. You may also experience lack of support from some people, but you will cope with that more easily than resistance from within yourself.

When you start to believe in yourself and in your life's work and form the view that stopping smoking will help you to fulfil your potential, the part of you that is dependent on nicotine and that does not want you to believe in yourself will protest. This part of you wants the status quo to persist and resists change.

We saw earlier the scientific support for following a systematic programme in recovering from any addiction. You know that breaking free from addictive behaviour can be as simple as doing the next thing on your plan. In Weeks One and Two, you analysed your smoking addiction and you decided you wanted done with it (or you wouldn't still be reading). Of course, it is one thing to analyse a problem and come up with a plan, and a different thing to put that plan into practice. Planning is one thing. Doing is another. While monitoring your smoking patterns this week, you have already begun to put in place your personal plan for quitting. You will conclude the planning phase at the end of next week, in time for Quit Day at the start of Week Five. But already you are into the doing or implementation phase in certain regards, such as your commitment to going to bed earlier, eating healthily, writing your morning journal and taking your weekly congé.

You can find yourself having planned your exit route from dependency deciding not to take the next practical step, which could be as simple as not going to bed on time. Or, having set your alarm clock, you choose not to get up after all; or you skip your morning journal. Or you decide that you are too busy this week to take your congé. Or you feel awkward about contacting your sponsor.

As an alcoholic taking this course said to me, going back on the booze starts long before the day he finds himself in a pub drinking himself stupid. Decisions he made in his daily life were the ones which led inexorably to his relapse.

Plan Your Week: An Exercise

If you do not already do so, take some time at the start of each week to plan the week ahead. Take a sheet of paper. Construct a grid for your weekly plan based on key words in your mission statement. For instance, if you are in a relationship or have children, these significant others are likely to feature in your mission statement, as, presumably, would you. So write down yourself, your spouse or partner, and the names of your children as columns or rows on your weekly plan (see Sample Weekly Plan opposite). You might also have a heading for friends, your home and for work, paid or voluntary. In each category, what do you want to do over the next week to promote your mission? For instance, under the heading for yourself, you might write down morning journal each day, weekly congé and do some of the activities for the week from *WW2SS*. As already mentioned, you are recommended to make an appointment with your doctor, ideally for early this week (the section on Zyban earlier in this chapter explains why). Another important task under the same category for this week is, of course, to track your smoking patterns in your smoking log. It's also recommended that you make an appointment with your dentist to have your teeth cleaned close to, or soon after, your Quit Date.

Sample Weekly Plan

Monday 8 April to Sunday 14 April	
Me	Make appointment to see doctor for early this week. Congé.
Spouse	Keep Friday night free for a date. Mind children so spouse can take congé.
Son	Help Bill with his homework. Take to football.
Daughter	Kate's martial arts class. Parent/Teacher meeting.
Friends	Invite Mary over.
Home/Garden	Vacuum and dust. Weed vegetable patch. Pay phone bill.
Work	Complete report.
	Plan Wednesday's meeting.
	Confirm training day.
	Review project.

© Joe Armstrong 2004 www.writeway2stopsmoking.com

Under your heading for spouse, you might include 'Keep Friday night free to watch a video together', or to go out for a meal together or see a movie at the cinema. Or, 'discuss with partner when each of us will take our congé' (I've found that spouses or partners appreciate their congé too!) For each of your children, you might like to record at least one thing you want to do with them, such as 'check out the local pitch 'n putt club' or 'go window shopping together'. Under your heading for 'home', you could specify a bill you need to pay, a fence that needs fixing, a window-cleaner to be telephoned. In other categories, you might name a friend you have not seen for some time under the 'friendship' heading and decide to give him or her a call.

The work heading can be divided into suitable subheadings, detailing what you want to achieve at work in the week ahead. What you write will depend on the nature of your work. Over time, the subheadings you use will change in accordance with your work and the amount of detail you want to put into your weekly plan.

When you have planned your week, check if it is in accordance with your mission statement. Are there any aspects of your mission statement that you are ignoring in the week ahead? For instance, some people find when they do this that whereas they say the most important things in their life are their own health and wellbeing, their spouse or partner and their children, in fact they've planned a week more or less totally focused on work. Nothing wrong with work, of course, but the plan can be a useful snapshot of whether we are, in fact, living our mission statement. So you might like to adjust your plan if some important element of your personal calling doesn't feature in it. Or if it's lopsided towards any one sector to the detriment of others. Incidentally, at the end of each week, when you are planning the following week, do take a look at what you had intended to do that week. You will rarely have done everything you'd intended to but patterns can emerge. For instance, you might find that the thing that always gets put on the long finger is time spent with your children. You could reflect upon this when writing your morning journal, confronting the week that you've actually lived with what you claim are your highest values. Recognising any discrepancies can motivate you to live your mission more authentically.

Do your plan for the week ahead now, if you haven't yet done so. In this exercise, you are recording *what* you want to do. Next, apportion a status to each activity, such as AAAAA for most important and urgent; AAAA for important but less urgent; AAA for less important and not urgent; AA for things you'd like to do but can wait and A for things that simply aren't that important or urgent. Now that you've listed what you want to do and prioritised each item, take out your diary and decide *when* you are going to do each thing, starting with the most important and working down to the least important. It might be clear to you at this stage that the AA and A items will simply need to wait for another week.

In doing this exercise, be sure to include the tools of your recovery, such as your congé. Remember to be specific. Not 'sometime on Friday' but, for instance, I'll have fun with my higher self on Friday at the leisure centre from 4.30 p.m. to 6.30 p.m.

Daily Plan

Each day, take a sheet of blank paper (or, if you do this exercise often enough, you will develop your own template and could photocopy it to save time each day). Write the day and date and subdivide the page into half-hourly intervals. Write down for each half-hour period what you want to do at that time. Be realistic. Do not try to do too much or you will become disheartened. Build in rest periods, for instance at 11 a.m. and 4 p.m. If possible, plan how you will relax for three- to five-minute mini-breaks at the end of each half-hour, such as by brief yoga exercises, breathing exercises, stretching, a short walk or running on the spot. Schedule in longer periods of physical exercise, such as a walk with the dog, a swim or a 20-minute workout. Make sure you have time set aside for your morning journal, family, meals (including digestion!), relaxation and sleep. Test your daily plan against your mission statement.

Below is a sample daily template. But remember it is only a sample, for one person. The beauty of the daily plan is that you can develop your own personalised template. As with the weekly plan, your daily plan can be a touchstone of your fidelity to your personal mission. It, combined with your weekly plan, is a testament to your lifestyle balance – or lack of it. Ask yourself whether you make time each day to 'visit' all the core aspects of yourself. Do you spend some time, each day, in your mind centre, some time in your body centre, some time attending to your emotions and feelings, and some time cultivating your spirituality? If you don't, you lack lifestyle balance, which is probably a major reason why you are smoking or may have other addictions or compulsions. Note that your morning journal can help readjust your priorities towards your personal mission and realign your daily activities. It is better to write your daily plan after your morning pages as it often shifts your priorities back on track towards your higher calling. The journal may be the only time in the day that you attend to your feelings, moods, values, priorities and spirituality. Another very important moment is to take even one minute at the end of the day to become thankful for the blessings of the day. If you write even five things down for which you are thankful, it can work on your consciousness to change depression into gratefulness, glumness into joy, misery into beatitude.

Sample Daily Plan

Day:	Date:	Year: 20__	
Time	**What**	**Done**	**Reward**
6 a.m.	Rise, Morning Journal		
6.30 a.m.	Daily plan. Jog/workout		
7 a.m.	Shower, Dress		

Sample Daily Plan (continued)

Day:	Date:	Year: 20__	
Time	**What**	**Done**	**Reward**
7.30 a.m.	Family Breakfast		
8 a.m.	Car pool/Commute to work		
9 a.m.	Post/emails		
9.30 a.m.	Work/meetings		
10 a.m.	Work/meetings		
10.30 a.m.	Work/meetings		
11 a.m.	Break/relax		
11.30 a.m.	Work/meetings		
Noon	Work/meetings		
12.30 p.m.	Physical exercise		
1 p.m.	Lunch		
1.30 p.m.	Siesta/'power nap'		
2 p.m.	Work/meetings		
2.30 p.m.	Work/meetings		
3 p.m.	Work/meetings		
3.30 p.m.	Work/meetings		
4 p.m.	Break/fresh air		
4.30 p.m.	Work/meetings		
5 p.m.	Commute home		
5.30 p.m.	Prepare meal		
6 p.m.	Family meal/wash up		
7 p.m.	Family fun/activity/relax		
8 p.m.	Relax with spouse/partner/call friends		
9 p.m.	Relax with spouse/partner/friends		
10 p.m.	Gratitude journal. Bed		

Belief in Your Body and Withdrawal Symptoms

One of the things that can keep you back from believing you can stop smoking is a misapprehension about withdrawal symptoms. Certainly, they can be distressing, although they are often worse in the anticipation than in reality. It matters how you *think* about withdrawal symptoms. If you think positively about them, you could conceivably *welcome* them, even be *thankful* for them, rather than dreading them.

Do you have faith in your body, in the wisdom of your body and in your capacity to heal yourself? Cigarettes have poisoned you, probably for many years. For some of you, you have been poisoning yourself for decades. When you stop smoking, you allow your body to begin a natural process of cleansing itself. For instance, you might develop a cough. This is your body's way of clearing out the harmful substances that have accumulated in your lungs. If you develop such a cough, be grateful for it because with each cough you are getting better. Any cough that you might develop will usually last only a few days or weeks but in some cases it could last for several months. Again, be grateful for your lungs' natural capacity to undo much of the harm of smoking. The cough will go away and, when it does, you will be the healthier for it. If you are concerned about your cough, or you feel it's going on too long, consult your doctor.

Smoking can be a form of self-forgetfulness, whereas you are called to self-awareness and self-knowledge. You are called to emerge as the strong person that you were born to be in the theatre of life, playing your distinctive role, for which nobody else can play understudy. Insofar as you may experience transitory physical discomforts while stopping smoking, know that, apart from healing you, such symptoms can awaken you to the marvel of your body. Let's face it, for years you have probably taken your body for granted. You have abused it, knowingly. Your only ticket for staying longer on this planet is your body. You are your body. In abusing it, you have damaged yourself. Now is a time of healing, a time when you can forgive yourself for the harm you have done to your wonderful body. The only way you can be yourself and do your life's work is in and through your body. If you are distressed by any symptom and have checked with your doctor that nothing else is wrong, say to yourself: 'Time will take this away.' And it will. Sooner than you think. Have faith in yourself, and in your body's ability to heal. We will take a closer look at withdrawal symptoms in Weeks Four and Five.

Transcendent Support

You are supported in your desire and intention to quit smoking and any other addiction not only by your conscious self but by your subconscious. And by what Jungian psychologists call the collective unconscious. If you are a person of faith, the saints and holy ones who have gone before you, including your loved ones faithfully departed, are willing you on, cheering and roaring for your success. They know you can do it. The forces of creation and healing are on your side. You were born with a purpose. We sing our best songs when we are attuned to that purpose. There is no way under God's heaven that you were born to smoke. Creation does not will its own destruction. In your high intention now to leave behind addictive behaviour, helpers beyond your knowing are supporting you. As well, of course, as those on earth! Whatever trials you may experience in the weeks ahead, know that you are protected from within and without. You will always find and be sustained by inner and outer sources of practical help.

Stopping smoking and other addictions to live your personal mission to the full is a practical and spiritual journey. You will discover untapped energies within yourself which defend and aid you. Seeming coincidences will occur to confirm you in your higher purpose, give you heart and show you the way. Be humble enough to accept these 'coincidences', as significant moments along the way of your recovery. Joseph Campbell in *The Hero with a Thousand Faces* talks of helpers, human and divine, sent to aid your high adventure. He speaks too of amulets received to strengthen you, such as a stone or ring (or a humble nicotine patch!) to offer strength and gladden your heart as you proceed on your high mission to fulfil your calling.

Do not despise or look down upon anyone's help for, as Christ said, he who is not against you is with you. The passage out of the constricted place of dependency can seem long and arduous. Many monsters, inner and outer, will assuredly lie in your path. It will not be easy. But, like Frodo in *The Lord of the Rings*, at no time will the challenge facing you be beyond you, with the help of your wit and those sent to help you.

Only you can make the decision to proceed further. That is your dignity. By advancing, you accept that, metaphorically, you may at times feel crushed, cut, torn or overwhelmed. But you can go forward with confidence, guided by your higher self to fulfil your mission, leaving behind addictive thinking and behaviour for good. Follow the personal discipline of going to bed early, waking early and writing your journal. Take each congé. Read the chapters. Do the activities. Write your personal affirmations. Repeat them daily. Talk to your sponsor. And regularly use the technique outlined in the following exercise.

Thinking like a Non-smoker: An Exercise

Thought precedes action. Even though you are to continue to smoke until Week Five, you can already start to think as if you have quit. Think of how good it feels not to have your tongue coated with smoke. Yes, you can think this even while you smoke a cigarette. Think what if feels like for your lungs to be free from tar. Think what it is like for your body to have evacuated tobacco-related carcinogens and to feel so well physically, mentally and spiritually. Think of how great it is to have regained self-control, with the help of your higher self. Think how much you enjoy acting in a non-addictive way. Think how good it feels to know you can cope with problems without needing recourse to cigarettes or other dependencies. Enjoy the sensation of living your personal mission to the full and of having moved on from addictive thinking and behaviour. Savour these thoughts, enjoy them and know that by Day One of Week Five your actions will be in accordance with them.

Activities for Week Three

1. Make that appointment with your doctor, ideally ensuring that the consultation takes place *early this* week and certainly in advance of your Quit Date on Day One of Week Five. Tell your doctor you are taking this programme. Your doctor can discuss nicotine replacement therapy and other treatment options with you. There are so many products out there that it can be confusing and your doctor can advise you about the most appropriate one for you in light of your medical condition and smoking patterns. You could also ask the doctor to give you a general medical check-up and seek advice, if you have not already done so, about a physical exercise schedule appropriate for your age and state of health. If you have particular problems with other addictions, your doctor should be able to put you in touch with accredited counselling or therapy services. Your doctor may also know of any local support groups such as Alcoholics Anonymous which may be of help to you.

2. Make an appointment with your dentist. If possible, have your teeth professionally cleaned on or soon after your Quit Date. It's a very good time to have a dental check-up, given that you are

going to give such a boost to your oral health, appearance and aura by stopping smoking.

3.   What are the three proudest achievements of your life to date? Write about them in your journal.

4.   What would you love to achieve in the next five years? What simple, practical thing can you do this week that will move you closer to your goal? Decide when you will do it and just do it.

5.   Visualisation: What would it feel like to fulfil yourself completely? What would you be doing? How would you think, feel, decide and act? Make the picture as vivid as possible. Write about it in your journal or, if you prefer, draw or paint a picture. Alternatively, make a collage of pictures culled from old magazines, evoking as well as you can what you imagine fulfilling yourself completely would feel like.

6.   Write a letter to your higher power, asking for help as you progress further towards living your personal mission to the full, and leaving behind addictive thinking and behaviour along the way. Be thankful for the supports you already receive, known and unknown. Thank your higher power for the people who are assisting you in your aims and goals. You might regard this as a prayer, invoking the help of your higher power to help you create the work you were sent to do and to gain the courage to take the next step you are being asked to take.

7.   Be sure to take physical exercise this week, and some exercise every day. Breathe in fresh air, even if it is only by opening your window and breathing deeply for three minutes. Make time for five-minute periods for stretching, yoga or body awareness.

8.   Monitor how often you mentally step out of tasks at work or at home for moments of self-awareness. It might mean stopping what you are engaged in, doing the body awareness exercise presented in this chapter or, if you are driving, reducing your speed by 10 per cent.

9.   Look at your mission statement. Test whether you are living it today. For instance, if in your mission statement you have said that a positive relationship with your spouse and children is central to your personal mission and yet today you have spent, or intend to spend, very little time with them, what can you do about that? If you smoke in the presence of your children, what kind of modelling is that for them? If you smoke behind their backs, what are you teaching them? By smoking, they are much more likely to smoke too, apart at all from the damage being done to their health by inhaling your smoke. And as a recent official EU study showed, merely opening windows or even installing high-tech ventilation systems do not work. They do not remove the threat to other people.

10. Remember to meet or talk to your sponsor to discuss your progress. Contact a friend who will nurture you.

Review of Week Three

1. Did you do your morning journal every day last week? What was it like for you?

2. Did you take your congé? What did you do? Did you enjoy it? Did you avoid smoking during it?

3. Did you see your doctor to discuss nicotine replacement therapy and other options? If you have had the consultation already, have you decided to use nicotine replacement therapy or other treatments? If you have decided, under medical advice, to use Zyban, have you started taking it yet? If you are going to use nicotine replacement therapy, have you been to the pharmacist to stock up on your chosen product?

4. Did you arrange to see your dentist?

5. Did you meet or speak with your sponsor? Say how that has helped you.

6. Have any seeming coincidences happened in the last week to encourage you in your pursuit of your mission statement? If you noticed anything, write down what happened and how it strengthened you.

WEEK

4

Discovery

This week you continue to plan for how you will stop smoking and acting out other addictions from Day One of Week Five. You will start to eliminate some cigarettes this week. A simple review of your higher goals will strengthen your motivation. We look at withdrawal symptoms so you know what to expect and we suggest how to think positively about them. The technique of visualisation is explained to help you plan how to manage situations, places, and moods without resorting to smoking from next week. By the end of this week you will have discarded all smoking paraphernalia from your home and work environment. We'll take a look at personal stress management, learn from any previous relapses, and a smoking meditation is offered.

Higher Goals

Look again at your mission statement. How are you doing in implementing it? Have you begun to take steps towards your aims and goals? We know it's hard to develop new healthy habits, just as it is hard to break bad ones. But how are you doing on your morning journal? Are you keeping it everyday? Or has the practice not worked for you yet. If it hasn't, maybe you're trying to write someone else's journal. Write your own one. Do it *your* way. But please *do* it. Quitting smoking in a sense is an exterior thing. Your morning journal is an interior thing. Write the forbidden things. Write the things you feel unable to say to people. Express your feelings. Plan your day. Do with it what you will but do it! The morning journal is the lifeblood of this approach to living your life and giving cigarettes the boot. If you find yourself resisting writing it, know that you are reluctant to hear *yourself*. But where else can you run? Wherever you go you are *thinking*, and the journal is simply writing down what you are thinking in the here and now. It's an act of respect for yourself. It's a way your higher self can increase, while your addictive self decreases. If you do not have time for it, you do not have time for yourself. If you will not make time for it, you will not make time for yourself. What do you fear might emerge if you let your real thoughts come out on the page? If you don't write them, the fear travels with you. Face your singularity with you pen and rejoice in it!

When tempted to smoke next week, choose your higher goals over the immediate gratification of a cigarette. For instance, decide whether you will choose the higher pleasure of increased self-esteem, greater confidence and enhanced personal discipline over the transitory pleasure of a cigarette. If you act out your addiction, you will have less personal and spiritual energy to relate with other people for the following 24 hours. The choice to abstain in any given moment from acting out an addiction constitutes a decision in favour of family, colleagues and self. The quality of your relationship with yourself and others will be tangibly different by choosing to abstain. Your choice isn't so much not to smoke or not to indulge in another addiction. It is rather a choice in favour of the vitality that comes from being true to your calling, which will enable you to be of greater service to others. In choosing not to smoke, you are trusting in your personal mission. You are taking a choice in the direction of realising your freedom, fulfilment and good fortune.

Belly of the Whale

This week, you might compare yourself to Jonah in the belly of the whale, an image used by Joseph Campbell in *The Hero with a Thousand Faces* to describe an important experience of the hero – and *you* are the hero here. You find yourself in a place of confinement and, let's face it, addictions confine and reduce your life considerably. But you're also in a place of confinement in another sense, not unlike when you were in your mother's womb. You fear life beyond the womb. You possibly cannot imagine a whole different existence played out without the familiar environment of smoking, the paraphernalia of smoking, the social scene of smoking, and the way you cope with your feelings by smoking. Of course, if the babe in the womb were to stay there, the womb would eventually threaten its very life.

But now, in a sense, you can prepare yourself for life beyond your present confinement. As you progress towards your new birth next week beyond thinking and acting like an addict, use this time well to prepare for your smokefree life that beckons. This week you may realise, if you don't already, that your higher self who is emerging has no need for addictive thinking or behaviour. Not unlike a monk in a cell, you can discover who you are and become more yourself. Seek solitude. Your passage to a life beyond acting out addictions is like a babe in the womb choosing to go down the birth canal. You were here before. That first birth was much harder than the one you now face. You can do it again. When the waters break, go down that passage. Beyond lies a life of manifold opportunity.

Change

Imagine you are helping someone else to get over an addiction. Carl Rogers, writing about how therapists can best help clients with addictions, said that a counsellor who is empathetic, warm and genuine provides the best environment for the addict to heal him or herself. Treat yourself as he described and you will more readily facilitate your own natural ability to break this addiction. Get behind your own skin. That's why the journal is so important. In it you listen empathetically to yourself in a non-judgemental way, allowing yourself to open up on the page. In your journal, your real life will be expressed; not the life you feel you 'should' be living. Renowned addiction experts William R. Miller and Stephen Rollnick show in *Motivational Interviewing: Preparing People to Change Addictive Behaviour* that empathy is crucial to changing addictive behaviour. Rather than blaming yourself, accept that you have become addicted to smoking and any other addiction. A good therapist would try to understand your feelings and thoughts non-judgementally, without criticising you or blaming you. As Miller and Rollnick say, empathetic "acceptance of people *as they are* seems to free them to change". This is also true for our attitude to ourselves. So accept what you write in your journal. Do not censor it, judge it or criticise it. That way, you are less likely to consider not smoking as a deprivation. You will come to a position, if you are not there already, where you have grown beyond the phase of your life where you acted out addictive thinking and you discover a far greater joy, serenity and exhilaration in your life without smoking.

Eliminate Important Cigarettes This Week

Last week you observed and recorded your smoking habit. You probably realised or confirmed that often you smoke when you are hardly even aware that you *are* smoking. At other times, you are much more self-aware of what you are doing. The American Lung Foundation suggests in its book by Edwin B. Fisher *7 Steps to a Smoke-Free Life* that you eliminate those cigarettes that you *always* smoke in certain situations, such as if you always smoke with a coffee or while talking on the phone. Choose to eliminate these cigarettes *this week*. By doing so, you break the association between certain activities and smoking.

Smoke with Total Awareness

B. Jack Gebhardt suggests an alternative approach in his intriguing and insightful book *The Enlightened Smoker's Guide to Quitting*, first mentioned in Week One. He suggests that if you smoke with total awareness, attending to and enjoying every last detail of the activity of smoking, even seeing it as a divine act, the whole phenomenon of smoking will strike you as so absurd that you may well stop it with relative ease.

Smoke with Total Awareness: An Exercise

Try to smoke a cigarette with complete awareness. Do it as you might a sacred act. Touch the cigarette with love. Smell it. See God in the tobacco ritual you are enacting. Strike the match or lighter with thanksgiving. Inhale the scent of sulphur or of the petrol from the struck lighter. Savour the scent of the lit cigarette. Taste it with every taste bud of which you can become aware, lingeringly. Inhale the smoke into your lungs as deeply you would the breath of life. Let the smoke rest inside you and exhale, slowly, meditatively.

Do likewise with each inhalation. Watch no telly. Read no book. Talk to no one. Commit your complete awareness to the act of smoking as to a sacrament, a meeting point, with Divinity. Make this cigarette your most aware smoke ever. When you are finished, slowly extinguish the cigarette, again with total attentiveness, conscious of the nicotine now in your bloodstream and the aftertaste in your mouth.

Bhagwan Shree Rajneesh suggests in Osho's *Meditation: The First and Last Freedom* that if you smoke with complete awareness "soon you will see the whole stupidity of it".

Faith

Prayer can remind you of the bigger picture. You may draw strength from the belief that you are supported by God – God within you, the creator God or your Higher Power. It might be a sense of your own best self willing you to choose wisely in this moment, desiring you to be freed of all addictions and dependencies, wanting you to stand up on your own two feet as you are. If you believe in God, ask for God's help. If you believe in guardian angels, ask your angel to light and guard, to rule and guide.

If you are a believer, gain strength from the conviction that you were born to be free. Nothing is too great a burden or too great an addiction to keep you from the inner freedom that is rightly yours as a child of God. Claim that freedom. Tell God as you understand him what you want, do what you must do and then have faith that God's strength will aid you.

Visualisation

The technique of visualisation can help you prepare for situations next week in which you would normally smoke. It is an established and proven technique in all sorts of fields of human endeavour, including sports training. The idea is you visualise in advance what will happen. The golfer, for instance, 'sees' the ball go into the hole in his or her imagination and then manifests that visualisation by the perfect putt. Professional runners can visualise their time in advance and look up to see precisely that time as they win their race. Likewise, visualisation is a technique you can use to anticipate situations, feelings, places and moods with which you might normally have smoked in the past. If in your imagination you can 'see' yourself thinking, feeling and acting differently, it can be so. Indeed, anything in the created world was first *thought* or *imagined* before it came into being, whether it is a sportswoman achieving her goal or an alcoholic enjoying a happy and fulfilled life in sobriety.

You can visualise situations in your journal, imagining with your pen the different ways you could think and behave. The more you use the technique of visualisation, the better prepared (literally) you will be to think and act like a non-smoker.

Visualisation: An Exercise

Look back over your smoking log and choose one situation in which you smoked last week. Imagine you go into a similar situation next week, after you've stopped smoking. Bring all your senses to bear on this. 'Hear', in your imagination, the sounds you will hear, 'see' what you will see. Bring your senses of taste, touch and smell in too, so you really feel you're there. Now become aware of how you imagine you will feel in that situation next week when you are not smoking. Visualise what you will do with your hands instead. Imagine how you will respond if anyone asks you why you're not smoking or if they offer you a cigarette. Make it as real as possible. You can, of course, do this exercise in your morning journal.

In your imagination, if you chose to use nicotine replacement products such as a patch or gum have you come prepared? Have you a patch on? Do you have gum in your purse or pocket? Can you visualise yourself holding your own with people who tease or upset you about not smoking? If you imagine being with people you can trust, can you visualise yourself expressing how you feel such as "I'm finding this awkward" or "I'd appreciate your support". Anticipate what you might think, feel and do if others light up. One option is that you can simply leave that place to safeguard your recovery. This can sometimes be the best thing to do if you have an acute craving. Or simply bring to mind that even *intense cravings last only a few minutes*. If you can stick it out for five minutes, you've cracked it. Other suggestions that work are to sip water and to breathe deeply. We look in more detail at coping with cravings later in this chapter.

Feelings

Last week in your smoking log you recorded, amongst other things, how you felt when you smoked. By now you have a record of a range of feelings which you associate with reaching for a cigarette or other tobacco products. You will, of course, continue to feel a wide range of human emotion from next week's Quit Date. Indeed, you may well come more in touch with your feelings. Your challenge will be to feel those feelings *without* reaching for a cigarette. If you feel anxious, lonely, awkward, happy, you are invited to really feel those emotions. Dare to let yourself feel as you really do! The wisdom of the Buddhist tradition would suggest that we experience whatever feeling we may have, whether uncomfortable or pleasant, and say 'This is anxiety' or 'This is loneliness' or 'This is bliss'. Thereby we wake up to the wonder of our existence rather than fleeing from our emotions through craving or compulsion.

So do not worry that you will have nothing to *do* when you're not smoking from Day One of next week – you'll have heaps to do!

Becoming aware of the feelings and thoughts you might be avoiding by smoking will give you lots to be working on. You can write about your feelings in your journal or in your pocket notebook, even if it's only to jot down one word, such as "tense". Or if it's not appropriate to reach for a pen, simply perform that Buddhist detachment exercise described above, namely step back in your mind from the experience, becoming aware of it by saying what it is, such as 'This is tension'. In short, try to become aware of and permit yourself to experience whatever feeling precedes the urge to smoke. Do not be embarrassed about reaching for a pen in public. Is that any more crazy than lighting up? And, depending on your company, it could lead to interesting conversations. So, whether you're alone or with others, write! Or, if needs be, disappear off to a more private place and, if only in a word, commit your pre-smoking feeling to paper.

Now, consider how healthy non-addicts or well-adjusted 'sober' addicts deal with their human emotions. They do not reach for a cigarette, pipe, or other drug. They become aware of how they are feeling, own and accept it and they don't let emotions dictate what they do. Instead, the *responsible* person (the person who is *able* to *respond*) uses emotions as a gateway into self-knowledge. For Socrates, that was the most important thing in life: to know yourself. Imagine yourself dealing with the same feelings six months or a year from now without even thinking of smoking. Can you remember how you dealt with such feelings before you started to get hooked on nicotine?

Feelings: An Exercise

In a private room, visualise yourself in a social situation where you would normally stand and smoke. Now, stand up and practice how to feel comfortable without a cigarette. Let your arms hang loose from your shoulders, falling naturally by your sides. Choose not to put your hands into your pockets or to hold anything in your hand. How does it feel? Do you feel exposed, vulnerable, or awkward? Stay with that feeling! Smoking won't cure it but writing about it in your journal or discussing it with your sponsor or just allowing yourself to feel it in your body is healthy. Stay with the feeling, even for a few minutes. Remember, even the most successful professional radio and television presenters and leading politicians practice their lines and how they will stand or gesticulate in advance. There is nothing false about this. You are simply becoming comfortable in your own skin – without the crutch of a cigarette, cigar or pipe. You can, if you like, substitute another object such as a pen or small stone, if you feel the need to hold something.

Situations

If possible, avoid difficult situations especially in your first few days and weeks following Quit Day. For instance, you could suggest activities with friends that are less likely to involve smoking, such as going to the cinema or a leisure centre or smokefree restaurant instead of a usual haunt where you tend to smoke. Happily, with new enlightened workplace regulations, there are more and more places where you can socialise without coming home reeking of cigarettes. This can only be good news for people who are moving on from addictive behaviour, as it is for the vast majority of people who don't smoke.

People

We have already looked at various strategies for dealing with other people and suggested you prepare things you might say to both supportive and unhelpful people. Possibly the most important thing to remember is that most people who relapse do so when offered a cigarette by a friend. You need to bear this in mind, especially if you are drinking with friends. We look at relapse in detail in Week Eight but for now remember that you do not have to explain yourself to anyone and you can choose to walk away from people who are trying to get you to relapse. I heard somewhere the delicious line that those who matter don't mind and those who mind don't matter.

Control your environment

Making a few simple changes to your home or work environment can help hugely in stopping smoking and staying stopped. For instance, if you always have a cigarette before going to bed at night, simply remove the ashtray from your bedside locker. But don't lock it away somewhere. Or bury it in the garden. (One client of mine buried his pipes in the garden on an earlier quit attempt.) Put *all* your smoking paraphernalia in the bin! Don't keep any of it 'just in case'. Or for 'guests'. Your home, car and workplace should become a smokefree zone. If a recent EU research report proved that even the most hi-tech ventilation systems do not protect you against cancer in rooms where people have smoked, why should you permit anyone to smoke in your home, car or workplace? By breaking your ashtrays, dumping your lighter and smashing your pipes you communicate your serious intention to the universe and, of course, to your psyche.

Controlling your environment is a highly important activity before your Quit Date next week so be sure to do it – thoroughly. No secret stashes anywhere. When you make it inconvenient to smoke by smashing ashtrays, ditching lighters and wrecking pipes you create the space for your higher self to resume command should you be overcome by acute craving. Yes and be sure to get rid of that packet you've kept in the car for the last while and to check *all* pockets and handbags.

If you always smoke with a coffee, choose tea instead next week. If you smoke after a meal, leave the table as soon as you've finished eating. If you can, take a siesta instead, or go for a short walk. Anticipate how you will reward yourself, how you will comfort yourself or how you will relax. Remember it is good, indeed necessary, to be kind to yourself. Just because you stop smoking doesn't mean you no longer have the needs which, up to now, you sought to satisfy by smoking. Sure, destroy all smoking paraphernalia but don't leave your home, car or workplace devoid of alternative treats. Part of preparing your environment is to ensure that you have some creature comforts to support you. In particular, make sure you can sip water wherever you are. Always carry a bottle of water with you in the car, keep it by your desk and sip frequently at home. Have non-fattening nibbles, such as dried or fresh fruit to hand. Use music too as a treat, to reward you during breaks. Or have a favourite cushion or recliner to relax into and a good book to hand.

Stresses

You can deal with stresses by trying the various relaxation techniques suggested in Week Three, such as alternate nostril breathing, yoga and avoiding caffeine. You can take 20 minutes out for physical exercise. Writing your morning journal will help you to cope with stress. It will calm you down, slow down your racing mind, and ground you. If you are a workaholic, now is the time to make simple choices leading towards a better work-life balance, such as going to bed earlier, not taking work home or making a rule that you don't accept business calls after a certain hour (not midnight!). Moving towards fulfilling your personal mission statement also reduces stress. You know when you are on the path, doing what you are meant to do. If you claim that your spouse, partner or children are important, choose to spend more time with them. Let go of any fears you might have about money. Trust that the universe will provide. If you believe in God, trust that God, who knows all that you need, will provide. Use mantras like "All I have is all I need" or "All shall be well and all manner of being shall be well" or "It's all working perfectly".

Alcohol

As we mentioned in Week Two, it can be prudent to avoid alcohol or at least cut down the amount you drink while you are stopping smoking. You probably know people who had given up smoking – but relapsed while drinking. We also suggested that it can be a good thing to avoid all mood-altering substances and processes while you are working to move on from your addiction to nicotine or any other addiction. This is particularly important next week.

First Three Rules: Plan, Plan, Plan

If you fail to plan you plan to fail. Now that you have analysed your smoking and the situations, feelings, places, and moods you associate with smoking, you need to leave nothing to chance. Plan now for how you will deal with each situation that could arise from Day One of next week.

For each situation in which you currently smoke, devise a specific plan for not smoking. Copy the following table into your journal, with a line for each situation in which you would normally smoke. Complete it, naming the time and place you would normally smoke, who (if anyone) might be with you, and what you plan to do to avoid smoking in each situation from the start of next week. Three examples are given.

My Short-term Plan

Places I normally smoke	Times	People	What I will do
Example: In bed, listening to the radio	7 a.m.	With Chris	Rise at 6.55 a.m. and do yoga for 10 minutes or workout
Example: In car, going to work	8.25 a.m.	Alone	Make sure there are no cigarettes or matches in car
Example: Lunch	1 p.m.	Work colleagues	Meet Ken for lunch. He doesn't smoke.
1			
2			
3			

My Short-term Plan (continued)

Places I normally smoke	Times	People	What I will do
4			
5			
6			
7			
8			
9			
10			
11			
12			
13			
14			
15			
16			
17			
18			
19			
20			
21			
(Add more lines as required, ensuring you anticipate every scenario in which you might normally smoke.)			

Medium to Long-term Plan

Imagine you have been off cigarettes for three years. You know that ex-smokers can and do relapse (of course, many do not!). Perhaps you have relapsed before. If so, write down the circumstances in which you went back smoking before or in which other smokers you know did so. Where did the relapse take place? Who was present? Was alcohol a factor? Were there any particular feelings at play? When you stop smoking next week, what can you do to prevent a similar relapse? Fill in the table below or in your journal. Some examples are given.

My Medium to Long-term Plan

Situations in which I've relapsed before or where others did.	Times	People	What I will do to avoid relapse.
Example: At a wedding.	Evening.	With Mike.	I will abstain from alcohol at weddings *or* I'll not drink more than two glasses of wine.
Example: Feeling under pressure at work	Monday morning	Alone.	Monitor my work-life balance. My health and wellbeing come before my work. Take weekly sauna. Do daily morning journal & yoga.
1			
2			
3			
4			
5			

© Joe Armstrong 2004 www.writeway2stopsmoking.com

Withdrawal Symptoms

Forewarned is forearmed. If you know what may happen when you stop smoking, you will understand it more and so cope with it better. The most important thing to say about withdrawal symptoms is that, however unpleasant they may be, they are good for you. They're your body's way of healing itself. If you think about any withdrawal symptoms in this way, you might even welcome them as a sign that your healing is at hand.

Cough

Some ex-smokers develop a cough after they stop smoking. Your body delights in no longer having an acrid concoction of chemicals shoved into the lungs. A clear-out of tar and nasty stuff begins. The cough mightn't happen at all or it could last a few days, weeks or even months. Rather than moan, be glad that your lungs are doing a much-needed renovation. Soon they will work better than they have for years. Check with your doctor if you're worried about your cough.

Dizziness

Some ex-smokers feel dizzy at first. If you drive a car or operate machinery, you need to be careful not to crash or cause an accident. Any dizzy spells don't tend to last. It is always prudent to check such a symptom out with a doctor in case it is caused by some other health factor. Again, though, you should rejoice at this symptom as it indicates that your lungs are actually working properly again after perhaps years of abuse. The dizziness is most likely to be caused by new volumes of oxygen getting to your brain – the amount of oxygen you were meant to be getting all along but weren't because you were smoking! It's just that you're now unused to breathing as you should and your brain takes a little time to adjust. But consider how much happier your body, mind and spirit will be finally to be getting enough oxygen again. You will be a much more efficient human being, like a car after a good service.

Cravings

Depending on how heavy a smoker you have been, you will almost certainly experience cravings for nicotine, which is why nicotine replacement products and medication can help you. A craving is like an acute desire to succumb to your old addiction. It is a normal reaction to withdrawal from smoking.

The most acute cravings occur within the first three days after stopping smoking. But over the weeks and months ahead they will become less frequent and less intense. There are all sorts of tricks you can play on yourself to get over cravings. As already indicated, even the most acute craving only lasts three to five minutes. So you need to have some strategies to hand to get you over those intense cravings, especially in the early days of abstaining.

One is to bring to mind that *time* – and as short a time as up to five minutes – will deliver you from the craving. "In five minutes I'll feel better," is a simple thought you can repeat aloud or quietly during an acute craving. Clients of this programme have found sipping water a godsend to beat craving. If you are with a trusted friend, tell him or her that you're feeling an acute craving. If circumstances permit (and more might than you could expect) take out your pocket log and write about it. You might also be able to take a short walk or do something physical during a bout of craving. In short, try to distract yourself, do something, or get out of the situation in which you find yourself, such as going to a place where smoking isn't permitted or away from temptation where it is.

You can also fool yourself in a healthy way. Tell yourself you'll have a cigarette later. Again, by pre-planning your environment (that is, removing ashtrays, matches, cigarettes etc. from your car, home and workplace, or wherever else you might smoke), even if you succumb to the craving, you won't physically be able to smoke since you won't have any smoking paraphernalia to hand. You could also tell yourself that if you're ever to get over your addiction, you'll have to learn to cope with cravings and now is as good a time as any. By abstaining now, the frequency and acuteness of cravings will decrease. Mind you, even people who are years off tobacco products occasionally get a mild craving, as some ex-smokers who relapsed after many years can testify. Of course, a craving never means that you have to smoke. You are free and can plan how to manage cravings whether they occur next week or next year.

Irritability

Quitting smoking can leave you feeling raw, edgy and irritable. Tell people what you're doing and ask them to forgive you in advance if you are a bit off-form. Ask your nearest and dearest to understand and to give you a wide berth. If people love you, they should encourage you in your efforts and excuse you if for some days or even weeks you aren't your usual jolly self!

Sleep

Your normal sleeping pattern can become disrupted when you stop smoking. You could feel very sleepy or find it difficult to get to sleep. As with the other withdrawal symptoms, this too will pass.

Appetite and Weight Gain

Once you quit, you will probably find an increased interest in food. This is because you can taste food much better now and you want more of it. It's also because your body wants to be fed (now that the poison of cigarettes has been eliminated). Third, you might be tempted to snack more to have 'something to do with you hands'.

You can miss the oral gratification of smoking and seek substitutes. You can miss the ritual of smoking and counteract this by the ritual of eating.

It is normal to put on a few extra pounds when you quit smoking. Just as the air is finally getting properly to your brain, so too grub is finally doing what it's meant to do. The worst reason in the world for smoking is to lose weight or to avoid putting it on. Accept a slight weight gain as normal when quitting. Focus on life balance. For one, your health and good looks will benefit much more by abstaining from cigarettes. What's more, you will hopefully become more physically active, taking about 20 to 30 minutes of physical exercise each day. Ask your doctor what physical exercise routine would be suitable for you, given any diseases or conditions you might have. In quitting smoking, we also look at other addictions. If food addiction is a problem for you, now is the time to discuss this with your doctor. Be very careful not to replace cigarettes with fatty foods or sugary snacks. Do not pig out on crisps, cakes, biscuits, mayonnaise, full-fat dairy products or chocolate and, as a general rule, avoid fast-food restaurants. By eating a healthier diet you'll take the offensive in weight-control. Consider reading some books about healthy eating. Personally, I'm very persuaded by Dr Peter J. D'Adamo's *Eat Right for Your Type*, which presents individualised diets for staying healthy and achieving your ideal body weight based on your blood type. His more recent book *Live Right for Your Type* is also worth reading but it is a much more difficult book, whereas the first is a joy to read.

Countdown to Quit Day

Make sure that before your Quit Day on the first day of next week that you have ticked off as completed *each* of the following items in the Countdown to Quit Day Checklist.

Countdown to Quit Day Checklist

To Do	Done
Survey home, car, pockets, handbags etc. for any and all smoking paraphernalia, such as ashtrays, cigarette lighters, matches, cigarettes, cigars, pipes or chewing tobacco. Be ruthless: burn them or bin them (and make sure the bin is taken away!) Don't give them away as gifts. First, because they might come back to you if you relapse, suggesting lack of serious intent in the first place and, second, what friend would give a carcinogenic 'gift' to anyone?	

Countdown to Quit Day Checklist (continued)

To Do	Done
Buy fresh and dried fruit for snacks and a handy portable water container for sipping water throughout the day.	
Ensure you have your supply of appropriate-for-you nicotine replacement therapy or smoking cessation medication approved by your doctor, unless your doctor has advised otherwise.	
Confirm your appointment with your dentist.	
Get a moneybox or jam jar and decide to put into it each day from Quit Day the money you save by not smoking. Explore in your journal what you are going to do with that money. It must be a reward for *you*. Do not subsume it into normal family finances. Place ideas under the jar, or write them into your journal. (See Week Six under 'Money Log' for connecting money saved by not smoking with directly promoting your personal mission.)	
Ensure you do your journal each morning.	
Schedule next week's congé and keep to it.	
Schedule times for physical activity next week. For example: When will you take that walk? Where will you cycle?	
Schedule pleasurable activities each day, including healthy rewards such as buying a CD, going to a movie, or meeting a non-smoking friend for dinner.	
Practice alternate nostril breathing and/or other relaxation techniques. When in your day will you take mini-breaks and longer relaxation periods?	
Tell friends and colleagues that you are quitting. Ask them for their support. Visualise yourself dealing well with social banter about your quitting.	
Anticipate which friend or friends might be most likely to offer you a relapse cigarette and decide now how you will avoid it. Practice aloud saying 'No thanks'.	
Be sure to talk to your sponsor this week and next. If possible, have other smoking cessation supporters too, at home, at work, and socially. Ask for their support. They'll usually feel happy and honoured by your request.	
Carry the phone number of the Irish National Smokers' Quitline 1850 201 203 with you at all times or, in the United Kingdom, Quitline 0800 00 22 00, and the phone numbers of your sponsor and supporters.	
Carry in your handbag or pocket your pocket log and pen. Holding a pen can 'earth' your tension, much as holding a cigarette used to give you something to do with your hands.	
Plan to spend as much of next week as possible where smoking is not permitted.	
Spring clean your home. Wipe off any nicotine grime from windows, wash curtains, blinds and duvets, get the smell of stale smoke out of carpets and wardrobes. Start next week as you mean to go on, with clean and fresh sheets, clothes and hair.	
Re-read your mission statement and your reasons for wanting to stop smoking. Add any new reasons that occur to you.	

© Joe Armstrong 2004 www.writeway2stopsmoking.com

Activities for Week Four

1. Smoking is a very unnatural act. Try this week to reconnect with the natural world. Many of us insulate ourselves from the beauty of the earth. We drive cars rather than walking, surrounding ourselves in a metal shield rather than using our bodies to walk in the open air. We wear shoes rather than going barefoot, yet the simple pleasure of walking barefoot on grass or sand can literally ground us, connecting us with the earth from which we've come and to which we will return. Consider some ways that you could reconnect with the earth this week. Write them in your journal. Choose one to do today.

2. Be sure to use some affirmations this week. You could conclude your morning journal with a selected few. Use your own preferred affirmations or take some of the following: "This is a time of recovery and discovery". "I'm involved in a process of transformation." "I'm becoming more attuned with myself and the universe." "I'm caring for my body, my primary means of being in the world." "With the help of God, I'll move on from this addiction." "I am loveable as I am." "I no longer need to act out my addiction."

3. Write down three examples of times you accepted responsibility for your actions. For example: "I admitted that my injured knee was caused by not asking for help."

4. As a smoker, you might have handled anger by lighting up. From next week, you need to choose to handle anger more constructively. How will you handle anger at work or at home? In Week Nine, we shall explore assertiveness techniques and the Pinch/Crunch model of relationships but meanwhile do not despise the simple but effective tip of counting to 10. It really does work, since it gets you to use the logical/rational side of your brain, helping you to step back from inappropriate expressions of anger. Physical exercise will also help, even if it's only a walk around the block.

5. Fear can be a good thing. Over the next few weeks, be attentive to any reasonable fears you might have, such as an apprehension about dating someone whom you recently met. Quitting smoking is a really big life task. Don't complicate things right now by ignoring your fear. Think of a time that you're glad you respected your fear. For example: "I'm glad I didn't accept that job offer. It didn't feel right for me."

6. Reward yourself. You have worked hard on this programme. Take time out just for you. Play around with some art materials, listen to music instead of the news, or buy yourself a bunch of flowers.

7. Loneliness is part of life. It is an essential part of our humanity. Instead of reaching for a cigarette next time you feel lonely, reach for your pen and journal. Write about it. Spiritual writers talk of the journey from loneliness to solitude. If loneliness is perceived as a negative experience, it can be the gateway to a peaceful solitude, where you are at ease with yourself and the world. Consider where you stand on that journey.

8. Be alert to feelings of invincibility, superiority, depression, loneliness, anger or fear that you may be experiencing. Express your feelings on the page, thereby facing up to them and gaining power over them, rather than letting them control you.

9. Appreciate the vital importance of attaining and maintaining work-life balance, as a core goal in moving beyond addictive behaviour and towards the fulfilment of your life's mission.

Review of Week Four

1. Did you do your morning journal every day last week? What was it like for you?

2. Did you take your congé? What did you do? Did any aspect of it feel risky and, if so, are you glad you took the risk?

3. Did you meet your doctor to discuss nicotine replacement therapy and other options? Have you decided to use nicotine replacement therapy or other treatments, and do you have stocks to hand?

Road of Trials

Today, Day One of Week Five, you are a non-smoker. You have prepared very well for this day. It is a significant turning point in your life. This is a day of grace and blessing, even if your passage today down the birth canal to your new life is painful at first. For some, the birth is quick and simple. For others, there is struggle and distress. But nothing will happen today or for the next three days that you will not be given the strength to endure.

Threshold

At this turning point in your life, you leap into the unknown. Sure, you know from your preparation what you can expect, and we will take a more detailed look in this chapter than in Week Four at other withdrawal symptoms you may experience. Even if you quit smoking before, this time you are as well prepared as you can be. You know your reasons for wanting to stop smoking. You are willing to take the chance of believing in your personal mission. You have consulted with your doctor and are supported by any nicotine replacement products or medications you were advised or prescribed to use. You know that this is not only about stopping a disgusting habit. You know it's about daring to believe that you have a word to speak to the world and that, by your abstinence from addictive activity, the reason you were put on this planet will be made manifest.

Ask God's blessing on your ascent up the passage from addiction to abstinence and 'sobriety' from nicotine. Trust in your higher self to lead you beyond any other addictive activities too. Do not worry that your preparation has not been 'perfect'. Only your addictive self will whisper self-doubting thoughts to you at this stage. Your higher self knows you can do it. When you do it, your higher self will help with other obstacles as you reach for your authentic dreams and aspirations. Smoking has held you back. Other addictions have too. You can fear today the loss of your excuse for not achieving what you were sent to do. No longer will you be able to take refuge in defeatist thinking. You know now that you make your own luck. No longer do you choose to put off until tomorrow what lies within your power to do today. Now you appreciate the shortness of life. Increasingly, you realise that this is not a general truism but that *your* life is so short. Today is the day to live it to the full. No longer will you poison yourself. Your gift to the world is unfolding. Every second you succeed in choosing your authentic path over acting out any addiction, you are contributing to your own health and wellbeing and advancing your core aims and goals in life. You are also contributing to a universal hymn of hope. If you feel too weak to resist temptation, let your higher self act on your behalf. Imagine you are a teacher showing someone else how to do it. How to abstain, for the sake of something much greater. How to postpone the gratification for the sake of a far more satisfying and lasting pleasure, that of living and doing your personal vocation in life, in which you shine and flower and become the authentic, authoritative person in your field that you are called to be. Banish the block of perfectionism! Your preparation has been good enough. Now it is time to trust in your higher self or God who wills you to break free.

Helpers

We saw in Week Three how the hero embarked on a high mission is aided on the journey by amulets (tangible objects to help us) and supernatural helpers. Believe that you are that hero, as Joseph Campbell suggests you are in *The Hero with a Thousand Faces*. You can gain strength by carrying a personal amulet you may have been given. Sometimes when I run this programme I distribute humble pocket stones, possibly millions of years old, from which some participants draw strength. Fingering a simple stone during a craving for nicotine can give you something else to do with your hands, act to 'earth' any tension, and remind you of your personal mission, which you may begin to see as a divine commission. Respected spiritual traditions use stones such as rosary beads or worry beads. Of course, your amulet can be anything you wish, such as a medal, a photograph, a jewel. It could be a slip of paper inserted into your ATM cards, reminding you of why you want to stop smoking. As noted in Week Three, amulets need not be only symbolic; they can be practical appropriate-for-you nicotine replacement products much like a hero of old may have been given a sword or magical ring for protection.

Look to your mission statement and you may wake up to more helpers on your side than your realised. As I write this, my wife is considering ideas for the front cover. Downstairs, my children are quiet as mice respecting my need to complete this final draft on schedule. Editors are respecting my need for space to complete this book and, despite an 'impossible' deadline, I am still maintaining something close to work-life balance by doing my own morning journal, weekly congé, taking daily physical exercise and sufficient sleep, and somehow making time for family, relatives and friends.

You have your sponsor supporting you. You have your higher self willing you to succeed, knowing you can do this. If you believe in God then rely on the help of God or your angel to carry you through until your task is done. Insofar as this week and next might be hard, you can nevertheless be buoyed up and sustained by so many helpers, seen and unseen, at your side.

All heroes have to face their road of trials. At times this week you might feel totally alone. You might feel deserted by your supporters. You might accuse your amulets of being ineffective or not working. Just as a dying man might rant and rave unaware of the medical professionals and loving family accompanying him in his suffering, or even cursing them, know that you too are being supported. You are being bombarded with love this very moment, and the universe itself longs you to succeed in your high mission. (At its simplest your children, friends, colleagues and relations will thank you for clearer air.) Know that for every problem you face this week and beyond there is a solution within your reach.

Stripped Naked

These first three days of your new life as a non-smoker can be difficult. Your body craves nicotine. Your mind has grown to associate smoking with pleasure, escape and release from tension. Socially, although it is in fact a smokescreen, you thought of it as an icebreaker. If you had smoked for a very long time, smoking had become part of who you were. What you have left behind can feel like a wrenching from the ballast of your life, such as the client who smoked every hour on the hour, literally marking, for him, the passage of time. Standing without a cigarette, you can feel stripped naked, vulnerable before yourself and others. This is the week when you may have some dragons to slay. And no sooner have you slain one than another and yet another might well appear. At times this week, perhaps after you've triumphed, with the help of your higher self, over a sever bout of craving, you can glimpse the victory that awaits you. But then another craving can hit or you experience social awkwardness or other obstacles that seem to impede your way. Be thankful for preliminary victories and even transitory glimpses of the success that lies before you.

Other Withdrawal Symptoms

Last week we forewarned you about some of the withdrawal symptoms, such as a cough, dizziness, cravings, irritability, sleep disturbance, increased appetite and a small weight gain. You should be aware that there are other possible withdrawal symptoms so that, if they occur, you can relate them to your passage to a smokefree life. Remember too that all of these are good signs. It's your body's way of breathing a sigh of relief that the long years of abuse are over and your healing is at hand. Be patient. It took a long time for you to do the damage you've done to your body. By comparison, it takes a remarkably short time for the healing to occur. Naturally, if any symptom persists or concerns you, you should check it out with your doctor. In short, then, other possible withdrawal symptoms may include constipation, mouth ulcers, skin odours, palpitations, changes in body temperature, possible temporary changes to motor co-ordination (dexterity), watery eyes, and temporary difficulty concentrating. Stick with it. These symptoms are temporary. In fact, most withdrawal symptoms are over within three days. You can last that long! Your recovery, in every sense, is already underway.

Quick Tips from Quit Day to Day Three

- Distract yourself from withdrawal symptoms by keeping busy

- Have water and fruit to hand to sip and munch

- Carry your amulet (such as a stone, medal, beads etc.)

- Remember an acute craving lasts only up to five minutes

- Choose to do physical exercise, if only a short walk

- Work on your thinking – convert negative into positive thoughts, morose thinking into joyful thoughts

- Reward yourself in a healthy and enjoyable way

- Connect with your sponsor

- Use any nicotine replacement products or medication prescribed or recommended by your doctor or pharmacist

- Implement your strategies worked out last week

- Monitor the implementation of your strategies – what doesn't get monitored, doesn't get done

- Insofar as you can, avoid people who smoke in your presence

- Abstain from all other addictions

- Avoid all mood-altering substances and processes, especially for the next few days or weeks

- Re-read your mission statement

- Re-read the reasons you want to stop smoking. Add more reasons as you think of them

- Write three pages in your journal every morning, expressing your *thoughts* and *feelings* as you spontaneously write

- Have a really nice congé this week

- Buy in and keep to hand healthy snacks that don't put on weight

- If you become irritable, accept yourself, including your irritability. It will pass.

- Practice alternate nostril breathing and other relaxation techniques suggested in Week Three.

- If you have trouble sleeping, be assured you will re-establish a healthy sleeping pattern soon. Meanwhile, avoid coffee and other beverages containing caffeine. Cut them out completely or, if you find that too hard, reduce your intake. Don't take any drinks containing caffeine after 3 p.m.

- If you feel dizzy, don't drive or operate machinery.

- If you become constipated, drink lots of water and eat lots of fruit and roughage.

Emotions Bubbling to the Surface

Be gentle with yourself. As we explored last week, smoking is a mood-altering activity. Without the escape of acting out your addiction, your buried feelings and raw moods can more easily come to the surface. You may be unaccustomed to their intensity and be out of practice in how to deal with them. Over the coming weeks, you will become more at ease with your moods and feelings. For now, once again, be gentle with yourself.

Do not fear even your rawest emotions. They have been there all along but you haven't attended to them because you reached for a cigarette, cigar or pipe to avoid really noticing, let alone responding to, your emotive dimension. If you feel anxious, fretful, tearful, vulnerable, irritable, depressed or any other emotion, dare to feel it! Welcome the opportunity of letting your authentic feelings emerge, which they will do in your morning journal or pocket log. Have the courage to stand as you are in company feeling as you do. Abstaining from cigarettes is not causing the feelings. You have felt these feelings before but kept them at bay by smoking, thereby not giving yourself permission to really feel them. Now you can. You no longer need to hide your emotions behind a smokescreen. You are human! Rejoice in your singular humanity. Nobody else is quite like you. You have a gift to give to the world. What that gift is will become clearer as you disengage from your addictions and have the courage to feel how you feel and to write about it in your journal. Welcome emotional discomfort as a possible confirmation that you are on the right path. If the feelings are intense, and you feel worried by them, discuss this with your doctor who can reassure you or suggest some counselling or therapy.

Morning Journal, Morning Prayer

In recent years I have often found myself writing a prayer towards the end of my morning journal. In a sense, the whole journal is a prayer, a grounding in the self. A recognition of what's going on in my life. A slowing down. An opportunity for reflection and self-expression. An opportunity for solitude and silence.

It has almost become an established part of my morning journal by now, which I sometimes accidentally call my morning prayer. Perhaps the slip of the tongue is telling. The journal is a spiritual activity as well as a practical one. It promotes the health of the body, mind, emotions and spiritual life. So it is perhaps natural that a prayer should develop organically from whatever rambling thoughts precede it. A written prayer has a certain power. It is one thing to aspire towards self-fulfilment. It is another to ask your higher power that it may be so.

Entrust this week into the hands of the Creator God. Express your thoughts and fears. Come as you are, in the here and now. Ask for help and guidance. You might like to light a candle. (This should be safe so long as you truly have eliminated all smoking paraphernalia from your home! Prayer should not be an occasion of temptation!) Indeed, by striking a match to light a candle to aid your prayer, you are already setting up a new association for the sight and sound of a struck match, now an occasion of prayer and self-expression.

A prayer is a conversation with God or your higher power. You could see it as an attempt to awaken to the divinity within you, by which I mean the spark of the divine — all that is good, wise and creative — that you are. It could go along the lines of the following.

Creator God, I thank you for this moment. I thank you for your invitation to grow beyond addictive thinking and behaviour. I thank you for the challenge that I'm engaged in. I know the next few days and weeks might be difficult. But with your help I believe I can leave behind addictive ways for good.

I feel nervous. I'm not certain if I can do it. I fear it will be very tough. I sense you want me to do it. Indeed, I know you do. But I have tried before and failed. I don't know how I will cope without cigarettes or the pipe. I know you want me to succeed. Smoking is holding me back. It's a major obstacle stopping me becoming who you want me to become and doing what you want me to do.

With your help, I can succeed.

I pray too for those who are supporting me on my journey. I am thankful for my sponsor, for my friends and family, and all who care for me who want me to succeed.

I thank myself for embarking on this turning point in my life. I have worked hard. I pray it will not be in vain. Help me to take one day at a time, one hour at a time, one minute at a time. I pray that I will not only do what I must do in the coming days (abstain from smoking), but that I will thereby take real steps towards the fulfilment of my life purpose. Grant that I will achieve not only abstinence but 'sobriety' from cigarettes — not merely 'not smoking' but not even thinking about them and living my life to the full, enjoying freedom and good fortune.

I pray also for others who wish to stop smoking. I pray that my journey will somehow clear a path for them. Grant that in facing obstacles, I shall act as if blazing a trail for others to succeed after me. I thank you for the children whom I may not even know who may never smoke because of my example of living a happy, smokefree life. I ask forgiveness of the universe for anyone who has started or continued to smoke because I did.

I thank you in advance for the doors that will open to me once I stop smoking. By getting unstuck from my smoking addiction and any other addiction, I do the single biggest thing I can do to create my own luck. I thank you too for the inner doors that are already opening since embarking on this path of authenticity. The ultimate journey is the journey to the self and I no longer fear that self or what it might reveal.

Bless me now and over the days and weeks ahead, and teach me to live fully in the present moment. I recommit myself to looking after myself, working this programme, writing my journal, getting enough sleep, exercising, avoiding temptation when I can, eating well and rewarding myself with healthy treats and a great congé this week. Amen.

One Day at a Time

The phrase 'one day at a time' is associated with Twelve Step programmes, including Nicotine Anonymous. It is as valuable a phrase for those setting out to abstain from addictive thinking and behaviour as it is for those with several days', weeks' or even years' abstinence behind them. Any true philosophy or spiritual tradition speaks of the need to live in the now. Ironically, success in not acting out an addiction can be as big a barrier to doing this as a litany of failure. Success or failure really doesn't matter. What matters is the present moment: living in the now. The Christian tradition talks about the 'sacrament of the present moment'. Eastern spiritual traditions and philosophies speak of the value of 'awakening'. Yesterday is gone. Tomorrow never comes. All we have is this moment.

The Jesuit priest Anthony de Mello, most famous for his book *Sadhana: A Way to God* in which he fused Eastern and Western mysticism, presents many simple exercises for coming into the present. Techniques include body awareness exercises (such as that described in Week Three) and breathing exercises, in which you use your breath to summon your whole self into the here and now. A third technique is to focus on a particular sense such as hearing and to hear all sounds without identifying them and listen as if everything were a unified symphony.

Coming into the present, not being weighed down by successes or failures, trusting that, in this moment, you are being given the grace to resist your addiction, that is the essence of one day at a time.

Road of Trials or Trail of Joys?

While your first week, especially the first three days, may be tough, this is not always the case. In fact, it could – however unlikely it may sound – be a week of joy. We showed in Week One how to translate mental blocks into affirmations. If you're dreading your 11 o'clock morning break without smoking, write down that block in your journal or pocket log. Now, translate it into an affirmation. For instance, if you express the obstacle you envisage as 'I'm dreading taking a break without being able to enjoy a cigarette' your affirmation might be 'I will enjoy enhanced self-esteem by not smoking at break time.' Or you might affirm: 'The pleasure of not having to smoke will last longer than the self-absorbed escape of any cigarette.'

As mentioned in Week One, you can go further and do B. Jack Gebhardt's enlightenment exercise on any block. For instance, you might start off with the block 'I'm dreading the mental torture of being tempted to smoke but knowing I've quit'. You could strike out 'mental torture' and insert 'challenge'. That's better. Then you think 'Hey, let's strike out 'challenge' and insert 'game'. You could go still further and write 'fun time' instead of game. Having played with the negative thought, you've turned it into a playful opportunity.

If this all sounds like crazy mind games, as an addict you're already familiar with crazy thinking! Moreover, addiction primarily starts in the way you *think*. This is a creative way of changing how you think. Do not underestimate this. The mind can make a heaven of hell or a hell of heaven. How you *think* and changing your habitual and addictive way of thinking is at the heart of moving on from addictive behaviour. If you have ever relapsed into an addiction before, you know that your relapse occurred significantly earlier than the day you finally found yourself back in the pub or the bookies again. The relapse started in your *head*, possibly days or hours earlier.

So, if you are feeling heavy about the week ahead, write down in your journal how you're feeling. Practice playing with negative thinking, enjoying the challenge of reconstituting it as a positive or joyful thought. I could resent working very hard for the next two weeks, finishing off this book. I could think, 'There are my children downstairs on a Sunday. I should be engaging with them, relaxing with them, being Daddy to them.' Well, a lot of the time, I do. But not unlike the passage from the tomb of smoking to life beyond acting out addictions, I simply need to spend these last two intensive weeks on this book. The children are coping very well alone, learning responsibility, engaging with one another and doing minor house chores. They can learn too from my commitment to completing this important task with which I have been entrusted. If I take it one day at a time, just like quitting smokers must, I'll get there, with the help of my supporters and helpers and my higher self. By doing the work, I get through the labour of birth. By adopting a similar approach this week, you've nothing to lose but your slavery to nicotine.

Gebhardt goes so far as to suggest that you can transpose your *fear* of craving into the *joy* of craving. If this sounds mad, remember it's enjoying the *thought* that's at issue. Like birth, passage through that craving and other withdrawal symptoms, painful though it might be for a while, is the sure sign that you are headed for a new and expanded world and transformed sense of self in the not-too-distant future.

Physical Benefits Already

Just 20 minutes into your Quit Date on Day One this week your blood pressure already started to get healthier, as did your pulse rate and circulation. (One elderly smoker told me he quit when he was warned that otherwise both his legs would need to be amputated.) On Day Two of this week all nicotine from smoking has left your body! Already, your lungs begin expelling tar, mucus and toxins. By Day Three, you have eliminated carbon monoxide from your body. Already, your food tastes better and your sense of smell is recovering. Your breath is less laboured; your lungs are already more effective. More oxygen is pumping round your body and you will have more energy than you've had for years. No wonder many are rightly tempted to join a gym, walk more, take a bike ride or use the stairs instead of the lift.

Over the next few weeks, you will look and feel better. You'll be able to walk, cycle or swim further and better. Your circulation will continue to improve. Your lungs will continue to expel much of the garbage you put in there and you'll continue to breathe far better. Your stress levels will decline as you learn in the following weeks of this programme to deal with stresses in healthy ways. One short year from today, you will have reduced by 50 per cent the risk of your suffering a stroke or heart attack. Over the next five to 10 years, your high-risk status for developing lung cancer will decrease substantially. And each day you are saving hard-earned cash to enjoy or invest towards advancing your freedom, fulfilment and good fortune.

Not Even One

Let there be no ambiguity: you must never again take even one cigarette, cigar, chew or one smoke of a pipe. It is not an option for you. You cannot smoke one and leave it at that. You probably know people who were off cigarettes for months or even years only to relapse after they were offered a cigarette, possibly while they were drinking. Don't fool yourself. That 'just one' would climb, either in an orgy of smoking that night or incrementally, gradually smoking more and more until you're back to acting out your addiction as much as you did before. Just don't do it, ever. Not even one.

Stabilisation

You might find it difficult to believe this week but there will come a time when you will not even think about cigarettes. Imagine a time in the not-too-distant-future when you will stop being preoccupied by smoking or not smoking. Sooner than you think, as you work through this programme, you will be in a far better position to solve problems without smoking or acting out other addictions. Your body, as you know, is already recovering from the damage cigarettes have caused you. So too will your mind, emotions and spiritual life continue to recover as you continue to work this programme.

If you are also withdrawing from acting out an alcohol addiction, this week and next may be regarded as the acute phase of withdrawal. Post-acute withdrawal could last for six to 18 months. With tobacco, the acute withdrawal period, as we've seen, is usually over within three days, but naturally the emotional, social and spiritual recovery will take several months to come, which is why you will need to remain on your guard beyond the end of this programme. But this week, after Day Three, you can already focus on your mental, psychological and spiritual recovery. Keep focused on the fact that your long-term aim is 'sobriety' from nicotine and other addictions – living your singular life to the full without addictive thinking or behaviour. This week the focus is necessarily on abstinence. But your higher calling is a way of abundance, not deprivation; fulfilment, not fasting; and self-realisation. This is an important week. But when it is done your journey takes a new direction towards enjoying a balanced, responsible, adult lifestyle, fulfilling your personal mission.

Care for the Body

Your body is sacred. It is the vehicle for your being-in-the-world. Some religions and spiritual traditions regard the body as the Temple of the Holy Spirit. You are divine. You are called not only to give up smoking but to become proactive in promoting your body's health and wholeness. Holistic health means health of the whole person, body, mind and spirit. Holiness has the same word-root. Wholeness is a good word too for embracing that sense of a human being fully alive, physically, mentally, emotionally, and spiritually. Nurture your body with plenty of sleep, healthy food, physical exercise, mental exercise, relational wellbeing and spiritual calm, simplicity and contentment. Take time out for wonder and awe, which can be as simple as watching a cat move, listening to birdsong, or walking in a garden.

Care for the Body: An Exercise

In your journal, list about five things that block you from enjoying a more physically active life. Just a word or a phrase for each obstacle will do. When you have finished, ask if any of these challenges are also impeding your spiritual life and underline in your journal those that do. Reflect in your journal on the blocks that damage your physical and spiritual health. Can you plan some physical exercise for today?

Activities for Week Five

1. Take a little time to reflect on times of sadness in your life. Consider any damage that has resulted from your smoking or other addictions. List the losses: health, money, self-belief, opportunities missed, dreams unfulfilled, people or relationships damaged. Record in your journal if you feel sad for harm to yourself or to others. Write a few words about how you have been hurt by your addiction(s). Give examples. For instance: I regret the way my smoking and drinking often turned me in on myself, leaving me less attentive to my wife and children.

2. Be sure to take your congé this week!

3. You've made excellent plans and strategies to abstain. Make sure you put them into practice! Keep your eyes fixed on the aim of sobriety, not mere abstinence.

Review of Week Five

1. Did you do your morning journal every day this week? What was it like for you?

2. Did you take your congé? What did you do and did you enjoy it?

3. Did you meet or speak with your sponsor? If so, have you felt supported by your sponsor? Write about it.

WEEK

6

Inner Work

This week, we grow in self-acceptance and in acceptance of others as they are. With each victory over tobacco, your consciousness expands, just as a mountaineer sees more with each step taken up the mountain. You will continue to be tested but know that testing is needed to grow. Trust that the process is working, no matter how messy it might seem. As well as maintaining abstinence, you set your sights this week on your higher purpose of 'sobriety' – your life lived in fulfilment, harmony and self-actualisation.

Self-acceptance

Now in Week Six, we have the opportunity to admit our part in the mess of our addiction and in the mess of our life. All lives are a combination of order and chaos. Addiction brings chaos. Sure, we never asked to become addicted to nicotine. Certainly we never invited any other addiction to take away our freedom. And even though products were sold to us which were addictive, we chose at some level to buy them.

This is not a guilt trip. Far from it. It is simply coming to terms with the part we played in becoming addicted. We may not be solely responsible for our addiction but we are responsible for what we do about it. We need to accept the part we played in damaging our freedom, health, and relationships through smoking, for suppressing our genuine feelings while we smoked, and, due to our addiction, *getting stuck* in implementing our personal vocation in life.

The Book of Job

The book of Job in Judaeo-Christian literature is as good an exploration of the question 'Why do we suffer?' as has ever been written. The protagonist Job, who was once blessed with serenity, material wellbeing, wife and family, loses everything. He is brought from reactive anger and cursing God and the very day he was born to a mind-blowing realisation that no human can measure the will of God. At the end of the tortuous bereavement of his many losses, he comes to a wise and profound acceptance that suffering exists and is inevitable given the fragility of life and our mortal condition.

> *I know you can do everything,*
>
> *and all you command will come to pass.*
>
> *I have tried to comprehend things beyond me;*
>
> *things too mysterious for me, beyond my grasp.*
>
> *I heard of you by hear say,*
>
> *but now I have seen you.*
>
> *Therefore I take back what I have said,*
>
> *and repent in dust and ashes.*

> (Job 42:2-6)

Following this recognition of the majesty of God and the mystery of human suffering, God restored Job's prosperity, giving him twice as much as he had before. Supportive people care for him and Job's latter days were blessed even more than his earlier ones, with children, grandchildren and great-grandchildren. He lived until he was "old and full of years".

Like Job, part of our recovery from addiction and from having dawdled in getting on with our mission statement, is to be humble before the mystery of the cosmos and recognise pain that has befallen us, whether or not we had a part in causing it. Once we do so, we can experience an attitude shift that frees us from self-pity and complaining to live our lives to the full, ready and receptive to our manifold good fortune.

Simply Take the Next Step

Do what needs to be done. In any process, such as the journey you are on away from smoking and other addictions, we can feel overwhelmed by so much to be done. Or discouraged by so little apparent progress. Or cocky by the relative ease with which we have achieved something, thinking that all this planning and careful action was not required. That we would have got here anyway.

When you decided to do this programme, you announced to your higher self and to the universe your determination to leave behind addictive thinking and behaviour. You resolved, with others' help, to become 'sober'. Not just 'not smoking' but enjoying an immeasurably better quality of life. If you look back now at the past five weeks, you will see all sorts of things that have occurred which contributed to your increased wellness. Do not presume that these things 'just happened'. Perhaps, as one client did, you finally decided to get your back sorted out and visited a physiotherapist. You've been doing the exercises that were recommended and you feel much better. Or, as another client did, you took yourself off to a relaxation day in advance of your Quit Date. Or, as often happens, you have acted to resolve a blockage in a significant relationship.

You've been doing your morning journal, taking your weekly congé, getting enough sleep, eating better. You're taking better care of your appearance, aided by the fact that your hair, breath and clothes no longer reek of smoke. You are talking to at least one person in a more meaningful way than before, if 'only' to yourself in your journal; and almost certainly to others too like your sponsor and supporters.

With so much happening or already come to pass, focus simply on the next step you need to take, whatever that might be for you. I'll bet you know what it is. It might mean getting back to writing a full three pages of your journal, instead of skimping it. Some people taking this programme find that they enjoy so much the new balance in their life that they begin to take it for granted. They can let crucial tools drop, like the journal, and wonder, sometime later, how come they found themselves smoking again. Your addictive self has not gone away. There is nothing magic about this programme. It is you who do the work. If you let things drop, your addictive self will regain the initiative. Just because you are thinking less like an addict, you are not out of the woods yet. Don't think you've cracked an addiction in a week which held you in sway for years, possibly decades. Don't think the present stage of your recovery would have happened anyway, regardless of your hard work.

Keep working the programme. Recommit to your morning journal. Perhaps you learned last week how fragile is your new-found freedom from cigarettes. If you almost smoked, or reverted to any other addiction, analyse that moment in your journal, just as airline and accident investigators analyse 'near misses'. Maybe you asked a friend for a cigarette but she declined, saying how much she admired what you'd already achieved. Thank God or the universe for that friend. Perhaps your craving was so strong on an occasion that, had you not cleared out your smoking paraphernalia from car, home or workplace, you would have smoked again. Be thankful you ditched your smoking paraphernalia in Week Four. Keep it that way. Do not underestimate the crucial role keeping your environment a hindrance to your addictive self can be! And persist in breaking your associations between your addictive self and certain objects, activities, places and moods.

Your Addiction (and Slips) as Teacher

Pain can be a good teacher. You have been damaged by your addiction to smoking, not only physically but mentally, socially and spiritually too. You may have felt humiliated by your addiction to cigarettes or by other addictions. Your experience prior to this programme may have been of trying to quit but repeatedly failing to do so. As the quip goes, 'It's easy to quit smoking. I've done it lots of times.'

Your addictions can be your teacher. Through them, you learn your weakness. To err is human. You forget your humanity when you fail to appreciate your fundamental fragility and neediness. That is why you must not boast or feel superior to others if you have abstained from smoking since Quit Day. A relapse could be, at any moment, only seconds away. And when you hear of others who relapse, acknowledge the truism: 'There but for the grace of God go I.' And that is not in any way to undervalue your hard work of analysis in Weeks One and Two and of planning in Weeks Three and Four. Or your Herculean efforts last week. In short, be on your guard against any cockiness and do not forget that you remain addicted, despite your blessed successes since Quit Date.

If you do slip up and have a tobacco product, get yourself to your journal as quickly as possible. Write and write and write and write about it. Talk to your sponsor without delay. In Week Eight, we will explore a full-blown relapse and what to do about it. But for now, simply be sure not to 'blow the whole thing' if you do have a slip up. It is *not* OK to have a cigarette, *not even one*, as we stressed last week. It is *never* OK to put your hard-won recovery process upon which you are engaged at risk. It assaults your higher self and your great potential and that for which you were born to do. But it is more important to remain on course, to continue with this process, even if you have smoked again, confident that you can learn from a slip.

Your Addiction (and Slips) as Teacher: An Exercise

Write down five things you have learned about yourself because of your addiction to cigarettes, cigars or the pipe.

1._____

2._____

3._____

4._____

5._____

If you have had a slip or a near-slip (that is, if you smoked or almost did since your Quit Date) analyse the incident in as much detail as possible in your journal. You may find it helpful to complete the following Slips or Near Slips Analysis fiche.

Slips or Near Slips Analysis

	What happened?	**What I could do to avoid the slip next time**
Where were you?		
Who were you with?		
How were you feeling?		
What was your mood?		
What were you thinking?		
Did you do anything earlier which set yourself up for the slip?		
Did you do your morning journal that morning? If so, did you write a full three pages?		
Had you been doing your morning journal faithfully for the previous week?		

Slips or Near Slips Analysis (continued)

	What happened?	What I could do to avoid the slip next time
Did you take your weekly congé?		
Have you been getting enough sleep?		
Have you been losing your new work-life balance, e.g., by working too hard?		
Were you drinking alcohol at the time?		
Anything else?		
Conclude this exercise by answering the following question: What are you prepared to do to prevent another slip or near-slip?		

© Joe Armstrong 2004 www.writeway2stopsmoking.com

Identify your Achilles' Heel

As mentioned earlier, if you slip and have a cigarette, or almost do, you may find that your decision to smoke began many hours beforehand, for instance in deciding not to do your morning journal that day. Or by changing your route to pass your one-time favourite tobacconist. Or you diced with fire, going to a place where people smoked or you drank too much alcohol (or any) too early in your recovery. At some point you began to think again like an addict.

Stepping Back from your Thoughts

As ever, it really is with thought that you need to work. For instance, if you find yourself tempted to smoke, realise that you are choosing your thoughts. You could choose different thoughts. Addicts can obsess or fantasise about their addictions. Insofar as they do, and by wallowing in such thinking and fantasising, they set themselves up for a fall, even though the act of smoking might not happen immediately. The liberating realisation is that you do actually *choose* your thoughts.

The fact is that the smoker may like thinking about smoking so much that by indulging in fantasies of smoking it can be only a matter of time before they light up again. Next time you find yourself about to indulge in a smoking fantasy, choose to think of different things. You could think about the reasons you set out on this path to stop smoking or simply think of anything else. You are not a slave to your thoughts. You determine which thoughts to entertain and which thoughts not to follow. Write in your journal other things that you could choose to think about instead of following obsessional smoking fantasies. When you realise you choose your thoughts, it can be a real breakthrough!

Thinking Less About Smoking

Last week we introduced what addiction experts call the stabilisation stage of recovery, namely when you have recovered from the physical withdrawal symptoms, as you have for the most part by now, and you start to *think less often* about smoking. You are still very early in your recovery and so you have not yet reached stabilisation. But you may already find yourself thinking less frequently about smoking than you did at the start of Week Five. If, as is most likely, you find yourself still thinking of smoking, let that be a prudent reminder to you that you have more work and more recovery to do yet!

Stabilisation is categorised by being able to deal with problems you face without resorting to tobacco or other addictive substances or processes. Over the weeks ahead we will explore, for instance, problem-solving strategies which do not involve resorting to cigarettes or other addictions. Indeed, even at this stage you have done a lot of work towards further gaining or regaining such skills. Since embarking on this journey, you may have begun, for instance, to discover new ways to relax through your congé and specific relaxation methods presented in Week Three. Hopefully, you are enjoying physical exercise, making sure you get plenty of sleep and eating a healthy diet. With your improved quality of life, your relationships should also become more mutually enjoyable, supportive and healing, and we will look at specific ways this can come about in Week Nine. You may find you are being more authentically yourself and interacting with people more naturally and more in accordance with your higher self. Your daily journal is grounding you, helping you express first to yourself and then, if you choose, to other people, your real needs, hopes and fears, and dealing with them in an adult way (rather than resorting to addictive behaviour).

Now that you are abstinent, remember that you have a still more satisfying goal to achieve; namely 'sobriety' of thought, word and deed. Your achievable and tantalisingly close aim is a life lived to the full without cigarettes or other addictions, believing in yourself and doing and achieving what you were born to do.

Week Six Withdrawal Symptoms

Depending on how addicted you were (physically and/or psychologically), you might still be experiencing a bit of a storm this week. (If this is not your experience, skip this paragraph!) You might find it difficult to think clearly. You may feel muddled, or bereft, like someone possessed, confused or wrenched away from a close friend. You may feel emotionally fragile. You might feel weepy. You may find yourself shouting at people or feeling depressed or irritable. You could feel alarmed by violent feelings or impulses. (This is rare but I know smokers who inexplicably feel violent towards family or friends.) Remember, smoking has masked your emotions for a long time and if emotions have been intense then they could come more to the surface now that you are doing your best to live a more authentic life. Do not fear your emotions or thoughts. This is where the journal is a godsend because it helps us to express the riot of our minds. Our inexplicable emotions or crazy thoughts were there all along. *Stopping smoking didn't cause them.* Now, like an adult, we need to learn to accept them and deal with them responsibly. There is no shame in asking for help. Everyone is different. The stuff to emerge from your consciousness in your journal is you or a part of you. You may need to acknowledge stuff that you have repressed. You may need to forgive people who have hurt you. You may need to ask for forgiveness from those you have hurt. You may be worried that some of what you write or some of the thoughts or emotions you experience are so crazy that you need professional help. Some readers may need professional help and there should be no shame in seeking it. Indeed, this is another way in which your addiction can become your strength because in dealing with your addiction you can get to the bottom of any unresolved issues in your life. As someone who has had recourse to counselling myself at various times of my life, I recommend it heartily. It is almost always worth the money and, if money (or the lack of it) is an issue for you, your doctor may be able to direct you to free or inexpensive professional counselling or therapy.

Just because you quit smoking last week does not mean that you have as yet mastered healthier coping strategies for dealing with life's problems, challenges and crises. It would be unreasonable for anyone to expect you to have done so. Don't expect too much of yourself too soon. Indeed, even people who don't have the complication of being addicted to a substance, person or process, have to develop coping skills. You can too, by continuing to work this programme. Before last week, you probably coped with stress, at least in part, by smoking. So you might feel a bit wobbly for the next several weeks until you have further developed better coping skills. But you will. Have faith in yourself.

Physical withdrawal symptoms that may persist this week include constipation (drink lots of water and fruit to counteract it); a cough; a sore throat; sleep disruption; and fatigue. If you feel fatigued, that could simply be your body finding again its natural energy levels, freed from the artificial stimulants of cigarettes or other mood and energy-altering substances like alcohol and coffee. It's a bit like scraping the old paint or wallpaper off the wall. Once the toxins and artificial stimulants are gone, and you feed your body and mind with healthy food, physical exercise and sleep, your body will find its natural God-given energy rhythms again. As last week, don't worry if you have put on a little weight. So long as you eat wisely and don't substitute sweets, chocolate, biscuits and cake for your smoking, any weight increase will be minimal. If you feel you can't concentrate, that too will improve and become better than it was while you used to smoke.

Anger, Fear, Loneliness and Hunger

Use your journal to express any uncomfortable feelings, especially anger, fear and loneliness. If you can self-express on the page, you're much more likely to address your real needs and find someone else with whom you can share your humanity. It's an extraordinary thing but once we admit to something on the page, it's like as if the universe co-operates in our healing.

People recovering from addictive thinking and behaviour are advised within Twelve-Step programmes to avoid getting hungry. A recent smoker who took this programme confirmed the veracity of this advice. She found it crucial to avoid becoming hungry in the first couple of weeks of her abstinence from nicotine. If she did, she felt her recovery from nicotine addiction was in peril.

While keeping busy can help in the early days and weeks of abstinence, it is important not to work too hard. For instance, if you're too busy to take physical exercise, you're too busy; and setting yourself up for a fall. You owe it to yourself to take even 20 minutes physical exercise *today* (unless you've a medical condition preventing you from doing so or if your doctor has advised against it). It will improve your mood, self-esteem and dispel feelings of hopelessness or confusion. Just do it!

Pride Comes before a Fall

As we warned last week, success in remaining abstinent can itself become an obstacle to our recovery. Be on your guard against any feelings of pride, complacency or superiority. Many smokers find it easier than they had expected to abstain from tobacco products. So they begin to take silly risks. They *think* in a way which lets down their guard and they forget that an addiction that took years or decades to take hold will not release its captor after a couple of weeks' abstinence. The most effective way to relapse into your addiction is to forget that you remain addicted.

Just one cigarette is *never* OK.

Beware Feelings of Deprivation

Feeling deprived about not smoking is like a cured cancer patient who misses the attention she got in the cancer ward. When you stop smoking, you start to retake control of your life. Over the weeks ahead (and perhaps already), you might occasionally feel annoyed or surprised that people do not comment on the fact that you're *not* smoking. *You* are more aware that you are not smoking than they are. (Not smoking may be perfectly natural to them!)

If you feel deprived, explore those feelings of deprivation in your journal. Do not ignore them. Specify what you feel deprived *of* and compare it with what you wrote for your mental blocks to stopping smoking (or getting on with your life mission) in Week One. They haven't gone away, have they? But, hey, look at your work from Week One in which you translated those blocks into affirmations. You will see, for instance, that if you feel the loss of smoking as you 'best friend', that tobacco was, in fact, a false friend. Go further in your journal and write down the things you're happy to be 'deprived' of, like stale-smelling clothes, increased risk of cancer, and isolating yourself from spouse, colleagues or friends in order to feed your addiction. Now, consider the joy of regaining control of your life.

Life in Abundance

By the end of this week, you will be two weeks off tobacco products. It is time to truly set your sights on the fulfilment of your personal mission. I am regularly amazed at how, when someone sets out on this programme with the initial intention of trying to stop smoking, that, time and time again, wider life issues emerge. It shouldn't surprise me, given that the whole programme starts with the hero (that is, you) writing their mission statement. After all, from the outset we have said that your primary vocation is to fulfil your personal mission. Stopping smoking is done with a view to fulfilling your unrepeatable gift to the planet.

Stopping smoking can become your gateway to discovering the abundance of life, growth and possibilities that are open to you today. When you stop poisoning yourself, you gain a new sense of confidence about yourself, love, money, your work, your ambitions, your dreams and your contribution, even legacy, to the world. You become less fearful and dare to believe in yourself.

When you quit smoking for good and realise that you have succeeded for today with the help of God, you know that you can succeed at any authentic aim etched in your mission statement. That will be as distinctive and individual as you are. Whatever your dream is, it lies within your grasp. By getting unstuck from your addiction, fasten your seat belt while the universe co-operates with you towards the fulfilment of your higher aims and goals.

Whether or not you believe in God, you may be taken by Jesus' advice not to worry about what you are to eat or how you are to be clothed. To paraphrase: 'Look at the birds of the air. They do not sow or reap or gather into barns yet they have all that they need. And you are much more important than they are.'

Already in stopping smoking, you are saving money. Your financial wellbeing is becoming more abundant. You are investing in your health, happiness and independence from addictions. You are investing in your personal mission. You are being brought closer to doing what you were born to do, or to doing it in a more authentic way. You were born to do something great and only you can do it. Even if you have a litany of successes behind you, by quitting smoking and other addictions you can discover how vast remains your untapped potential. Already you are thinking differently than the person acting out an addiction. You are growing in self-control and trust in your higher self. You are choosing your higher values, rather than being stuck mindlessly gratifying an addiction. Who you are, your wonderful, singular self, is emerging more each day. Go for it!

Daily Luxuries and Rewards

Use at least some of the money you save by not smoking on rewarding yourself and indulging in a little luxury. Be prepared to pamper yourself a bit. It might be that you buy yourself a flash walking stick if you're into hill walking. Or luxuriate in a Jacuzzi once a week. Or put aside what you save and install your own Jacuzzi! (You could afford it sooner than you might think.) Each day, if possible, have some little luxury to look forward to. It could be that you buy a luxury brand breakfast cereal or splash out on some other product that costs more than the basic model. As a non-smoker, there is no need for 'poverty thinking'. The universe is abundant. Sure, the earth's resources need to be shared equally. But give yourself permission to enjoy some measure of abundance, to expand your mind and self-esteem.

Money Log

It is a good idea to consider tracking your money on a daily basis to find out, if you don't already know, where it all goes. You could set aside some pages in your pocket notebook to record every cent you spend. By doing this, you will discover the detail of your spending habits. You could put expenditure into categories such as food, education, insurance, transport, etc. Work out how much you earn after tax per hour. Then, instead of merely saying how much money you spend on your various categories per month, decide how many hours you had to work to buy those things or services. If you reckon it wasn't worth having to work for six hours to buy a specific item, you'll find it easier to pass it by. If you haven't already done so, work out how much you used to spend on cigarettes. Look at your mission statement. Is there something in there that could do with a bit of money to get the ball rolling or to bring it to completion? If you can make a direct link between money saved by not smoking or acting out other addictions and promoting your personal mission, you fulfil your higher purposes with every cigarette not smoked!

Write down how much money, at today's prices, you would have spent on cigarettes over the next five, 10 and 25 years had you not embarked on this programme. A sample is done for you. Write your own savings in the bottom row, calculated from the average number of cigarettes, cigars or other tobacco products you used to smoke.

Approx. cost of cigarettes	Day	Week	3-months	Year	10 years	25 years
20	€6	€42	€546	€2,184	€21,840	€54,600

Calculate at today's after-tax income how many hours you used to have to work to feed your smoking habit. Now you can see you are not only saving a lot of money but heaps of time too by not smoking (plus the extra longevity you could enjoy by being smokefree plus your improved quality of life). When you are doing what you were born to do, life, including your work, feels more like a holiday. And with the money you're saving by not smoking, you could factor in actual vacation time too. Consider how the time saved by not having to work to feed your addiction frees up time to spend on the people mentioned in your mission statement, including yourself. Anticipate fewer complaints from those nearest and dearest to you that you don't spend enough time with them. Think time, relaxation, and quality relationships. In short, you can live a lot more, work a lot less; rather than working a lot and living a little. Write down five things that you might spend your money on now that you are not burning it up in smoke or acting out other addictions.

Internal Home Decorations

Many people dread the disruption caused by painting rooms in their house. Old paint or wallpaper may need to be stripped off the walls, furniture moved out, a period of disruption follows. But the benefits after the disruption make the temporary chaos worthwhile. Likewise, in quitting smoking since Day One of Week Five, you have initiated a major repair job for your body, mind, emotions and spirit. The benefits make it worthwhile but you can forget the benefits if you're feeling rotten or nervous or out-of-sorts right now. Count your blessings. Think of at least five benefits you are enjoying since stopping smoking. Write them down.

Already your cravings, which we looked at last week, are becoming less frequent and less intense. Of course cravings *can* still be intense. But six months from now you will have no cravings for cigarettes and, if you do, they will be very rare and mild.

Week Six Checklist

Alternate Nostril Breathing (See Week 3) – are you doing it? It takes about as long as smoking a cigarette and is much more effective in calming you down. It doesn't damage anyone's lungs, clothes, hair or contentment, whether practised alone or in public.
Visualisation (See Week 4) – do not neglect to practice visualisation, for instance, to re-imagine a situation in which you slipped or almost did. Continue to use it to prepare to not smoking in as yet unfamiliar scenarios for you.

Week Six Checklist (continued)

Rewards – remember to reward yourself in a regular, visible, tangible way.
Vigilance – remain on your guard like a hawk, avoiding complacency, pride and superiority.
Thinking – remember any slips begin not with the act itself but with addictive thinking indulged in earlier. Focus not so much on any individual slip but on the thinking you did possibly hours or days previously which led to your slip.
Journal – write your three pages faithfully each morning. Do not think your progress would have happened anyway. Continue to ground yourself daily using pen and paper. To skip it is to put your recovery in jeopardy.

© Joe Armstrong 2004 www.writeway2stopsmoking.com

Activities for Week Six

1. Keep a money log for the next week, or, if you feel up to it, for a month. When you shop, work out the real cost of items in terms of the number of hours you had to work to buy it after tax. Was that purchase worth so much time working? Are there other categories where you don't spend enough money, such as on hobbies, relaxation or entertaining friends? Are you spending your money in the pursuit of your personal mission? Remind yourself how much money you will save over the next year and decade now that you have stopped smoking. Once again, how much time will you *not* have to work just to feed your nicotine or any other addiction?

2. You have been cleaning out your body during Weeks Five and Six. You have been cleansing your mind, ridding it of addictive thinking. Now, why not also have a clear out of your living space? Clutter is stuck energy. An untidy desk or drawer saps your personal vitality. Go around your house with a pen and paper and notice areas that need to be de-cluttered. Here's the rule. If you haven't used it for two years and if you do not love it, it goes. Bin it, recycle it or give it away. Beware the imaginary character 'Justin Casey' who begs you to keep stuff '*just in case*'. Don't listen to him. You've been given the guideline above. Put it into practice. Ask yourself: 'Do I really want to carry this around for the rest of my life?' If not, it's time to part with it. When you de-clutter even one drawer, you can feel a weight has been lifted from you. Try it. Don't attempt to de-clutter the whole house or workspace in one go. Do ten minutes at a time. You may find you want to keep at it for longer. Don't be afraid of

letting stuff go. When you do so, you create space in your life, work and finances for new things to come in.

3. Phone, write, text or email three important people in your life who have contributed to your growth whom you haven't heard from for a long time. Don't let awkwardness get in your way. Simply contact them and say hi.

4. Re-read your personal mission and see if you have detected any movement or change in your sense of moving towards your higher aims and goals. Be open to 'co-incidences' which aid the promotion of your personal mission.

5. In Week One you wrote your story of addiction, involving tobacco and any other addiction. Now, explore your 'happy' memories of addiction. Did these numb your self-awareness and thwart the emergence of your authentic self? Did they merely disguise how dysfunctional your life had become? If possible, share your story with your sponsor or with another trusted person.

Review of Week Six

1. Did you do your morning journal every day last week? What was it like for you?

2. Did you reward yourself each day with some healthy luxury? Did you take your congé? What did you do? Are your congés teaching you anything about pleasure and fun? Are they re-awakening authentic joy in your life?

3. Did you connect with your sponsor this week? Has that been fruitful?

4. Have you been open to synchronicity this week? Has anything happened to confirm you on your journey?

WEEK

7

The Big Picture

You are now in early recovery from your addiction. While you should not expect temptation to disappear this week nor for several weeks or months yet, you will probably find any bouts of craving are less frequent and less intense than before. They are, of course, still real and dangerous. By now you might have experienced some moments of what we might call 'grace' where, were it not for some external assistance, you might have fallen back to acting out your addiction. Let such moments be an opportunity for you to appreciate that each battle is part of a wider war – which, with your higher self, you can win.

Just as the person emerging from the cave of addiction realises that there is a whole different world outside of which they had been unaware or forgotten, you might this week find a shifting perspective from fear to trust, from self-criticism to self-listening. This week you are invited to focus even more on your thinking. You will explore the purposes that nicotine served for you. Having two weeks of behavioural success under our belt, we attend more to the change that needs to come about in our thinking and feeling. The trials of quitting tobacco are akin to our apprenticeship for adult responsibility, wisdom and love. Come as you are. There is no perfect way for your arrival at this point. However you have come and by whatever route, you are here now. Well done and read on.

Attitudes and Beliefs about Tobacco

You are invited to change your old attitudes and beliefs about nicotine. If *only* your behaviour has changed with old attitudes and beliefs intact, you set yourself up for relapse. 'Only!' you might understandably protest. It's no mean thing to have stopped smoking and to have stayed stopped for two weeks! Indeed it is not. Who should you thank for this achievement? Primarily you, that's who; and your higher self at work in you. However, your challenge now is to undergo the *metanoia* mentioned in the Introduction, that is, the change of mind and heart, as well as ongoing behavioural change, as you continue the new direction upon which you have embarked. If you began this programme 'simply' to stop smoking, you know by now that your higher objective also includes living a balanced, healthy lifestyle without even thinking of smoking or other addictions. Our destination is, as we said from the outset, to live under the domain of your higher self, enjoying a mentally, physically, emotionally and spiritually fulfilling life. Now that you have become abstinent, your goal is to maintain that abstinence *and* to advance towards 'sobriety' from all addictive thinking, feeling and behaviour. A conversion of mind and heart, if you like – and you wondered why we needed 12 weeks!

Your Thinking

You are doing very well, with the help of your higher self, to have abstained from nicotine since your Quit Date. Even if you have had a slip, or near slip, count the number of cigarettes which you did *not* have rather than the one or two you might have slipped up on. Hey! If you're still reading, still on the way, you've done great! You know the devastation wrought to your body and mind by smoking. By the way, don't fool yourself: shifting from cigarettes to cigars, pipe smoking or chewing tobacco is your addictive self regaining control. It is simply not an option. Indeed, people rightly take this course from the outset to stop pipe and cigar smoking. Do not substitute your habitual tobacco activity for any other tobacco activity! It's abstinence and sobriety we seek, not an equally nasty substitution.

One of the challenges posed by the goal of 'sobriety' is that it might not seem as tangible as the more measurable achievement of abstinence. What is at stake is that your higher self, rather than your addictive self, is in charge. Your addictive self thinks crazy thoughts. Your addictive self cannot cope with your authentic feelings. Your addictive self leads you into self-defeating behaviours.

Distinguishing your Higher Self from your Addictive Self

You could not have come this far unless you were getting in touch with your higher self, the part of you that does not need to smoke and never did need to; the part of you that has no need for addictive thinking or acting out. As you read this sentence, your higher self and your addictive self are operative within you. In recent weeks you have been attending more and more to your higher self. You have dared to believe in your higher calling. At other times, your addictive self holds sway, even still! If a week is a long time in politics, five minutes can seem like an eternity as both parts of you tussle to assert themselves. One second you can feel emboldened, your spirits lift, you believe the promises held out to you by your higher self. The next you hit the wall, just like in a marathon. Everything is an effort. You feel like blowing the whole thing. You want to go back to leading the habitual life to which you had become accustomed. You crave nicotine. You feel fearful of the future without cigarettes or other addictive escapades. You deny you *are* addicted. And what's wrong with a cigarette anyway, you think. You could be doing much worse. That, of course, is your addictive self talking.

   You need to know at any given time whether it's your higher self or your addictive self who is 'talking'. Even though in recent weeks you have operated more under the influence of your higher self, your addictive self remains close. It is there by your shoulder now, ready to pull you back into addictive behaviour. That same addictive self tells you that your high mission in life is a load of cobblers. It will usually be subtler than that, but the message and effect is the same. Indeed, unless you advance one more step towards *acting as if* you believed in your higher mission and purpose, your addictive self will have very little to do!

Acting As If You Believed in Your Higher Purpose

Ask yourself 'What would I do today if I really believed in my higher mission? What single thing would I do right now to take another step towards my ultimate aims and goals?' Make sure you *do* at least one thing today to move you in the direction of fulfilling your mission statement. It could be you will discuss an important matter with your spouse or partner. Or you might enrol tonight for an evening class. You might invite a friend over or unplug the phone while you complete that short story you've been writing. Whatever single step it is, do it. Pause awhile and write down in your journal *one* thing that you will do *today* to advance your higher purpose.

Acting As If I Believed in my Higher Mission

> **Complete the following sentence:**
>
> One thing I will do today to advance my higher purpose, that is, to fulfil what I have written as my personal mission in my mission statement, is to
>
> ....
> ....
> ....
> ....

© Joe Armstrong 2004 www.writeway2stopsmoking.com

Your Addictive Self and Your Higher Self: An Exercise

1. In your journal, describe and/or draw a picture, using crayons or colouring pens, of your addictive self.

2. See if you can come up with 12 descriptive words or phrases to describe your addictive self. Try to come up with your own words. For example, irresponsible, dependent, uncontrolled, childish, difficult to manage, greedy, self-indulgent, wasteful, self-damaging, self-defeating, not centred, lacking in serenity, selfish, reckless.

3. How do you feel when you become aware that you are acting out of your addictive self or when you sense other people are observing you while controlled by an addiction? See if you can come up with eight to 12 descriptive words or phrases in your journal. For example, ashamed, vulnerable, letting myself down, unreliable, a fake, a bore, uninspired, impulsive, uncontrolled, weak, embarrassed, humiliated, naked.

4. Repeat exercises 1 to 3, but this time focusing on your higher self. Describe and/or draw your higher self. Do you notice a different energy while drawing your higher self? Have you used different colours? Now, write down up to 12 descriptive words for your higher self. For example, grounded, realistic, authentic, grateful, trusting, hopeful, thoughtful, self-disciplined, self-assertive, rested, listening, reflective, serene, contented, self-aware. Finally, write down 8 to 12 descriptive words of how you

feel when you act out of your higher self. For example, confident, happy, peaceful, courageous, ambitious for worthwhile aims and objectives, encouraged, self-accepting, accepting of others, non-competitive, attuned to higher purpose, present in the here-and-now, fulfilled.

Dialogue

Your higher self and the addictive self can operate independently of one another and never, as it were, seem to talk to each other. In another sense, they're talking to, or at, one another most of the time! Just when you really believe you're on track towards your personal mission, you're addictive self butts in, deflates your hope, tells you you're being silly and will never amount to anything much. Or, under the influence of your higher self you reach out in a difficult relationship to attempt a reconciliation and wham! Your addictive self wants none of it and prefers to revert to type, operating out of your past unhappy history together rather than a mutually respectful commitment to a better beat.

In Week One of this programme you looked at your motivation to stop smoking and other addictions. In Week Two you looked at the extent to which you may have wanted to keep smoking or acting out other addictions. We noted then that resolving this ambivalence is the heart of the matter. Even though you are now abstinent, you know that your ambivalence has not gone away. Your addictive self remains active within you. But you don't need to stay stuck in any rut. Recognise any continued ambivalence to staying stopped. I believe the best way of resolving residual ambivalence is to pro-actively pursue your personal mission. Smoking kept you stuck from fulfilling your life to the full. Now that you have stopped smoking and other addictions, dare to believe that your singularity really is worth working for. And use your experience of quitting smoking and other compulsions as the fuel to get you there.

You are much more likely to stay off cigarettes for good if you can become aware at any time of whether your *thinking* manifests your addictive self or your higher self. Note the word is '*thinking*'. Of course it's obvious when you're *acting* out of your addictive self because you rationalise that you don't need to keep your journal anymore, you can stay up late, skip congés, eat poorly, overwork, ignore family and friends, stop taking physical exercise. When you do this, reverting to smoking is merely a matter of time. Note that you can superficially appear to *act* 'sober' by not smoking but *think* like an addict. And, as we know, thinking precedes action.

This is another reason why the journal is such a central tool in stopping smoking and other addictions because you 'see' yourself thinking on the page. Your journal slows you down. It helps you to become reflective. It gently eases you towards greater self-awareness. You can more easily notice when your addictive self may be gaining the upper hand in your thinking. That way, you can take corrective action, get grounded in your higher self and ask for help.

In the following exercise, you are like the director in a play with two characters, your addictive self and your higher self. You can get the best out of your actors by quietening down for a minute. Possibly do a relaxation exercise such as one of those described in Week Three or an exercise suggested in Week Five for coming into the present moment. Now, try to get a dialogue – a simple conversation – going between your addictive self and your higher self. Do it in your journal. If this sounds silly, well, give it a go. It is a recognised, respected and effective psychological technique for personal growth. Try it and see where it leads.

Dialogue: An Exercise

Become quiet and calm. Relax. Come into the present moment. When you're ready, write the dialogue as you think it, spontaneously, just as in a conversation between two people. There is no 'right' way of doing it. Both aspects of yourself are operative, so start off with whoever seems to want to talk first. An example is done for you.

Addicted Self: Hey Kate. Let's get a fag and light up and have some pleasure. You'd love to. Just one! Hmm! I can taste it already. Inhale. Hell, I've missed you.

Higher Self: I'm glad I didn't listen to you earlier. I got up and went out for a walk, got some fresh air, then did some work. I know that you turn me inwards. You hinder my capacity to function authentically. I prefer to delay my gratification.

Addicted Self: Oh, Katie! Get that ciggie out. I know you're dying to. You can smell it already. You're a born smoker. You'll never give up. Stop kidding yourself. Hey, have a smoke now.

Higher Self: Life isn't about immediate gratification. Where you sow, you reap. I know from experience that I prefer to channel my energy into my work, life and relationships. I look forward to seeing M. later. By not smoking now, I believe I'll be able to be more myself later, thereby strengthening our relationship.

Addicted Self: Such a dreary drip! Drip, drip, drip. Seize the hour! A third of the planet smokes! Why not you?! You know you're going to relapse anyway, so why put yourself through all that abstinence nonsense?

Higher Self: I don't know I'm going to relapse. I hope I do not. I know that I do not need to relapse. And even if I do that too can be part of the process. All that matters is now. And for now, I'm choosing my higher values. By not smoking, I've more confidence, a different vibe. I'm not only not smoking — I'm taking tentative steps to fulfilling my mission in life.

Addicted Self: Where did you learn that silliness?

Higher Self: It's not silly. It's true. I believe it. I've a mission in life. I know what I want to do and achieve. I know I've a long way to go but I'm putting my feet firmly on the ground and I'm getting there.

The above is just one possible dialogue. Your dialogue will necessarily be different and as original as you are. Just let the conversation begin. If you're at a loss what to write some morning in your journal, strike up a conversation between your addicted self and your higher self.

You need to keep aware of addictive thinking to prevent any rear-guard assault by your addictive self. Regularly step back from your thoughts and ask 'Who is thinking this – my addicted self or my higher self?' If it's your addicted self, don't ignore it. Explore what's going on in your journal. And if you're in a situation in which you could smoke or revert to another addictive activity, get out of there fast. Other strategies, as suggested in Week Four, include drinking water and reminding yourself that craving and temptation pass within minutes. Temptation, of course, can last for hours if you cultivate it. But, as you know, you choose your thoughts and have no need to entertain smoking fantasies.

Do not neglect deep breathing as another tool in your armoury to defeat temptation. Become attentive to your breathing. Breathe out your anxiety, addictive thinking and temptation, and breathe in peace, harmony, health and your higher calling. Breathe from your stomach, that is, deep breathing in which your diaphragm expels air rather than shallow breathing only from your chest. Start by exhaling, drawing in your tummy and pushing up your diaphragm. Then inhale, with your diaphragm drawing air deep into your stomach. As you breathe out think of yourself expelling addictive thoughts. As you breathe in, pick a word such as 'serenity'. Get into the rhythm of your breath, expelling craving or temptation and inhaling who you are deep down, someone free from addictive thinking and behaviour and fulfilling your wonderful higher mission.

Your Story of Addiction Revisited

In Week One you wrote your story of addiction, including your addiction to smoking and any other addictive substance or process, from your first cigarette to the start of this programme. It often amazes me how people fail to connect addictive behaviour with blockages to their aims and goals in life. This book's sub-title is *How to Get Your Life Unstuck*. Getting unstuck is in essence what this book is helping you to do. Having reflected, in Week One, on your story of addiction, it is now time to scrutinise that story. If you skipped that exercise, why not do it now? Or you could add to what you wrote in Week One. Break it down into the stages of your life, from early childhood, primary school, adolescence/second-level education, early adulthood/college/first job, subsequent jobs, career changes, marriage/relationships/friendships, and significant events to the present day.

My Life and Addiction

Stages in My Life	My Addictive Behaviour at this Time

© Joe Armstrong 2004 www.writeway2stopsmoking.com

Try, where possible, to weave your story of addiction into your life as it unfolded. See whether each stage helped you to live your personal mission or whether it contrived to block your path to self-actualisation. You might find it useful to see the correlation between the different stages or stepping stones of your life and your addictive behaviour at each stage. If you represent this graphically, the correlation might become more apparent. Try to do your own first and then look at the sample opposite.

My Life and Addition (Sample)

Stages in My Life	My Addictive Behaviour at this Time
Early childhood. Tension at home.	Dad drank & smoked. Mother didn't.
Bullied at school. Lonely.	
Adolescence.	Compulsive sexual activity. First smoke.
Early adulthood	Addicted to chocolate and caffeine. Smoking 20+ a day.
Accountancy firm	Smoking 40 a day.
Sabbatical. Travelled to Asia. Met John.	10 a day, sometimes less.
Got married. Children born.	Quit smoking.
Rough time in relationship.	Back to 20+ a day. Drinking too much.

© Joe Armstrong 2004 www.writeway2stopsmoking.com

The purpose of this exercise is to see for yourself the negative part smoking and any other addiction has had on you, physically, mentally, emotionally and spiritually. It didn't solve problems. It caused more. Rather than daring to believe in your mission statement, you withdrew into yourself and acted out an addiction. You were less and less available to live your life's calling. You retreated into a fantasy world rather than dealing with life.

Ask yourself what problems smoking seemed to solve. Sure, addictions *always* make matters worse. But what did smoking or other addictions *seem* to empower you with that you felt you didn't otherwise have? Do you sometimes still feel the need for that fake empowerment? How do you feel admitting to yourself certain perceived inadequacies *without* resorting to smoking or other addictions? Do you feel vulnerable without them? Allow yourself to feel those uncomfortable feelings, write about them in your journal, talk about them to your sponsor, a friend or a counsellor.

Moral Inventory

You have done a lot of writing about your life and your story of addiction this week. You have looked at how acting out your addictions have made matters worse. How they have damaged your body, damaged your free will, stymied your personal mission, disengaged you from other people. By smoking you have collaborated in your own 'getting stuck' in life, rather than moving on to fulfil the mission you were born to do. Your addictive behaviour has damaged your self-regard, been a bad example for others, especially children, and possibly caused diseases in, and certainly discomfort for, other people. As is increasingly well known, passive smoking or second-hand smoke or environmental tobacco smoke (ETS) causes strokes and lung cancer in non-smokers. It worsens non-smokers' pre-existing conditions such as asthma and emphysema. It weakens non-smokers' arteries, leading to possible heart attack and angina. It is associated with sudden infant death syndrome (cot death). It leaves unpleasant smells in non-smokers' hair, can sting their eyes, and cause them nose irritations. ETS is possibly associated with children's brain tumours, and causes and exacerbates asthma and ear infections in children, as well as wheezing, coughs and irritations. It is possibly associated with lymphoma. None of this is made up. It is authenticated by the World Health Organisation, and published in *The Tobacco Atlas*, by Dr Judith Mackay and Dr Michael Eriksen.

In short, people who have acted out a tobacco addiction and any other addiction benefit from doing a moral inventory of how their addictive thinking and behaviour have harmed themselves and others. Within Twelve Step programmes, including Alcoholics Anonymous and Nicotine Anonymous, the addict is invited to share with another person a written moral inventory of themselves as they are, warts and all. Likewise within Christian churches the practice of a general confession is seen as an important moment of acceptance, healing and grace, often made in conjunction with a major turning point in the person's life. In doing this programme, you are at such a key moment in your life. So take your journal. Do your moral inventory of how smoking has harmed you and others and then find someone, possibly your sponsor, with whom to share it. You do not have to go into the minutiae of everything you're ashamed of. The focus here is on healing, not guilt. You are closing a chapter on self-damage and damage to others, with your eyes fixed, with confidence, on your personal mission. It is enough to discuss your moral inventory with another person in general terms, and to listen to their words of hope and healing.

Activities for Week Seven

1. Write down five of your weaknesses. Now write down how each one could become your strength.

2. Look at your weaknesses again. See if you can identify the good parts of each weakness and the bad parts of each weakness. Decide to keep their good aspects and to give up their bad aspects.

3. Be aware of how your weaknesses come into play in your daily life. Resolve to become sufficiently self-aware to notice when your weaknesses come into play as you go through your day. Write about them in your journal. Record the good and the bad consequences of your weaknesses as they manifest in the daily round.

4. Look at your mission statement. What weakness is preventing you from fulfilling any aspect of your personal mission? What practical steps could you take to remove this block to your personal fulfilment? For instance, if it concerns a job or career change, find out what studies you need to do. If it involves treating yourself better, decide how you will do so, such as recognising and respecting your feelings in your journal. If it involves resolving an issue in a relationship, decide that you at least *want* to fix the relationship. There'll be more on relationships in Week Nine.

5. Write a one-week action plan for *one* aspect of your personal mission. For instance, if in Activity 4 above, you wrote that you needed to find out how to get a qualification, write down specific steps you could take in the week ahead to move that on. For instance, you might decide to ring up a school or college, seek out a careers advisor, or check it out on the Internet.

6. Listen to some music that you love this week.

7. Play with crayons or colouring pens. Doodle, and see what emerges.

8. You are discovering the peaceful inner power to say 'No' to smoking, 'No' to other addictions and 'No' to acting out your character defects. Be thankful for this.

9. Stay on your guard still. Monitor your lifestyle balance. If you feel any cravings this week, they originate in your mind, not your body. So deal with your mind – write your journal. Avoid temptations and, insofar as you can, avoid smokers and places where smoking takes place. Be abstemious still in your use of alcohol or, better, avoid alcohol for some time yet. Your recovery is still early and fragile. Be gentle with yourself.

10. Remember: your eyes are not set on deprivation but on abundance!

Review of Week Seven

1.   Did you do your morning journal every day last week? What was it like for you?

2.   Did you take your congé? What did you do and did you enjoy it?

3.   Did you speak with your sponsor? Did you share with him or her, or with another person, your moral inventory? What was the experience like for you?

Relapse

This week we explore the nature of relapse and the part it can play in stopping acting out of our addictions. Given that you began this journey in order to quit smoking, you might find it surprising that an unintended slip or a full-blown relapse *can* often be a necessary part of the cycle towards living your personal mission to the full. Of course, it does not have to be. People do succeed in permanently exiting their addictive behaviour on their first attempt. However, the reality is that many people need to try a number of times before they finally succeed in abandoning addictive thinking and behaviour for good.

This is not, of course, to encourage you to smoke again! Rather, it is an opportunity for you to understand better the nature of addiction, to know what to do in the event of a relapse and to raise your game, as it were, to a higher strategy for ultimate success.

The Spiral of Change

Two renowned and highly respected addiction cessation experts, J.O. Prochaska and C.C. DiClemente, are perhaps most famous for their "stages of change" model of how people leave behind addictive thinking and behaviour. Their indispensable insight is represented in Figure 1 on the following page.

The Stages of Change

Figure 1:

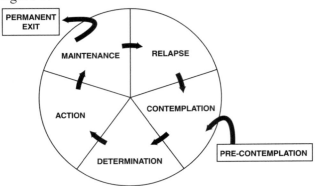

© Joe Armstrong 2004 www.writeway2stopsmoking.com
© Prochaska and DiClemente 1982

This is the model used by the Irish Cancer Society, the Irish Heart Foundation, the Irish College of General Practitioners, the World Health Organisation, and counsellors with the British charity QUIT are also trained in this model. However, I prefer to visually represent the model as a spiral, rather than a circle, because, as Prochaska and DiClemente and other smoking cessation experts agree, even if you relapse you are *not* back where you started, even if it feels that way (see Figure 2).

The Spiral of Change

Figure 2:

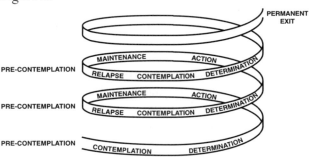

© Joe Armstrong 2004 www.writeway2stopsmoking.com
adapted from © Prochaska and DiClemente 1982

With the image of an ascending spiral, we have what I believe is a truer representation of the process. It is somewhat like the experience of walking in a labyrinth (not a maze). A maze can be frustrating because you can go down cul de sacs. But there are no cul-de-sacs in a labyrinth. While walking a labyrinth, you circle your intended destination, sometimes moving clockwise, sometimes anticlockwise; at times moving inwards, closer to your goal, again moving further out, even to the point of returning – almost – to the vantage point from which you set off at the start of the journey. But that 'almost' is so important. When you come back *as if* to where you started, while it can appear that you are now just as far away from your goal as when you first headed out, in fact you are much further on than that. You had to come back here in order to proceed further. You are *not* back where you started! In order to get here, you had to pass along the route of the labyrinth, through a less direct route than you could have imagined. In fact, when you get to the point where it seems that you're essentially back where you set out from, *all you need to do is to take the next step.* By doing do, sooner than you imagined possible and sooner by far than you feared, you find yourself progressing to the heart of the labyrinth and arriving at your destination. For us, the destination is permanent exit from the cycle of addictive thinking and behaviour *and* the purposeful pursuit of our personal mission, higher values and life goals. Incidentally, I recommend anyone who has the opportunity to do so to actually walk the curving paths of a labyrinth. It is a practical and spiritual learning tool for how we arrive at any worthwhile goal. Physically walking it becomes a metaphor for moving towards the achievement of our personal mission, and any intermediary goal to that end.

Stages of Change and Your Journey through this Programme

The *pre-contemplation* stage represents smokers who probably know smoking is bad for them but they are not actively involved in, or considering, an attempt to quit. They might think of it occasionally, but not enough to seriously consider changing their behaviour. *Contemplation* comes next. You might have been at the contemplation stage when you chose to read this book. Perhaps a doctor said something to you. Or you appreciated how silly it was to smoke. Maybe you were tired of smelling of cigarettes or you just felt the time was right to try to quit. You might still have been in the contemplation stage during the first two weeks of this programme. Indeed, the first fortnight was designed to enable you to resolve the contemplation stage. You will remember that after two weeks you reached a turning point where you weighed whether your motivation to stop smoking was greater than your motivation to continue on the fags, cigars or pipe. Hence, you were brought to what Prochaska and DiClemente and other smoking cessation experts call the decisional balance. In short, by continuing with the programme, you showed that you wanted to stop smoking and other addictions *more* than you wanted to stay smoking. Your resolution of that turning point brought you into the *determination* phase. You spent Weeks Three and Four planning your exit strategies, first by observing your smoking patterns and then by preparing to change them. On Day One of Week Five you began the *action* stage: you stopped smoking. You had, of course, been acting in lots of ways already, not least in writing your morning journal, taking your congé, becoming aware of your smoking habits, de-cluttering your environment of smoking paraphernalia, and visiting your doctor, dentist and pharmacist. But from your Quit Date you actually stopped the addictive behaviour. You coped with the intensive withdrawal period of the first three days when your body still craved nicotine. You took each day, or each minute, at a time. You worked on your lifestyle balance, such as taking care not to get hungry, eating healthily and regularly. You balanced your day with periods of work, rest, reflection and play. You realised that if you did not 'visit' each aspect of a balanced lifestyle (body, mind, feelings, and spirit) each day you were setting yourself up for a fall. Each day you took time out for physical exercise; applied your mind to something; became aware of your feelings, often through your journal in the first instance. You opened up your human spirit to your higher self. You continue to do all this, ensuring you live a balanced lifestyle each day. If the focus in Weeks Five and Six was supporting you in your abstinence, Week Seven and this chapter guide you through early recovery, where you are moving gradually into the *maintenance* stage, and help you to prevent a *relapse*.

Throughout this programme you have realised that quitting smoking and other addictions is your secondary goal: your primary goal is to live your unique life to the full. To do so you realise that poisoning your body, mind and spirit with cigarettes, cigars or pipe-smoking or by any other addiction can have no place in your personal mission. You know that smoking made you 'stuck'.

Your challenge now more than ever is to *believe* in your *personal mission*; to believe that you were put on this planet to do something that nobody but you could do, or that nobody but you could do in the way that you were born to do it. All you wanted to do was give up smoking and here you are confronting your ultimate purpose in life!

You have written your personal mission. Look at it again now. *That's* what you're about. You know smoking and other addictions conflict with it. Look again at your higher values contained in your mission statement. I'll bet you have things like enjoying each day, getting on well with others, being healthy. They too are what your life is about. They are what your life can be and increasingly *is* about *today*. In the moment of temptation, choose your higher mission above the immediate gratification of a cigarette or other addiction. Choose higher personal energy above the deflation of personal energy which invariably follows self-indulgence in any addiction.

Moving as you are now into the maintenance phase, it is important not to perceive it as a passive stage, simply marking time or fixing things that break. No! The power of your addiction is close by, waiting for its chance to regain control. You have worked so very hard to get to where you are. There is nothing inevitable about your continued abstinence from smoking but neither is there any such thing as an inevitable relapse (even if you relapsed before). If you feel that it is only a matter of time before you relapse, you need to take another look at the blocks to quitting exercise in Week One. For instance, if your addictive self is whispering

> *You won't succeed. You'll be back on the fags again sooner or later, so why struggle? Have one now! Most people who try to quit fail. And they're not that much harm for you, you know. Those so-called health enthusiasts are just anti-smoking. Anti-personal freedom. You've the right to smoke, if you want to. And of course you want to. Enough of this abstinence nonsense. Light up! Come back to me, my old friend! Can't you taste me?*

As in Week One, you can translate this addictive thinking into affirmations.

> *With the help of my higher power, I can succeed. By keeping a balanced lifestyle I can succeed. By facing my feelings in my journal, including my feelings about a relapse, I can succeed. By re-writing my blocks into affirmations, as I'm doing now, I can succeed. By taking it a day at a time, I can succeed. By keeping in touch with my sponsor, I can succeed. By believing in my personal mission, I can succeed.*
>
> *There is nothing inevitable about me going back on cigarettes, sooner or later. I am free. I choose my present and my future. I choose not to smoke. With the help of my higher*

*self I can succeed in implementing that choice. I am prepared
to struggle because I believe I can live a life free from acting
out my addictions. I do not need to smoke. If most people who
try fail, I am not most people. I am me. And even if I do fail,
if I have a slip or even a full-blown relapse, I shall 'get myself
up, dust myself off and start all over again'. Except I
wouldn't be starting over from scratch. I'd be still engaged in
the process and still learning. Even if I do slip or relapse, I
shall not blow the whole thing. Ultimately, it is not whether I
succeed or fail that matters but whether I try. I shall try after
each success and try after any failure. By the grace of my
higher power, I have done very well so far. I trust in my
higher self, that part of me that never needed to smoke and
never will need to think or act out addictions. I trust in my
higher self who wants me to continue to get 'unstuck'. I trust
in my higher self and in my higher values. I choose my
personal mission over the immediate and false gratification of
a cigarette, pipe or cigar.*

*As for health enthusiasts, they are right to be anti-
smoking. No creature on earth knowingly takes noxious fumes
into its body, nor chemicals that damage, retard and kill. I
no longer want to be what is increasingly becoming akin to a
social pariah. I want my freedom back and I want to keep my
new-found freedom! Hey, addictive self: don't you dare tell
me you want me to have the 'freedom' to smoke. Smoking, by
its addictive nature, is the antithesis to freedom. I cannot
have even one. You rob me of my freedom. If I want personal
freedom, the last thing I need to do is to smoke. I do not have
the 'right' to smoke. I do not have the right to damage my
body, mind and spirit nor to cause lung cancer in others. Nor
do I have the right to communicate to children that smoking
is all right. Smoking is not all right. It is never all right.
And on 'wanting' to, it is only my addictive self that wants to
smoke. My higher self wants much better things for me and
has in mind for me far better pleasures and joys than my
addictive self could contemplate! You were never my friend.
You were an abusive 'friend', a false 'friend', a freedom-
robbing, body-damaging, feelings- and mind- and spirit-
stunting enemy. There is no reason on this planet why I would
want to taste you again, no more than I would want to be ill,
nor have tar in my lungs nor limbs amputated! I want only
the delicious, lingering taste of freedom from you!*

How to Cause a Relapse

As a person dependent on nicotine, (and remember *your addiction does not go away simply because you have become abstinent!*) is there anything you could do to *cause* a relapse? Terence T. Gorski in his brilliant and insightful book *Passages Through Recovery: An Action Plan for Preventing Relapse* answers: "You don't have to do anything. Stop using alcohol and other drugs, but continue to live your life the way you always have. Your disease will do the rest. It will trigger a series of automatic and habitual reactions to life's problems that will create so much pain and discomfort that a return to chemical use will seem like a positive option."

The same, of course, applies to smoking. If you abstain from smoking or other addictions but do not change your thinking, behaviour and lifestyle, it is only a matter of time before you start smoking again or reverting to another addiction or becoming addicted to a new substance or process. That's why the focus of this book has been to analyse, plan and execute your goal of stopping smoking in the context of lifestyle changes and awakening to your higher self. As shown in Week Seven, guard against relapse by becoming aware of when your character defects are in play and work, with the help of your higher self, to redeem them.

Relapse

For all your good intentions and despite your best efforts to date, it is, of course, possible that you might relapse. For Prochaska and DiClemente and other addiction experts, this can be a normal part of the *process* of giving up smoking and other addictions. So, if you do slip – and, as you know, this is *not* inevitable – how you *think* about the lapse is crucial.

After so much effort over the past several weeks, you *could* feel crushed by a relapse. You *could* blow the whole thing. You *could* tell yourself your journey thus far was a waste of time. You *could* let your addictive self regain the upper hand, banishing your higher self to the shadows for years to come, or forever. You *could* dismiss the immense progress you have made over the past several weeks, reinterpreting your growth from the cynical perspective of addictive thinking.

You could, of course, think very differently about any slip or relapse. A slip, by the way, might be where your habit of smoking was so strong that one day you find yourself smoking again, having, as it were, momentarily forgotten your higher purpose. Your higher self can understand such as slip as a minor aberration on your ascent from the cave of addiction. Certainly there is no such thing as a safe cigarette, least of all now that you have been doing so well in reaching for your higher purpose. If you are smoking out of forgetfulness of your higher purpose, out of sheer power of a dying habit, stamp it out immediately. You're addictive self might echo that catch-phrase of BBC television's *Mastermind* series: 'I've started so I'll finish.' Don't let your addicted self fool you with this ruse. Just say No! As before, leave where you are. Remind yourself a craving will pass within five minutes. Drink water. Breathe deeply, using your breath to ground you in your higher mission, expelling addictive thinking, inhaling calm. If you finish it, you'll have to come back at a later stage to face this same challenge again and it won't be any easier then. So let's deal with it now. In short, if, God forbid, you start, you *don't* have to finish it. Extinguish it.

A relapse may well start from a slip. Which is why you commit yourself to *not even one*. If you relapse, analyse in your journal the thinking, feeling and circumstances that led to it. You could use the following questions to guide your analysis of the relapse. Where were you? What were you doing? Were you drinking alcohol? Who were you with? You already know that most people who relapse do so in the company of a friend who smokes. What is going on in your life right now? How do you perceive your personal mission? If some knock or setback has occurred which eroded your self-belief, say what it is. Has any new circumstance arisen in your life? How were you *feeling* about yourself when you chose to smoke? What feelings or new mood did you hope smoking would induce? How did you feel after you had smoked? What stresses, if any, were you under at work or at home?

We have seen that Prochaska and DiClemente and cessation experts across the globe see relapse as part of the process of giving up an addiction. If you relapse, there was something else that you needed to learn before your could proceed to permanently exit your addictive thinking and behaviour. William R. Miller and Stephen Rollnick in *Motivational Interviewing: Preparing People to Change Addictive Behaviour* say: "Each slip or relapse brings you one step closer to recovery." Of course this is not to encourage people to slip or relapse in order to learn more, nor is it an excuse for going back to addictive thinking and behaviour! Rather, it is a positive and effective way of thinking about a slip or relapse. If you relapse, you need to try to discover what you can learn from the apparent failure. You may need to cast off the false belief that you could do it all by yourself.

Some smokers, when they experience the first flush of abstaining from cigarettes, forget how difficult it has been and how vulnerable they remain to reverting to the addiction. They might look down on those who continue to smoke when, but for the grace of God and their analysis, planning and hard work, they too would have been smoking all along. Maybe they forgot that they remained addicted and always would remain so, or they may have stopped using the tools which had aided them to abstain from smoking: the morning journal, congé, regular exercise, a balanced lifestyle of food, sleep, work, rest, prayer and play.

You Still Cannot have 'Just One'

Some people relapse in order to learn the hardest way that they cannot have 'just one'. But, like being knocked down by a car, this is one piece of information it is better to accept as true without having to personally verify it. Think how many smokers would not be smoking now if, after a period of abstinence, their addictive selves hadn't fooled them into thinking they could have just one. You *cannot* take '*just one*'. If you do, sooner or later, with each successive 'one', you will find yourself smoking more until your addictive self holds sway again. Your higher self *never* needs *even one*. Your higher self calls you not to try *any*, no, not even *one*.

As B. Jack Gebhardt says in *The Enlightened Smoker's Guide to Quitting*: 'The reason having "just one" is so dangerous is not because of the cigarette itself but because it is very difficult to smoke and still enjoy all your thoughts about yourself.' By smoking even one cigarette, you will feel poorly about yourself. You will have less energy to move towards the completion of your personal mission. When you were smoking, you smoked because you felt you needed to. But smoking does not satisfy *any* authentic need you have. Instead of yielding to the insatiable desires of your addictive self, assert your higher values, aims and goals. In a real sense, your personal mission is fulfilled with every choice in favour of your higher mission.

Dealing with Inner Resistance

If you feel your addictive self is coming to the fore, try another dialogue between your addictive self and higher self as you did in Week Seven. If you skipped that exercise last week, you might like to try it now. You can spot inner resistance if your addictive self is arguing a lot, interrupting your higher self, denying you are addicted or ignoring valid points made by your higher self. Don't be worried if you encounter resistance from your addictive self. In fact, Miller and Rollnick in *Motivational Interviewing: Preparing People to Change Addictive Behaviour* argue that resistance is an opportunity because "it is on this stage that the drama of change unfolds". So write creative dialogues between your addictive self and higher self in your journal, confident that, by so doing, you are expressing on the page the very heart of the fight for your authenticity, healing and growth.

Feeling Disheartened

If you relapse, you can, of course, feel disheartened. The danger is that you slunk back into the cave of addiction, lick your wounds, and stay there. You can feel humiliated personally and socially, or welcomed too readily back by the company of smokers, who feel consoled in their own impotence by your resumed smoking.

It can, indeed, be the mark of the man or the woman, who can say, despite a relapse, that the higher self is better to aspire towards than the addictive self which gloats in your return. It can seem harder to set out again on the journey to abstinence and 'sobriety' from smoking and other addictions while humbled by relapse. You can understandably be tempted to wallow for a while in the relapse. And there you could stay for the rest of your life. Alternatively, you could realise that there was indeed something else you had to learn, learn it and appreciate that the next stage on the spiral of change is contemplation (see Figure 1 earlier in this chapter).

What I suggest is that *if* you have a slip or full-blown relapse, to *continue to work the programme*. Continue to do your morning journal, just as for the first four weeks you did so even though you hadn't given up smoking yet. Continue to take your weekly congé. Continue to talk to your sponsor. Continue to work through the suggested exercises and activities in this book. Continue your pursuit for a balanced lifestyle, every day. Most of all, continue to read and meditate upon your personal mission, which is your primary aim. And be confident that, despite the apparent setback, it is still all working perfectly. That this relapse, too, is part of the process.

The research shows that most people make three to five attempts to stop smoking before succeeding to permanently exit the cycle. As with other addictions, few succeed on their first attempt. Note that the permanent exit happens when people get to the maintenance stage, which is where you are now (unless you have relapsed). So the maintenance stage is far from a boring one. It is the phase from which you will either never smoke again or relapse until you return to a similar point on the addictive cycle again. So the maintenance stage, where you hopefully are now, is full of opportunity. If you think you've 'arrived' because you haven't smoked for three weeks, well, you haven't quite yet. (This isn't a *12-week* programme for nothing!). To use a pregnancy image, you are approaching the end of the second trimester. But the third trimester of gestation, the gestation for the reign of your higher self, needs more time and work by you before your new more authentic self can be born.

Sure you *could* abandon the programme now and not go back to smoking, just as premature babies can and do survive. But it's risky. And it's far better to stay within the womb to become stronger and improve your chances not only of survival but of flourishing in an often difficult world. You've more growing to do! You need to become more yourself. Indeed, you are learning that yourself and your higher self are one; and that your addictive self is a false self, intent on stunting your personal growth and mission.

Relapse: Don't Minimise Successes

If you relapse, do not let addictive thinking reduce your considerable successes. Don't let your addictive self reduce your fine achievement to nothing special. Neither should you let your addictive self tell you that there is no point in trying again anytime soon. Write down the number of healthy things that you have done, bidden by your higher self, over the past several weeks. In your journal, recognise the release of energy you have experienced. Bring to mind the confidence you have felt. Recall experiences of better self-esteem. Be grateful for any physical benefits you experienced such as breathing better, being able to climb stairs or play sports more ably. Be thankful for your improved skin, the extra sparkle in your eyes, the congés you have enjoyed, the insights gained through your morning journal. All of that and so much more is and remains real, even if you relapse. Be thankful for everything, even for the relapse. Your higher self works with you where you are. Write about any feelings of discouragement, humiliation, anger, or disappointment in your journal. Remember how you progressed before your Quit Date. You can continue to progress even after a relapse.

If you relapse, do you pick another Quit Date? That will become clear to you as you continue with your morning journal. You will know yourself what is best to do. It may be that you need to sort out something else in your lifestyle balance, which you can continue to explore in your journal. You may need some counselling to resolve some issue such as career direction, sexual identity, marriage, solitude or your spiritual life. Whatever it is that you have yet to learn will become apparent by continuing to trust your higher self as you express your innermost self in your journal. Perhaps you will find out that all that went wrong was some small deficiency in your plan to quit smoking. No matter how thorough you were in your planning in Weeks Three and Four, perhaps you overlooked something. Now is your opportunity to rectify the plan so that you can be even more confident when you abstain from smoking again, shortly. Remember the process of walking the labyrinth. Sometimes when you arrive back seemingly where you started, you realise that you have in fact come a long way and by simply taking the next step you quickly advance towards fulfilling your higher purpose.

One Day at a Time

As we saw before, one of the challenges presented if you relapse after a period of successfully abstaining from cigarettes or any other addiction is that you can feel a bit oppressed *by* your past *success*. You know the achievement that represented and, like a successful marathon runner contemplating a new race, you might feel like you're not up to trying again anytime soon. You forget that your secret to that success was precisely to take one day at a time, just as the runner must take one step at a time. So forget about oppressive thoughts like 'Can I go another full seven days without smoking?' or however long you abstained for. Rather ask: *'Can I go one more minute without smoking?'* If you focus on the present, you come again into 'the sacrament of the present moment'. *The most important time in your whole long life is now.* This minute. Pride can get in the way and think: 'I'm not up to doing it again for a long period.' Wisdom intervenes and says: 'I don't need to.' I can abstain for this minute. Just for now.' So long as you live in the now, rather than being oppressed by past successes or failures, you can gain the courage to simply take your next humble step forward. And right away you're back on track! Ultimately, it's the journey that matters, not reaching the destination. The only reality is *now*.

Getting Back on Track

When the time is right, and probably sooner than you expect, you'll know when to abstain again. So long as you continue to work the programme, you can explore in your journal the kinds of things you did in Weeks One to Seven. Consider what you did well and anything you might have undervalued or not implemented as you'd intended. For instance, did you avoid using nicotine replacement products or medication recommended by your doctor? Did you never quite get into the journal and so skimped on it, writing only two rather than the three pages recommended each morning? It is on the third page that the interesting stuff often emerges, once you've had the chance to get important but nevertheless more superficial stuff out of the way on the first two pages. Did you cut back on physical exercise, sleep or proper food? Did you neglect yourself, or your family or friends? Did work take over? Or did you try to fool yourself by smoking cigars while congratulating yourself for quitting cigarettes? Lastly, if you relapsed while drinking alcohol, are you altogether sure that alcohol might not be an area you need to look at? Whether or not you decide that it too is a problem area for you, might your higher self be suggesting that you try abstaining from alcohol for a while until you have established yourself as a non-smoker living your singular life to the full? If you find the prospect of abstinence from alcohol or any other mood-altering substance or process unthinkable for an extended period, you could invite your higher self to shed light on this reluctance in your journal. You could discover all sorts of unexpected joys by taking the journey further to include abstinence from such substances or processes for a period. Consider the benefits and perceived losses of such a venture by doing exercises similar to those which you did in Weeks One and Two. I repeat it is not a question of giving up alcohol forever, but rather for a period of your choosing.

One factor that can lead to relapse is a reluctance to look at *all* addictions and habits, or *possible* addictions, simultaneously. If you're not addicted to whatever it is you don't want to give up, consider giving it up and exploring where it leads you. You could learn so much more than you could possibly anticipate and be invigorated physically, mentally and spiritually by so doing.

When getting back on track, remember the simple strategies you used, and which worked, before. Things like eating a piece of fruit, drinking lots of water, moving out of an environment where you might smoke, and reminding yourself that craving only lasts three-to-five minutes.

Other Addictions: An Exercise

In your journal, write your spontaneous response to the suggestion that you abstain from some other mood-altering substance or process. Keep writing. Be spontaneous. Go with the flow. See what emerges. Be aware of your thoughts, feelings, energy, attractions, and resistance. See if there is any denial operative in what you write. How free are you of all mood-altering substances and processes that you use? Ask your higher self, who wants nothing but your personal good, for guidance and insight.

Acknowledging Injuries: An Exercise

Part of the healing that you may need to do at this stage of your journey is to acknowledge injuries, including self-inflicted injuries. This is a time of healing in your life. Your body has been getting better. Your emotions have been re-awakening, now that you are no longer numbing your feelings with tobacco. Your authentic mood is coming to the surface, now that you have stopped using mood-altering substances or processes. You will probably find you have a normal range of human emotions and moods. Some smokers, removed from the artificial stimulus of mood-altering dependencies might sense they need some professional medical or therapeutic help. Do not fear whatever emerges. With the bubbling to the surface of feelings, perhaps long suppressed or ignored by you, comes the opportunity for a gracious healing of body, mind, feelings and spirit.

Explore any area of personal injury in your journal. Include physical damages done to, or by you, to yourself (for instance, but not exclusively, through smoking). Look at violations done by others or by yourself to your personal mission. For instance, perhaps you knew what you wanted to do with your life career-wise but remained in a job you hated, or which wasn't quite you, for fear that your dream could not come true. Maybe you were given the opportunity to try out some long-held dream but you turned it down. Count your losses, visited upon you or self-inflicted. Be gentle with yourself!

Discarding Dysfunctional Ways

If, while you were at the mercy of your addictive self, you used to handle problems in a dysfunctional way, you are now called to try more adult and effective ways of dealing with stresses and crises. In particular, beware feelings of superiority, anger, jealousy, fear, resentment, or depression. Take one simple step towards putting right anything that is lacking in your current coping strategies. It could be as simple as going to bed earlier tonight or taking more time over a meal, digesting your food properly. Or stopping work, even though it isn't 'perfect'. Or repeating silently or aloud an affirmation. Or, if you're feeling tense, doing a relaxation exercise for five minutes.

No Excuses

If you have blocked the pursuit of your personal mission, using excuses like you're too old, or you've too many financial or family commitments, or you lack the necessary knowledge, connections, skills or experience, stop making such excuses! Maybe you've had countless setbacks or started out with innumerable disadvantages, but these can in fact be turned to your advantage. If you really *want* to achieve your personal mission you really *can*, with the help of God. If you can't go through the wall, go around it. If the conventional route isn't working for you, find an unconventional route. No excuses! Go for it! No one expects you to achieve your life's goals overnight. But you always know even one simple thing you could do right now to move you towards where you need to be. It will be a practical, measurable, simple thing, maybe like turning on (or off!) your computer, making a phone call, or buying goal-specific materials in a local shop. Go do it!

Activities for Week Eight

1. Sit in a relaxed position, your feet firmly on the ground, palms opened on your lap. Become aware of your muscles, tensing and relaxing the body from toes to head. Focus on your breathing, exhaling hurts, injuries, regrets, and breathing in serenity, peace, acceptance, hope. Try to let go of any pain in your life. Your desire to quit smoking and other addictions permanently and to fulfil your personal mission is held in the palm of God's hand. Let your higher power 'hold' your successes and failures, your abstinence and lapses. Now is the time to abstain from smoking. *Not 'for ever' (which never comes and is oppressive to contemplate) but just 'for now'.*

2. Write down a dream you aspire to but have not yet fulfilled. Imagine yourself at the end of your life having accomplished this grand dream. To get there, what would you need to do in the next five years? What would you need to do within the next twelve months? To move towards your goal, what do you need to

do within the next month? What do you need to do this week? What one thing can you do today to move towards fulfilling your dream?

Review of Week Eight

1. Did you do your morning journal every day last week? What was it like for you?

2. Did you take your congé? What did you do? How are your congés helping you wake up to joy?

3. Did you speak with your sponsor and other supporters of your authentic self? How have they helped you?

4. Has anything happened in the last week, or since the start of this programme, which is nudging you towards a great dream you have for your life?

The Power Within

This week we recognise that sustained freedom from acting out our addiction to smoking or other compulsions lies within ourselves. Stopping smoking and other addictions is not an ego-trip but a spiritual quest. We need to forgive ourselves and others, and show compassion to ourselves and others. We learn that we can cope well when we focus on one thought at a time. We look at stress. We recognise the reality of inner healing and we work on gaining or regaining enhanced social skills and discovering or rediscovering quality relationships without resorting to any addictions.

Tricks

In the journey of the mythic hero as elucidated by Joseph Campbell – and you are, of course, that hero here – the protagonist must trick opponents out of their treasure. Whether it is *Jack and the Beanstalk*, *The Lord of the Rings*, or the Harry Potter stories, the hero tricks the enemy to solve seemingly intractable problems. Likewise, you have been learning tricks to beat the habit and addiction of smoking. One of those tricks, as you've been practising, is to live completely in the present moment. By doing this, you know you can climb any mountain since the only step that matters is the one you're taking *now*. As Campbell and other spiritual teachers, traditions and religions, including Christianity, teach, immortality is present in the here and now. In a real sense your abstinence and 'sobriety' is already achieved *in this moment*. Likewise, your personal mission is being completed even as you read this sentence. All you need to do is to listen to it; co-operate with it; and let your true story emerge. Don't try to manipulate any outcomes. Simply listen, especially in your journal, and let who you are as a person who has outgrown addictive thinking and acting emerge.

Dysfunctional Families of Origin

Often, addicts come from dysfunctional families. This can, of course, be as true for smokers as for people with other addictions. Consider in your journal problems you now have to deal with that began while growing up in your family of origin. Write down one or two of them. You could also consider the blessings that have come by being born into your family. When you've done that, think about any unresolved issues from your childhood, such as unresolved pain or hurt. To balance that again, you might also think of things to be thankful for by being born into your family.

In getting to this point of the programme, you have recovered from much of the damage done to you by cigarettes. You have begun to think, feel and act differently now that you are more attuned to your higher self than when you were at the beck and call of your addictive self. You have been countering poor lifestyle balance with an improved work-life balance, keeping a daily check on your body, mind, emotions and spirit. You are well and truly into the maintenance stage, in which you consolidate your learning that there is no such thing as a safe cigarette. You need constantly to be on your guard against being hi-jacked or sabotaged by your addictive self. Of course, your journal is key to this in that you slow yourself down and hear yourself thinking. When addictive thoughts or feelings or actions emerge, do not ignore them but let your higher self engage them on the page in dialogue.

One-month Watershed

You start this week with one month's smokefree thinking and behaviour under your belt. You have now become physically withdrawn from your addiction. This is true for most people, although some symptoms could linger.

Mind you, an insurance company might not accept that you are, as yet, a non-smoker. But by living each day one day at a time, in less than a year from now they may so regard you. You might still be struck at how normal people regard your non-smoking, as if long-time non-smokers don't appreciate the gargantuan efforts you've put into analysing, planning, stopping, and staying stopped. Then again, isn't it wonderful that people no longer have to regret your company because of your smoking, conscious of the carcinogenic threat it used to pose for them or their loved ones. You can be sure they appreciate no longer reeking of smoke after spending time with you.

Feelings Unrelated to Smoking

One of the things you need to be aware of is a tendency of many former smokers to attribute to smoking something which is, in fact, not related to it at all. For instance, if certain emotions bubble to the surface, it is all too easy to think that you wouldn't have these uncomfortable feelings if you were still smoking. In a sense, you're right. Smoking often dulled your awareness of how you were feeling deep down.

But now that you are steadily embarked on the path to self-actualisation and fulfilment, you realise that numbing out feelings is not a responsible or adult way of life. Your feelings, even your uncomfortable ones, are gifts, sent to your conscious mind to be listened to, respected and responded to. They are telling you something you need to hear. They can help you get unstuck. Rather than blaming the absence of cigarettes for being put in touch with these feelings, be thankful for even uncomfortable feelings because you need to deal with them.

Indeed, that old feeling you used to get – and possibly still do – of wanting to have a cigarette can become an opportunity for you to grow in self-knowledge and advance towards personal fulfilment. Instead of stopping at the urge to have a cigarette and giving in to it, as you did in the past, now you can transcend that urge and examine the feelings that lie behind it. For instance, if you feel frustrated at work or in a relationship, the real issue is to resolve that frustration in an adult way. Smoking clearly does nothing to solve the actual problem: it simply suppresses it or buries it. The problem remains to be tackled! So, if you feel the urge to smoke or act out any other addiction, see if you can write down in your pocket log or morning journal the feeling that lies behind that urge.

Perhaps you're not happy in your work. Maybe there are issues in personal relationships you need to face and resolve. Maybe there are issues of self-esteem and personal worth you are being called to explore and work with. Just as stopping smoking allowed you to breathe better, your feelings could be telling you that something in your life needs to change, such as within a relationship, or at work, or in the way you treat yourself. Possibly you don't respect yourself or recognise or respond to your personal needs enough. You may be being called to honour yourself. You cannot love others until you love yourself.

You cannot emerge as your unique self – the unrepeatable human person whom you alone are with a singular mission to fulfil which no one else can do as well as you – without encountering your emotive self. So do not interpret any new level of awareness of your feelings as a negative thing. Quite the contrary, by working with whatever bubbles up from your sub-conscious you will be better equipped to advance further towards your personal calling. As Sarah Litvinoff says in *The Essential Guide to Stopping Smoking*:

> Sometimes you are affected by symptoms that seem to be connected to quitting smoking long after it is likely to be the case. You need to evaluate what you are feeling, and whether, in fact, it has anything to do with smoking at all.

Your Long-forgotten Purpose: An Exercise

Now that you have abstained from cigarettes, cigars or the pipe for a month, a real fear can emerge. Whether you feel called to be an artist, a musician, an electrician, or whatever, a fear of success and a fear of failure can seize you. When you smoked or indulged in other addictions, you could forget your higher life purpose. Now that you have stopped acting out your addictions with the help of your higher power, you can feel exposed and fearful. You can shudder at the responsibility of taking your personal mission seriously. It can be a fearsome thing to believe in yourself. You can fear that you're not up to the lofty ideals of your mission statement. You're too old, too young, too unskilled, too skilled, or you just don't want the responsibility of working to bring about that to which you feel (or fear!) you have been called. But if you do not proceed towards your higher purpose, you may well sidle back into addictive thinking and behaviour.

Here your journal can come into its own. Having written your mission statement and done so well as to arrive at this point of abstinence from addictive behaviour, how do you feel deep down about fulfilling your personal mission? Write about it. Take a few minutes and express how you feel about your higher calling. Are you clearer what it is? If you don't know where you're headed, you won't recognise it even if you've arrived! Have you written your six-month plan to move in the direction of your calling?

Beware Stress

Just as you need to avoid getting hungry, you must also employ 24-hour personal stress antennae. For instance, if you are working too hard, you are in danger of feeling 'entitled' to a cigarette. Sure, you're entitled to relax. Or to take time out. To breathe in a relaxing, restorative, calming way such as by alternate nostril breathing or deep breathing. Sure you are entitled to make time for physical exercise, which will help you manage your stress levels and enhance your mood and self-esteem, and counter depression. But only addictive thinking could ever lead you to thinking you're 'entitled' to a cigarette (or acting out any other addiction).

If you're losing your life balance you need to shout stop! Your health and wellbeing, mental, physical, emotional, social and spiritual, is more important than anything that's causing you stress. This is not selfishness. It is healthy self-love, without which you would soon be back in the cave of addiction.

Symptoms of Stress

If you notice any of the following signs of stress at this remove from your Quit Date in Week Five, please believe that giving up cigarettes is *not* causing them. There is nothing wrong with experiencing these signs. What is wrong is to conclude erroneously that (a) they're caused by not smoking or (b) they would be cured by smoking. In fact, as members of Alcoholics Anonymous say, there is no problem that a drink will not make worse. Since abstaining from cigarettes is no longer the cause of the following, you will need to examine your lifestyle, thinking, attitudes and behaviour to discover their true cause.

- Irritability, shouting

- Arriving late at work

- Taking sick days

- Loss of motivation

- Neglect of personal appearance

- Isolation

- Mood changes

- Disproportionate responses

- Cynicism

- Tears, weeping

- Changes in behaviour

Impact of Stress

Stress can have negative consequences for your personal life, your work and your health. It can lead to:

- a loss of work-life balance

- lack of personal fulfilment

- increased addictive behaviour or relapse after period of abstinence

- poor sleep

- loss of appetite

- less time or energy for partner and family members

- disturbed relationships

- sexual problems

- low self-esteem and poor morale

- decreased creativity

- lower productivity

- accidents

- heart disease

- aches and pains, such as back pain

- stomach and bowel complaints

- poor concentration and thinking

- reduced ability to learn

- headaches

- anxiety

- depression

- mental health problems

- suicide

What to Do about Stress

As we've said, the last thing you should do is reach for a cigarette, other tobacco products or act out any other addiction. That would only make you feel *more* stressful, not less. You would feel annoyed with yourself, disappointed and quite possibly depressed for having relapsed to addictive thinking and behaviour.

Stressors (things that we feel stressed about) have an objective and a subjective element to them. For instance, one person might feel stressed at the idea of speaking in public but the same person might love dogs. Another person might relish public debate but quiver at the sight of a poodle. On the other hand, some things would be stressful to most people, such as divorce, bereavement, loss of a job, financial problems, or the diagnosis that your child or partner has a serious illness.

Stress arises when the demands placed upon you seem greater than your coping skills. However, coping skills can be learned. And objectively stressful situations can be modified to become less stress inducing. For instance, stress at work can be caused by poor job design, a bad person/job fit, work-life imbalance, lacking control over your work, poor communication, job insecurity or an unpleasant or unhealthy working environment. All of these things can be changed within organisations, and indeed employers are obliged to do so in light of health and safety legislation in developed countries requiring employers to take all reasonable steps to ensure the health and safety of their employees. Like giving up smoking, change doesn't happen overnight. Problems need to be analysed, solutions planned for and implementation must take place and be monitored carefully. Ultimately though if, for instance, the ethos of an organisation conflicts with your own, you may need to consider alternative employment. This may require you facing fears about being true to yourself, taking a calculated risk, becoming clearer about your mission, and being brave enough to face whatever fears you have. It can be very hard to leave behind the security of employment, and possibly a permanent, pensionable position for the more tentative and uncharted journey of responding to your higher self, perhaps by trying a new job, a new career or setting up a venture on your own. But those who take the lonely and courageous road of responding to what they believe they were put on this planet to do never regret it.

Quick Tips for Stress Reduction

- Achieve and maintain work-life balance

- Each day 'visit' the mind, body, emotions and spirit

- Eat healthily

- Take regular physical exercise

- Write your journal every day

- Learn to say 'No'

- Take time out just for you, in your weekly congé and, daily, take time out to relax.

- Develop and enjoy mutually satisfying interdependent relationships, where neither party is the sole 'giver' or 'helper' but each enjoys supporting and being supported

- Know how your feel and express your emotions in your journal and with your partner or trusted friends

- At work, ensure:

  1. workers are respected and valued

  2. culture of blame avoided

  3. sensible work schedules

4. demands within workers' coping skills

5. workers have measure of control over their work

6. no bullying or harassment

7. change carefully managed

8. adequate training for the job

9. supportive relationships

10. roles clearly defined

- If stress is too great, you may need to consider asking for professional help. There is no shame in this. Simply talk to your doctor who should be able to arrange a consultation with a therapist or counsellor.

Visualisation and Dealing with Smokers

In Week Four, we looked at visualisation as a practical and effective tool in helping you prepare for situations in which you used to smoke. As we've seen, it is also useful in exploring near misses, or actual slips. In your imagination, you can visit or revisit a scene and decide how you would handle a similar situation the next time.

If you have been avoiding places and people you used to socialise with in order to give yourself a better chance to stop smoking, you may feel it's time to get back to your old social network. Before you do so, ask if you really need to. Make your choice on the basis of whether returning to old haunts is in keeping with your higher self. If most of your friends smoke, you might have a very limited social network, given that many more people don't smoke than do. After all, approximately two people don't smoke for every one that does. That's a lot of potential friends out there. Moreover, by hanging out with friends who smoke, you may be more tempted to slide back down into the cave of addiction. And your higher self does not want you to be susceptible to the carcinogenic effect on you of their second-hand smoke. And do you really want to smell of other people's smoke?

If, while you smoked, you were not listening to your higher self as well as you do now, might you not consider that many smokers too are stuck? That they are trapped in their addiction and comforting one another rather than emerging into the more challenging adult world beyond the cave? Imagine if, instead of spending so much time with people who are addicted, you spent more time with people who are actively pursuing their personal calling? People who respect themselves enough not to poison their bodies and reduce their personal freedom through acting out addictions. This is not to suggest that all non-smokers are in active pursuit of their higher calling, or that all smokers are not. After all, it was your response to the call of your higher self *when you were a smoker* that has brought you this far; and for the first four weeks of this programme you still smoked. God accepts us as we are, smokers and non-smokers alike.

However, if you must return to the scenes of former crimes, as it were, then use visualisation to prepare you. What you imagine will be close to your actual experience of going back to former places or mixing again with smokers whom you've seen less in recent weeks. Anticipate people who will try to get you to smoke, people whose lives played out in obedience to their addicted selves are affronted by your courage and progress in responding to your higher self. In your imagination, feel how you will be feeling and *be worried if you feel superior or better than anyone else*. You have done what you have done, despite all your hard work, by the grace of God.

Visualisation and Dealing with Smokers: An Exercise

Take some minutes now to imagine going back to an old haunt where you used to smoke, or meeting up with smokers with whom you always smoked. Use your five senses, making the scene real in your mind by sight, hearing, touch, taste and scent. What's the mood of the people? What is being said? What might someone say to tempt you to smoke? In your imagination, how do you respond? How do you feel when you smell others' cigarette smoke? What do you want to do if you feel pressurised or jeered and what do you 'see' yourself doing in your imagination? Decide what you will say. Do you walk away, break a cigarette, or ask someone to respect your choice? When you do meet your smoker friends, you will be better prepared against temptation just as a golfer who visualises each hole in advance will perform much better than those who don't use visualisation.

Weight Gain

As we mentioned in Week Four, you can expect to put on a few pounds after quitting smoking. But if you are putting on more than just a few, it is almost certainly because of your diet or lack of physical exercise. As a rule, it is good to cut back on full-fat dairy products, and avoiding things like biscuits, cakes, and mayonnaise. By taking fruit instead of confectionery for snacks, you will be surprised how quickly you can attain a healthy body weight.

You are what you eat. Think twice before you put anything into your body. Eating is not only a physical activity. It also feeds (or fails to nourish or actually damages), your mind, emotions and spirit. The way you eat is also important. Take sufficient time for a meal. Don't rush. Put down the fork or spoon between mouthfuls. If possible, don't listen to the news while eating and don't watch television while eating. Taste your food. Chew each mouthful, remembering that the mouth is the first organ of digestion. Swallowing food insufficiently chewed gives your other digestive organs more work to do than they should have to do. Moreover, taking your time over a meal helps you appreciate and become grateful for the food you eat. When you are grateful for the blessing of good food, you are less likely to abuse your body with unhealthy food. Ideally, don't drink while eating, as that can interfere with your digestive juices, including those of your mouth, which will break down foods better without other liquids competing with their function.

Taking time over a meal is also a way of reducing stress in your life. It slows you down. If you can take a short siesta of 10 to 15 minutes after your midday meal, all the better. If you find your breakfasts are rushed, get up earlier. Try not to eat too late at night and, if you are taking alcohol, it is better to have a drink earlier in the evening than later as alcohol actually inhibits sound sleep. It is a good practice to pause to become thankful for food before and after eating. As such, dining becomes a holistic experience and a counterpoint to stress. If your lifestyle doesn't allow such an approach to eating, then you might need to re-examine your lifestyle. Few things are more basic in life than eating. If you cannot do so fundamental a daily activity without pause, awareness and gratitude, you might reflect in your journal if your higher self has a better way for you.

Temporary Journals and Filing

Now is a time for vigilance: redouble your commitment to your morning journal. If you are travelling or away from home, take some blank single sheets of paper with you for your journal and staple them into it on your return. If you are going away for a longer period, take a smaller more compact journal with you. Keep all your journals, storing them away carefully and safely. You can write on their front cover the period they cover. You really don't ever need to read them, although they can be interesting and insightful if browsed after a number of years.

Social Interaction

Many smokers began to smoke as a way of feeling accepted within a group. Some people feel awkward socially and smoking was literally a kind of smokescreen they erected to pass off their discomfort. Like so often in life when we take a wrong turn or mistake, when we give up smoking we can find ourselves back there, this time trying to meet the challenge in a more responsible, adult way. Try if you can to define the problem. For instance, maybe you find it hard to speak honestly or openly in conversation. Perhaps you speak with a monotonous or overly quiet voice. Maybe your body language is askew. Maybe you don't think of smiling or you've problems with eye contact. Maybe you've never learned to shake hands in a wholesome, welcoming, confident way. All these problems can be overcome.

Perhaps your self-esteem is two inches high. That too can be worked on. Indeed, insofar as you are responding to your higher self, you will already have found yourself growing in confidence and with a sense of purpose. There are so many ways to gain or regain social skills. Once you identify the problem, if this is an area you need to work on, then you are already on your way to finding the solution. Writing about your self-esteem in your journal will help. You could consider counselling as social skills challenges can have as their root some unresolved childhood trauma or ongoing conflict.

You can also use the skill of visualisation to anticipate social interaction, trying out new initiatives in your imagination. It might be as simple as smiling more.

Remember that people love talking about themselves so you could get people to do just that. Say positive, up-building things to people. Treat other people as you would like them to treat you. You might also consider that a person shy in one social context could be gregarious in another. Perhaps you are like a fish out of water and your higher self could be suggesting that you could be more yourself in a different social setting. For instance, perhaps you associate with people for whom material success is very important but your higher self may be inviting you to associate with people who share better values. When you feel grounded in who you are, which happens day-by-day through your journal, and as you reach for your personal mission and maintain your abstinence from tobacco and any other dependencies, you may be surprised at your growing facility to express your authentic voice in any social setting.

Niggles, Pinches and Crunches

There is a model of human relationships which holds that if you share your 'niggles', you will have fewer 'pinches'. And if you deal with pinches, you are likely to have very few, if any, 'crunches'. Typically, however, people ignore niggles – small things that bother them about their relationships. By ignoring them, they don't go away! They build up and subsequently mutate into a pinch – a more serious disagreement. If these in turn are left to fester unresolved, you are brewing up a serious conflict situation. When you get to a crunch point, it all comes out, usually in an atmosphere of high emotion, low rationality and poor listening.

There are excellent books and resources written on the pinch/crunch model of relationships such as Margaret Vincent's *Love Needs Learning: A Relationship Course for Young People.* Niggles, in fact, are an opportunity for relationships to deepen. You should welcome them! They show your relationship is alive. Indeed, if you don't experience niggles, the relationship might need some to waken it up! A niggle healthily recognised and expressed could be something as simple as 'I'm bothered that I'm left to pick clothes from the floor that I didn't put there.'

Listening is paramount within the pinch/crunch model. In the first instance, listening to yourself. Not ignoring the niggle. Again, the journal is great here because you'll find yourself expressing minor irritations that need to be dealt with. When expressing a niggle, it's important to pick an appropriate time. Not while your partner is dashing out to work, or deadbeat after a hard day at the office. When the time is appropriate, the niggle needs to be aired sensitively, in a non-accusing way. Now is not the time for either party to bring up heaps of things from the past. This is not a 'but-what-about-when-you-did-such-and-such-a-thing' exercise. Be specific. Focus on the one thing that gave rise to the niggle. We will look in the section on assertiveness (below) how this is best done. The point here is to search for a win-win solution. You're not looking for an 'I-was-right-You-were-wrong' situation, nor do you want to win while the other person loses. Unless you both feel like winners at the end, and that the niggle has been resolved to both persons' satisfaction, then the work is not yet complete.

Assertiveness

An excellent device for being assertive is to use the formula: "When you... I felt... because..." This really is a winning formula for dealing with conflict. Conflict, which can be defined as a clash of two intentions, is not a bad word. It is essential and inevitable in human relationships. It is how you deal with conflict that matters. Of course, you know that smoking or resorting to other addictions solves nothing but only creates new problems.

Here's an example of the formula offered above. "*When you* didn't do the dishes *I felt* it was unfair *because* I had cooked." This is assertiveness because it expresses your feeling about someone else's behaviour in a non-aggressive way. So long as you have chosen your time astutely – not while your partner is in the middle of a tight work deadline or dealing with screaming children – you trust that you will reach a mutually satisfactory outcome to the niggle. It may be that the other party *was* taking you for granted and this niggle reminds both of you that relationships go wrong when that occurs. Or it might emerge that they intended to do the dishes or pick up the clothes but needed to do something else first or it slipped their mind. Wherever the conversation leads, so long as it is done in a non-threatening, sensitive way, with both parties focused on arriving at a win-win solution, then the niggle and the process of discussing it and coming to a solution will actually *deepen* and *strengthen* the relationship. Communicating niggles is also a great way of realising that your partner is not a mind reader, nor should he or she be expected to be one.

Fear and Your Personal Mission

We have suggested throughout that being 'stuck' smoking cigarettes was in some way associated with being stuck in progressing towards your personal mission. Blocks to living your higher calling are often rooted in fear. Have a look at experiences you have had in the past of seeking self-fulfilment. Can you think of experiences which you regard as setbacks which could be looked at differently? Perhaps you worked really hard on something but it seemed to go no-where. Maybe you got negative feedback which discouraged you. Or you heard only the negative and ignored positive reactions. We can all-too-easily erect blocks from within ourselves to the pursuit of our personal mission. Maybe we wanted to be successful too fast, without doing much needed preparatory work. Or maybe we feared success and looked for excuses not to proceed.

Fear and Your Personal Mission:
An Exercise

1. Have you had opportunities to advance your personal mission which you declined? This isn't a blame game. Just a reality check. Write about one or two such incidences in your journal. What did you fear? What was holding you back?

2. Once again: this isn't a blame game. So, what can you do now to prepare yourself for your next big break? Remember the old maxim: chance favours the prepared.

3. In your journal, write down any fears you have about your personal mission.

Activities for Week Nine

1. Now that you have stopped smoking, beware a possible feeling of disappointment. It has been one thing to stamp out the cigarettes, cigars or to discard the pipe. It's another to live your life to the full. Quitting smoking is a tool for personal growth and change: it is not the end of the road in itself. Do you need to take a look at your marriage or primary relationship, or explore your career or job? Is there something missing? Would you consider doing marriage counselling or therapy? Are you open to reviewing your career with a career analyst? Will you do so? When? Are you willing to do any course or programme of study that could benefit you?

2. Have you apologised to people whom you have hurt by your smoking? Do you feel able to do so? Are you willing to make restitution if possible, if your offences warrant it? For instance, have you directly or indirectly influenced others to smoke? Do you need to say sorry to people whose clothes and hair you polluted, or who might have contracted lung cancer because of your smoking? Do you need to ask forgiveness of yourself for the harm you have done your body, mind and spirit? Redemption doesn't involve forgetfulness: it involves remembering and forgiving.

3. Once again: do you accept yourself as you are right now? What do you accept about yourself? What do you not accept? How might it feel if you *totally* accepted yourself in this moment? Write how you would feel in your journal.

4. Crises will still happen even now that you've quit smoking. To prevent reverting to addictive behaviour under pressure, do not ignore crises when they occur. Deal with them. Write about all that's going on in your journal. Express your feelings and thoughts. Explore possible solutions. Name your fears. Face them. Maintain or redouble your efforts to achieve a balanced lifestyle. Don't think: 'I haven't time for my journal in this crisis.' Or: 'I'll skip my walk/cycle/swim.' Or: 'I need to eat fast or skip meals.' Or: 'I just don't have time for my congé.' Quite the contrary! In a crisis, commit afresh to the tools for balanced living.

5. Write a personal prayer to your higher power to use in a crisis or stressful time.

6. Daily *examen*. It is a good idea to end each day with a few quiet moments of reflection. Become aware of any shifts in your mood during the day that is ending. Recall things for which you are grateful, specifically writing down at least five things for which you are thankful. Feel free to write down many more than this. Ask yourself if you spent some time that day attentive to your body, mind, emotions and spirituality. Did you achieve a good balance between work, rest, prayer and play? Who has done most of your thinking today, your addictive self or your higher self?

Review of Week Nine

1. Did you do your morning journal every day last week? What was it like for you?

2. Did you take your congé? What did you do? How did it change you?

3. Did you meet or speak with your sponsor? Write about what you discussed.

10

Called to Serve

This week we look at how the lessons we are learning can help other people. It is suggested that we *avoid* becoming a zealot – acting in a way that is over-eager for others to discover the path we have taken. We are cautioned not to nag others or in any way to feel superior to them. Rather, we are called to support others and respect their freedom. Ex-smokers can renew the community. We must learn to do all we do from the perspective of serenity, a humble self-knowledge and love.

Avoid Becoming a Zealot

A danger for the person recovering from their addiction to smoking is a temptation to become an anti-smoking zealot. It's understandable, for sure. You have learned how bad cigarettes, cigars and pipe smoking are for you. You realise the dangers they create for the smoker and those who must breathe air in places where smoking takes place. You appreciate how easy it is to lose one's freedom to nicotine and you know how hard it can be to regain that freedom. But you must proceed from here humbly, remembering that at any moment you are, perhaps, only moments away from reverting to acting out your addiction. Do not become puffed up with pride, which, as you have been reminded, comes before a fall. Of course you have worked very hard to get to this day and your active participation was essential. But instead of feeling superior, which you are not, rather feel grateful. Be thankful to your higher self for calling you from the cave of addiction. By the grace of God you have emerged from that pit. By grace, and your response to the divinity within you, you remain outside the cave.

If you are tempted to change the world, or, more particularly, to change other people, recall the wise words of Jesus: "First remove the beam from your own eye. Then you will see clearly enough to remove the speck from your brother's eye." Or, as Joseph Campbell put it in *The Hero with a Thousand Faces*: "Instead of clearing his own heart the zealot tries to clear the world." So, do not feel superior. Remember again the dictum: "There but for the grace of God go I."

Your Third Turning Point: Retreat or Return

So far in this programme, you have made two major turning points. After Week Two, you decided to proceed with your aim of quitting smoking for good, as a subsidiary goal to responding to your personal mission in life. You could have chosen to remain smoking but you choose to journey further through this programme in response to your higher self.

In Week Five, you quit smoking. In advance of that you analysed what you needed to do and planned how you would do it. You held off quitting until you reached your appointed date. You went through the Road of Trials of the first few days off cigarettes and, in short, you proceeded apace from then to here. But your second turning point wasn't so much your Quit Date as the discovery in Week Six that the journey from being slave to an addiction to emerging from that cave of addiction is the realisation that you had important inner work to do. You grew in self-acceptance and acceptance of others. Your consciousness expanded with every victory. You learned that testing was a necessary part of personal growth and that how you think and feel is vital.

Having realised the importance of inner work, you proceeded in Week Seven focusing more on your thinking. You learned that the trials of stopping smoking were akin to an apprenticeship in adult responsibility, wisdom and love. You explored the purposes nicotine served in your life and you focused on the importance of listening and receptivity.

In Week Eight you explored the spiral of addiction, looking at relapse as part of the learning process. You looked at the need to stay focused on your personal mission and on staying smokefree. You appreciated the discipline of the programme (morning journal, weekly congé, regular physical exercise, healthy diet, enough sleep, affirmations, talking to sponsor, etc.). Last week you focused on your inner power and the realisation that freedom from acting out addictions lies within yourself, with the help of God. You looked at the need for forgiveness and compassion for yourself and others. You recognised that you needed to attend to important matters such as a satisfying career, initiating and sustaining significant relationships, and recovering or discovering enhanced social skills including assertiveness, rather than aggression or withdrawal into addictive behaviour.

After all that inner reflection, people can sometimes be reluctant to get back out into the world as it were and serve others. Just as your higher self invited you on this inner journey, you are now being called to return to renew the community. Your turning point now – your third since coming on this journey 10 weeks ago – is to decide whether to retreat or return. How you are to serve others you can glean, if you do not already know it, by unpacking your personal mission statement. You were not sent to this earth only to become yourself or to serve yourself: your mission will include a personal call to service. The human community relies on you alone to fulfil your mission and humanity itself will be the less if you fail to carry it out.

Being at Peace with Smokers and Non-smokers

You start being of service to others not by doing anything for them but by how you *think* about them. The phrase 'love the sinner, not the sin' can seem, and be, terribly arrogant. But there is wisdom in it, so long as one doesn't condescend to the smoker. If, as a former smoker, you judge those who still smoke, that creates an obstacle between you and them. You have listened very well to yourself in your morning journal. Use your journal too to explore your thinking about other people: smokers and non-smokers alike, alcoholics and non-drinkers, and all addicts and non-addicts too. Try to meet people and enjoy them where they are without preconception, judgement, superiority or inferiority, or the desire to change them. Accept other people as they are, as you have been gaining, or regaining, your own self-acceptance. By the same token, help other people to enjoy being with you by your own self-acceptance.

How You Can Help Others

Once you sort out your thinking so that you're not looking down on others because of what you have been gifted with, you can be of practical help to others. You can share with them the journey you took towards stopping smoking, the aids you benefited from along the way and where you are on your still unfinished journey.

The greatest way you can help others is by living your own personal mission to the full. Part of that mission, you know, is to stay off cigarettes, cigars and the pipe, and to avoid acting out any other addiction. When temptation hits, part of your motivation for staying smokefree can be your mission to other people. By living a balanced lifestyle and dealing with the problems you ignored while you smoked (such as working too hard, poor assertiveness skills or ignoring important issues in your relationships or career), you become a better model for others. By doing your journal, taking time out for your congé, enjoying physical exercise, eating healthily, doing relaxation exercises, you show yourself to be pro-active in nurturing your physical, mental, emotional and spiritual life. By declining excessive workloads or excessive money, you choose your higher path, just as by taking certain calculated risks in the direction of your personal mission you fulfil your journey with every step.

To those who have been given much, much will be expected. Do not underestimate the part you could play in helping others to leave behind addictive thinking and behaviour. You might, for instance, be willing to become a sponsor for someone else who is trying to quit smoking. Indeed, some of you could become ambassadors for *WW2SS*, guiding other people through this programme, thereby being of real service to others while you also consolidate and master all that you have already learned and practised. As someone once said, if you truly want to learn something, teach it.

In helping others with their affirmations, you can see the importance of your own. In pointing out to others their successes, you will see more clearly your own achievements. If you ask the person you are sponsoring to give you feedback, it can be a great way of enhancing your confidence. Sponsoring another person or guiding people through this programme can help you to realise that you are still on your own journey. You depend, at any moment, on your higher self to keep you from relapse and you respond to your higher self as you move ever closer to fulfilling your personal mission in life.

Timing is Everything

You know from your own journey of quitting smoking that timing is everything. Nobody else can force the pace towards your turning away from smoking. You saw in Week Eight that when you were at the pre-contemplation stage, there was no point anyone trying to talk to you about preparing for the action stage. You simply weren't ready. You didn't want to know. Likewise your concerns now that you are at the maintenance stage are very different than they were in Weeks One and Two. And they are different from your practical preparatory time for quitting (Weeks Three and Four) or when you stopped smoking in Week Five.

In short, don't try to browbeat anyone into quitting. Don't nag. Don't lecture anyone. As you will remember, while you smoked you knew it was bad for your health but you still did it. Remembering that everyone has their addictive self and higher self, refrain from forcing the smoker into a position of reacting out of their addictive self. If you act out the role of their higher self, they are more likely to play the role of their addictive self. Don't play such a game. It is self-defeating and unhelpful. As Miller and Rollnick observe regarding encountering resistance in an another person in *Motivational Interviewing: Preparing People to Change Addictive Behaviour*: "If you speak these same lines, as others have done, the script will come to the same conclusion as before."

You can help smokers best by listening actively to them, that is, by reflecting back to them what they say. (We will look at active listening in detail in Week 11.) If it is their addictive self speaking and that aspect is reflected back to them their higher self may perceive through the self-deceit of addiction. Likewise, by reflecting back any aspect of their higher self which may be evident such as 'I really would love to stop smoking but I can't. I've tried so often' you reflect back the aspiration of their higher self. For example, in the above instance you might say: 'You really would love to stop smoking.'

By doing this, you perform a similar function to that which your journal provides for you. The person hears again, through you, what they themselves have said. It slows them down from tearing away onto the next thing. You provide an opportunity for reflection. You have really heard their higher self and believe in their higher path.

Likewise, insofar as they express why they like to smoke, you reflect that back to them too, without judgement. By refusing to play the role of persuader but rather choosing to actively listen, the person has a better chance of hearing their own higher self. At the end of the day, that is the only way they will want, or be able, to quit when the time is right for them. Moreover, by empathising and truly listening to them without judgement, you can hasten the day that they might move from pre-contemplation to actively thinking about quitting.

You can support people who are in the process of stopping smoking by being there for them, encouraging them and affirming them. Depending on your relationship with them, that can include hugs, celebrations, or just lots of verbal encouragement. No person's passage from addictive thinking and behaviour is identical to yours so avoid telling them what will happen next because you cannot be sure. They are on their own journey. If you found it easier than you expected, don't assume your friend will too. If you were depressed and emotional, that might not be the other person's experience. If you're dealing with someone in Week Five who is having a difficult time and who might feel irritable, don't criticise them. And obviously don't encourage them to go back on cigarettes so they'll be less prickly! They should get over any feelings of irritability or depressed mood within a few days. Thereafter, they have some re-adjustment and learning to do, just as you did. Encourage people in Week Five to expend their energy at the gym or simply by taking a walk.

If someone relapses, help them to see it as part of the process of quitting. Encourage them not the 'blow the whole thing' but to continue on their path towards 'sobriety' and self-fulfilment. Remind them it is not, ultimately, about success or failure but about trying. Console them that they had something else to learn and are now better equipped to succeed on their next attempt.

Recovery is a Process

A real danger for you at this point is that you could feel you've beaten your addiction. You have not. You remain addicted to nicotine. Nor has your addictive self gone away. It is lying in the wings, waiting its opportunity to unseat the greater influence your higher self is now playing in your life. As with so many other worthwhile things in life, unless you are moving forward, you will slide back. That is why is it now more important than ever that you keep writing your morning journal and continuing to use the other tools recommended in this programme: your weekly congé, regular physical exercise, a healthy diet, enough sleep, an active social life ideally with addiction-free friends, and ongoing awareness of your thinking and emotions. To which list we add this week: helping and being of service to others.

If you stop being pro-active about your recovery and the maintenance of your smokefree status, you will soon find yourself unprepared to cope with increased stress or crises. Addictive thinking will seep back in. If you're wise – and you are – you might decide now to schedule regular 'sobriety' check-ups between yourself and your sponsor. Write it in your diary. For this year, pencil in a review date with your sponsor for three months from when you quit smoking. Have another review six months down the line and another on your first anniversary of not smoking. You could schedule an annual review on the anniversary of your Quit Date each year.

Problem Management

Naturally, problems don't go away just because you've stopped smoking or acting out any other addiction. The difference is that you can meet the challenge to manage problems as a more responsible adult. It is not what happens to you which is the yardstick of your growth but how you handle it. Using your journal, you express how you feel in any situation. From there you can learn to approach problems with the self-confidence of your higher self rather than the insecurity, fear and escapism of your addictive self.

If you have a problem, do not deny it. Rather, recognise that there is a problem to be solved. If you fail to recognise a challenge, you may revert to addictive thinking and, eventually, behaviour. Left unchecked, you could relapse or take up a new addiction. As with smoking, acting out other addictions might seem to relieve temporarily some stress but it cannot solve the original problem and will make matters worse. As Terence T. Gorski says in *Passages Through Recovery: An Action Plan for Preventing Relapse*: "Never underestimate the great number of people recovering from chemical dependencies who have simply traded chemical addiction for another compulsion."

Needless to say, your journal is the surest way of keeping you aware of problems as they arise. As you know, writing your morning journal slows you down. It confronts you with what is really going on in your life. It expresses what you feel and think. It is a unique instrument for personal growth and development. I doubt if anyone could write a daily journal of three pages each morning and manage to fool themselves into denying or evading any problems they face. The journal doesn't make the problems go away. It enables us to face them and creatively consider possible solutions.

Problem Solving

If, instead of seeing 'problems' we saw opportunities, we might approach 'problems' in a much better way. You've lost your job; someone dear to you is ill; you have a complaint to deal with; you're spending more than you earn; you feel lonely. Whatever your presenting 'problem' is, believe that, from the perspective of your higher self, this challenge has been sent your way for you to grow as a person. Sure, that can sound glib. But there is much wisdom in it. And it is not only a clever way of thinking about problems. It is the *truth* of how we are as humans. In Eastern thinking, there is a phrase: 'Good luck, bad luck, who knows?' If you play with this you can perceive that *anything* that happens to us, no matter how seemingly grave the calamity, can be turned around, by accepting it gladly as an opportunity for personal growth. You fail to be offered a job for which you were interviewed? Well, that opens up the possibility of moving to a new location and there you go on to live out your personal mission more fully than you could have done had you been offered that job. If you believe, with Shakespeare, that a hidden destiny guides our ends then you will see apparent bad luck as your higher self actually looking out for you. Or, like Job in the Judaeo-Christian scriptures, you declare: "Naked I came from my mother's womb, naked I shall return. The Lord gave; the Lord has taken back. Blessed be the name of the Lord. If we take gladness from the hands of the Lord, must we not take sorrow too?"

Practical Problem Solving

When faced with a problem (for which we might *think* 'opportunity'), invite your higher self to see how this challenge can move you forward towards the fulfilment of your personal mission. For instance, lots of people who lose their job later rejoice for that crisis because it forced them to realise that life was short and that *now* is always the right time to do what you *want* to do with your life.

When confronted with a challenge, ask yourself if you could solve it by considering 'outside the box' solutions, even if they seem silly.

For instance, if you feel the problem is that you must replace the job that earned you such-and-such an amount per year, a creative off-the-wall idea might be not to earn any money at all. This can free you to consider what you would *like* to do with the rest of your life if you didn't have to work for a living. If you recognise what you would like to do, you might discover you can earn your living doing that. Or that, since you'd enjoy what you do, you wouldn't need to earn as much to compensate for working at something you didn't enjoy. Indeed, when you're putting your energy into doing what you *want* to do, you may be more likely to earn more than working at something you don't like.

Another way of dealing with the problem/opportunity might be to come up with an alternative. So, for instance, you substitute one accountancy job for another one. A third approach is to examine the challenge from a different perspective. For instance, you might imagine yourself exploring this time in your life from the vantage-point of you looking back at it in 20 years' time. What might that older and possibly wiser self suggest? A fourth way of tackling it is to ask whether this problem needs to be fixed at all. For instance, if the comedian Ken Dodd ever wished as a youngster that his teeth were less prominent, as an adult he realised they were an intrinsic part of his artistic act. The 'problem', if it were ever conceived as such, of prominent teeth in fact helped him become the artist he was called to be. It became his signature in many ways. A fifth way of looking at problems/opportunities is to reduce the problem. For instance, if you're spending more than you earn, you could perhaps spend less instead of only tackling the problem by earning more. Or someone else might earn some too and you could pool resources.

Sometimes your higher self might communicate with you through a lived-out metaphor. 'A what?' I hear you say. Well, if you almost choke one day over your dinner, you might reflect whether you are taking on more than you can chew in your work (and not only on your fork). That you need to work less and spend more time with your family. Indeed, here dreams can be most helpful. I was once told of an aspiring minister of religion who rarely if ever could remember his dreams but could remember a dream image of pastel colours. By playing with the word *pastel*, he realised that he didn't feel *bold* about his *pastoral* work. By working with the dream, the student discovered his vocation lay elsewhere other than within the ordained ministry. If you recall any dreams, do record them in your journal!

Experiences of the Desert

While most people when they get as far as you have in this programme feel thrilled to be off cigarettes for so long, just occasionally people wonder why they bothered. Any excitement of their first successes seems a dim memory. Life hasn't changed very much. They get up, go to the same boring job or live in the same old stultifying marriage. They might not feel particularly better about themselves. They feel barren, dry, like a desert.

This too is an opportunity. Don't be tempted to think 'I might as well be smoking'. You have cleared the decks and, perhaps, discovered an underlying problem. That could be a problem with your faithfulness to your higher mission. It could be a lack of faithfulness to yourself and your personal growth and development. Perhaps you are unearthing the fact that you do not love your work or realising that the most important relationship in your life doesn't feel very life giving.

The solution, of course, is not to go back on the fags but to explore this discontent in your journal or with your sponsor or with a professional counsellor or therapist. Experiences of the desert can precede important personal insight and profound life-enhancing decisions. That is not to say that you will leave your partner or change your job! You might discover new life in old relationships, new wine in old wineskins!

Flowers in the Desert: An Exercise

If you are experiencing the desert as described above, setting yourself some ground rules could help some unexpected flowers to bloom in the wilderness. Look at your mission statement and see what element of it you could work on. For instance, if you'd love to live abroad you may need to learn a new language. If you'd love a career in music, you need to practice your preferred instrument. If you want to write a bestseller, you must set aside time to write and persist until the job is done!

Your ground rules could be to rise an hour earlier or spend at least 15 minutes a day working on your Big Idea, no matter how busy you are. You might decide that you won't eat breakfast until you've painted for an hour, practised your French or recorded your radio voice. Or, if it's part of your personal mission to spend lots of time with your family, a ground rule might be that you won't take work home at nights.

Activities for Week Ten

While you have done so well to abstain from nicotine since Week Five, you will never be 'out of the woods'. You may know of former smokers who relapsed after months, years or even decades.

1. In your journal, write down specific actions which you must avoid to continue to abstain from smoking. For instance: 'No drags or puffs from a cigarette'; 'No use of illegal drugs'. Some people also find they must add: 'No drinking alcohol'.

2. Write down behaviours likely to put your abstinence and 'sobriety' from nicotine or other addictions in danger. When you have finished recording your at-risk behaviours, put a two-column table in your journal, as in the example below. In the left-hand column, record the behaviours that put your sobriety at risk. In the corresponding right-hand column, say when you last performed that behaviour.

Risky Behaviours Audit

Behaviours Risky to My Sobriety	When I last Behaved like that
Drinking more than two small glasses of wine or having more than one pint of beer (or, for some, drinking any alcohol)	
Being in an environment where I used to smoke	
Socialising with smokers	
Working too hard	
Sleeping too little and getting tired and worn out	
Not eating properly or getting hungry	
Skipping my morning journal	
Not working responsibly with my emotions, especially anger and fear	
Feeling isolated and doing nothing about it	
Allowing my smokefree environment to be compromised, such as reintroduction of smoking paraphernalia into my home, work or car	

Risky Behaviours Audit (continued)

Behaviours Risky to My Sobriety	When I last Behaved like that
Failing to practice assertiveness	
Feeling depressed and not telling anyone	
Stopping my physical exercise	
Failing to keep on my guard against addictive thinking	
Ignoring my higher self by skipping my congé.	

© Joe Armstrong 2004 www.writeway2stopsmoking.com

By putting a date after each risky behaviour, it alerts you when you last put your recovery in jeopardy. If you continue with many at-risk behaviours, it can only be a matter of time before you relapse. By the same token, so long as the behaviours are not repeated and the greater the distance in time since you last performed risky behaviours, the more likely you are to maintain your abstinence and 'sobriety' from nicotine. A dated analysis such as the above can provide a powerful wake-up call and instil motivation to better maintain your nicotine-free status and further advance towards fulfilling your personal mission.

3. It is beneficial to explore to what extent you are keeping addictive thinking at bay. As you know, addictive thinking precedes addictive behaviour so you need to keep your addictive thinking 'detractor' wide-awake. This is where your journal can come into its own, where your higher self can alert you to any reversion to addictive fantasies, feelings or crazy thinking. List addictive thinking which you need to be watchful for. For example: 'Fantasising about smoking with a cup of coffee'; 'Reminiscing about smoking on holidays'.

4. Pro-active solutions: Write down what you will do to get back on track to responding to your higher self whenever specific actions or behaviours put your abstinence, 'sobriety' and personal mission in jeopardy. For instance:

- When I lose my work-life balance, I shall take physical exercise anyhow even though I feel there's no time for it

- When I feel tempted to smoke, I shall delay the gratification, choose my higher path and promise to treat myself to a more wholesome pleasure later (e.g., massage, extended congé, a personal luxury)

- When I begin fantasising about smoking, I'll contact my sponsor or arrange an outing with non-smoking friends.

Review of Week Ten

1. Did you do your morning journal every day last week? What was it like for you?

2. Did you take your congé? What did you do and did you enjoy it?

3. Did you meet or speak with your sponsor? Write any specific outcome from the conversation.

4. Do you feel you are living a more authentic life? Do you feel you are on your way to becoming who you were born to be?

Being a Non-smoker

This week we become more used to life as a non-smoker. We learn to cope with life's challenges without resorting to nicotine or other addictive behaviour. We grow in responsibility. We recognise the sustained benefits of our 'sobriety'. We are cautioned against sabotaging our higher calling and we're reminded that this is a path of growth and serenity. We look at dysfunctional families and consider the art of active listening. We monitor and audit our work-life balance as our surest way of remaining true to ourselves.

Being a Non-smoker

When you move to a new country, it takes time to find your feet. You're not used to the rules in this place. They might drive on the other side of the road, speak a foreign language, greet one another differently. Their accent or language might be difficult to understand. You don't even know the basics like where to shop and the range of produce might be new to you. You need to check if your ATM bank card works and how you go about finding the local doctor. It can be stressful at first. So many things are unfamiliar. Gradually, though, you get a feel for your new place. You feel more at home and know you can cope and live happily in this new environment.

In quitting smoking and any other addictions, it is as if you've moved to a new country. Things are done somewhat differently in the community of non-smokers and non-addicts. Having spent some six weeks in this 'new land', it's probably beginning to feel more comfortable and familiar to you. Perhaps you relish your new surroundings. Occasionally, you might long to be back down in the cave of addiction where everything was so familiar. But the longer you're in this new country of non-smokers the less often you long to return to the way you were before embarking on this journey.

Being a non-smoker involves living a balanced lifestyle which facilitates the growth of your physical, mental, emotional, social and spiritual health. This is the 'sobriety' from nicotine to which you aspire and which you are already fulfilling with every decision you make attuned to your higher self. You have already, with the help of God as you understand him, achieved abstinence. Be grateful for that and congratulate yourself for your hard work. But, yes, you have still more work to do as you dare to believe in yourself and your singular mission in life. You probably still have more preparation to do to plan for the good fortune you set out to seek. You *can* make your own luck. Get prepared! For it is the *prepared* who are blessed with good *luck* and good *fortune*.

In getting this far you have passed many milestones. These include:

- deciding to embark on the path of abstinence and 'sobriety'

- deciding to listen and respond to your higher self

- articulating and committing yourself to your personal mission

- embarking on the healing process, physically, mentally, emotionally, socially, and spiritually

- appreciating the power of your mind to think differently

- learning to think differently

- awakening increasingly to your feelings and emotional wellbeing

- changing your attitude to smoking and other mood-changing substances or processes

- devising, implementing and monitoring a more balanced lifestyle

- developing the capacity for responsible decision-making and behaviour

- healing what needs to be healed in your life, from childhood to now

- realising that you are called through daily growth to embody your higher self

- recognising that you have never 'arrived' but are always 'on the way'

- realising that you can never have another smoke

- committing to practising daily the tools of this programme which have fostered your growth: journal, work-life balance, weekly congé, healthy eating, regular exercise, proper sleep; awareness of your thoughts and feelings; avoidance of artificial mood-altering substances and processes; and fulfilling your personal mission, ever conscious of how easy it would be to slide back into addiction.

Responsibility

Even though you have not smoked since the end of Week Four, remember that you remain addicted and will always be addicted to tobacco. Smoking even one puff is a choice incompatible with your personal mission. You are responsible for what you do with your addiction. You are responsible for the way you think since you choose your thoughts and could think differently, as we examined in Weeks Five and Seven, noting that you choose whether to think from your addictive or your higher self.

You are also responsible for your feelings. As with thinking, you could choose to feel differently. Changes in how you feel will often follow changes in how you think about things. By re-thinking how you regard a situation, the feelings will often look after themselves. You are also, of course, responsible for all of your behaviour. When you assume responsibility for your thoughts, feelings and behaviour, you are well on the path towards healing, growth and the fulfilment of your higher mission.

Sustained Benefits of Not Smoking

Remember and appreciate how much better your health has become since quitting smoking as we mentioned in Week Five. Your blood pressure normalised within an hour after your final cigarette in Week Four. (You should, of course, regularly have your blood pressure checked.) Nicotine has now left your body. Your lungs have possibly by now finished their spring cleaning of your lungs (although for some people a cough could continue for some more weeks or months while tar and toxins continue to be expelled). Carbon monoxide has long since left your system. Your circulation is much better. You are more willing and able to take the stairs (a free exercise machine) rather than the lift. You've been able to taste food much better, your sense of smell has been enhanced, and your home, clothes and hair no long stink of stale smoke. Your concentration has improved, as you are not constantly thinking of when you'll have your next cigarette. You are more in touch with your feelings. You know yourself so much better than eleven weeks ago, because of all the hard work you've done. Your self-esteem has grown. Your eyes twinkle. Your social skills have matured as you no longer hide behind a smokescreen. You are living a more balanced lifestyle and realise that you need to monitor your wellbeing on a daily and weekly basis. You are taking regular exercise, sleeping better, eating better and you're more in touch with who you are. You are actively embarked upon your higher mission. You're acting as if you believed in yourself.

In less than a year from now you will have reduced by half your chances of suffering a heart attack or stroke. In a few years you will have reduced it further to that of your fellow non-smokers. By continuing doing what you're doing, you will reduce your likelihood of getting lung cancer and other smoking-related diseases such as cancer of the mouth or throat.

Don't Sabotage Your Higher Calling

Your personal mission is not negotiable. Sure, at times, like Hamlet, you procrastinate about your long-forgotten purpose. But consider that it will find you. As the poet of Psalm 139 prays: 'Where can I run from your love? If I climb to the heavens you are there. If I dive to the depths of the ocean, you are there too.' If you neglect your calling to take courageous steps in the direction of your higher purpose and personal mission, then things start to go pear-shaped. If you ignore your personal mission, you will probably return to smoking or some other addiction. Don't negate your calling. Do not reduce it. Respond to it. Dare to believe in yourself and in the purpose for which you were sent. And use the tools of this programme to co-operate with your higher power to bring it about. If you do not do your daily journal and weekly congé, you will be like an aircraft without radar, or a traveller without a map. You are more important than any work, familial or relational demand that is being placed upon you. Respect yourself and your divine mission. Trust the universe. Do not act out of fear. Dare to believe that the dreams of your heart *can* and will be fulfilled, and indeed, *are* being fulfilled, even as you read this. Be filled with confidence in your mission, as was Christ at the beginning of his when he prayed, quoting the prophet Isaiah: "The Spirit of the Lord is upon me. He has anointed me to bring good news to the poor. He sent me to proclaim liberty to captives and sight to the blind, to let the oppressed go free, and to proclaim a year of favour."

Growth and Process

If Rome wasn't built in a day, neither will your life mission! Sure, you can get weary when you have worked on your aims and goals for possibly years and seem to be getting nowhere fast. Of course you can feel discouraged at times. At such times, recall moments along your path when you felt encouraged. It is so easy to forget these moments of recognition, confirmation and hope. Think of one time when you felt affirmed in your personal mission. What happened? In one sentence, write down how you grew in self-belief in your mission.

Serenity

A good definition of serenity is to accept willingly whatever may come to pass. It's the perspective of our friend Job in the Judaeo-Christian scriptures: accepting even affliction by seeing the bigger picture of the vastness of the universe and a belief that God has reasons beyond human comprehension. It is well expressed by the Christian mystic Julian of Norwich who described it thus: "All shall be well and all manner of being shall be well."

It is the prayer within the Christian tradition of personal abandonment to the will of God, not in a resigned way but with a willing and active acceptance, as did Christ on the cross: "Father, into your hands I entrust my spirit."

Dysfunctional Families and Functional Families

Given that smoking damages people physically, mentally, psychologically, socially and spiritually, and that smoking can never be a choice supported by one's higher self, smoking must be regarded as a dysfunctional act. As is *often* the case with alcoholics, compulsive gamblers and other addicts, although it must be stressed it is *not always* the case, many smokers came from dysfunctional families. Unless they resolve any dysfunction, they too can carry that forward into new families which they are part of or found.

In dysfunctional families, people learn that it may not be safe to reveal who they are. This is why their higher self and personal mission is often buried so that the individual doesn't know why they were sent into this world. Latent talents lie untapped or undiscovered. Emotions, if shared, are dismissed or ridiculed. People have trouble admitting to themselves how they're feeling. Individuals don't feel heard and, eventually, give up trying to express who they are deep down. That is why the journal can be such a powerful tool for getting us in touch with who we are meant to be, who we were born to be.

In a functional family, people's authenticity is fostered, welcomed and celebrated. The singular identity of each member of the family can emerge. People don't fear revealing who they are or, if they do, they face the fear and self-reveal anyway. In functional families, there is no need to pretend an identity or to play a role or set up a smokescreen (metaphorically or literally). Conflict is resolved through discussion and dialogue. Everyone seeks a win-win solution. All family members trust that their feelings and point of view will be respected and responded to. Individuals can promptly admit to problems as they are, without minimising or exaggerating them. Age-appropriate decision-making is respected and people are given the freedom to make mistakes. The culture within functional families supports the process by which decisions are arrived at. It is understood that questions need to be asked, rationally and dispassionately; that understanding needs to be arrived at. Further questions are explored testing that comprehension is complete and accurate, and so judgements are formed. This in turn leads to well-founded decisions duly carried out. Indeed, as the philosopher Bernard Lonergan has stated, it is at the level of decision and action that we emerge as people. Our individuality becomes manifest when we act in accordance with our honest judgement. All along this process, we recognise and name our feelings, pleasant and unpleasant, and can communicate them effectively to family members.

Active Listening

Dr Thomas Gordon in his classic book *Parent Effectiveness Training* famously listed blocks to listening. These blocks are equally relevant whether applied to listening to others or when listening to ourselves in our morning journal. His "Typical Twelve" responses, reproduced below, constitute the *opposite* to listening, and yet consider how very often such responses occur where listening is supposedly taking place:

1. Ordering, directing, commanding

2. Warning, admonishing, threatening

3. Exhorting, Moralising, Preaching

4. Advising, Giving Solutions or Suggestions

5. Lecturing, Teaching, Giving Logical Arguments

6. Judging, Criticising, Disagreeing, Blaming

7. Praising, Agreeing

8. Name-calling, Ridiculing, Shaming

9. Interpreting, Analysing, Diagnosing

10. Reassuring, Sympathising, Consoling, Supporting

11. Probing, Questioning, Interrogating

12. Withdrawing, Distracting, Humouring, Diverting

With so vast a catalogue of what is *not* listening, what *is* listening? Note that even seemingly positive things like cheering up people, trying to get people thinking more positively, or consoling, praising or agreeing with people are *blocks* to listening. Dr Gordon urges us to try to get to the feeling behind what someone says to us, (an approach equally applicable towards ourselves when writing our journal). He gives the example of a child who asks its mother 'When's dinner ready?' She might respond (avoiding the typical twelve blocks) by saying: "You're very hungry". Active listening takes place when you reflect back to the other person (or to yourself in your journal) the feeling behind what is being said.

William R. Miller and Stephen Rollnick in *Motivational Interviewing: Preparing People to Change Addictive Behaviour* suggest that you feed back to the person what you believe they mean in the form of a statement (rather than a question). For instance, "You're feeling uncomfortable," rather than "You're feeling uncomfortable?" This allows the other person to explore whatever is going on inside himself or herself and it avoids probably wrong assumptions being made by the listener. The aim of reflective listening is to enable the person who is speaking to express what they want to do. In short, active listening is a powerful tool to enable one's authentic higher self to come out.

Become aware of whether you are using any of the blocks to listening as listed above in your conversations with others and also in your journal writing. By practising active listening, you will have a tool to help you put yourself and others at ease in conversations. You will no longer need the smokescreen of a cigarette and you will increase the effectiveness of your morning journal as a vehicle for your higher self to emerge.

Counselling

Last week, we looked at some practical problem solving techniques. However, sometimes, perhaps due to being raised in our family of origin, we get stuck in trying to resolve personal problems/opportunities. If this is the case for you, do consider seeking professional help to remove whatever may be holding you back from dealing with problems/opportunities. There is no shame in doing this. Indeed, people who recognise they need help are to be commended. If you feel blocked or repeatedly procrastinate about a problem in your life, what is there to lose by exploring the issue with a professional therapist or counsellor? It could turn out to be the making of you.

Work-life Balance

No longer battling so much now with the false allure of addiction, we focus more and more in our daily life on personal growth. We are in the process of unlearning self-destructive dysfunctional thinking, feelings and habits developed over years of smoking or earlier in life. But we must retain a constant vigilance not to slip back into addictive thinking. The addictive self could regain the initiative by regaining control of our thinking. So, stay awake! Detect crazy thinking in your journal. Do not ignore it. Each day, review your behaviour. Have you put work before your personal wellbeing? Have you skipped a siesta even though you badly needed one because you felt you could not take 10 minutes away from chores or other duties? Have you skipped a congé recently? How faithfully have you been writing your morning journal? Do you put it before other demands clambering for your attention? Have you been cutting back on night-time sleep because of family demands? Did you take time out today for physical exercise? Did you eat your meals today slowly and with awareness, with the news off and listening, perhaps, to tranquil music? Take a look at yourself in the mirror. Have you been too busy or too disorganised to have a haircut or look you best? How highly do your rate your current investment in personal care and personal growth? Have you been listening to yourself? Have you taken the time to really listen to others or are blocks to listening getting in the way of hearing the other person or yourself?

If you spot a problem, a hole in the dike as it were, you need to fix it there and then. Don't say: 'I just don't have time for all that right now'. With addictive thinking, 'tomorrow' is the adverb of the defeated. So, as soon as you realise that you're neglecting yourself in any of the ways indicated above, stop what you are doing and fix it. Ask yourself: "Which is more important right now, to fulfil some impossible deadline or to be true to my personal mission?" If what you are doing is not attuned to your personal mission, then why do it at all? Get back on track. Focus on your higher calling and the call of your higher self. Obey that self. The rest is not important.

Your objective is to develop and maintain a top quality work-life balance, constantly attuned to your higher self and mission. Your priority is not to earn more money or get top grades. Your ideal is not perfection. Your aim is personal growth and self-knowledge; becoming yourself; fulfilling your higher purpose; initiating, sustaining and growing authentic relationships, primarily with yourself and with everyone you meet.

Work-life Balance Monitoring

Over the past 10-plus weeks you have improved your lifestyle balance. You now know that when you lose a healthy work-life balance, you leave yourself vulnerable to acting out your addiction(s). This remains the case, and will continue to do so.

Therefore you need not only achieve but maintain a balanced lifestyle.

Your health and wellbeing is more important than any demands that are being placed on you (or that you are placing on yourself) at work or at home. If you are too busy to enjoy a balanced lifestyle, you are too busy! It is *not* virtuous to continue being overextended. If you do, you are simply choosing to revert to smoking or other addictions by an indirect route. Loss of balance will lead to higher stress levels, which in turn will seem to justify reverting to old ways. Soon, you find yourself rationalising and denying that it's such a bad thing to smoke after all or that, since you've done so well, surely you could have *just one*. A relapse is caused not so much by the first cigarette after a period of abstinence but by failing to take corrective steps before the lapse to prioritise your health, wellbeing and personal mission.

Work-life Balance Checklist

	Yes	No
Am I doing my journal every morning?		
Am I taking my weekly congé?		
Am I getting enough sleep?		
Am I eating a healthy diet?		
Am I avoiding alcohol and other mood-altering substances?		
If I am drinking alcohol, am I drinking moderately?		
Am I taking time out to relax each day?		
Do I take sufficient physical exercise every day?		
Am I asserting my needs in a healthy way?		
Am I enjoying interdependent relationships, at home, at work and socially?		
Am I being authentic and asserting my real needs?		
Am I keeping work in perspective?		
Am I prioritising what I need to do at home and work and doing first things first?		
Am I managing my finances responsibly?		
Am I monitoring my thinking, recognising whether it is my addictive self or my higher self that is at work?		
Am I consulting with my sponsor and other supporters?		

© Joe Armstrong 2004 www.writeway2stopsmoking.com

Work-life Balance Audit

Use the Work-life Balance Checklist above to do an audit of your life as it is now.

Journal

If you are not making time for your morning journal, you are neglecting yourself. You need this time alone every morning, just as you need a shower or to brush your teeth. It grounds you. Can you afford a day in which you're not centred? You express yourself, including your deepest needs, hope and fears, thoughts and emotions. This is a tool for your authenticity and healing. Neglect it at your peril.

Congé

You need this time alone once a week to re-charge your batteries. If you are too busy to take it, you are losing your life balance. Nothing, not even what appears to be a good cause, should take over. Granted, you might not be able to do it 52 weeks a year. But if you've missed, say, two on the trot, this is a warning sign that your lifestyle balance is off keel. Unless you correct it, you will be vulnerable to reverting to smoking and other addictions. It is not a monthly congé. It is a weekly congé. If you like you could try to have a full day's congé every three months but this would supplement, not substitute, the weekly congé.

Sleep

If you don't get enough sleep, you cannot function at your best. By sleeping, you repair your body, mind and soul. Skip it or cut back on it and it is only a matter of time before you get physically or mentally sick or revert to addictive thinking or behaviour.

Healthy Food

You are what you eat. Food is the fuel of your body, mind and soul. If you eat nourishing food, you will be nourished. If you skimp on your food, eat fatty, junk foods or neglect to eat properly for your age, state of health, level of physical exercise and, some would argue, for your blood type, then you cannot flourish.

Alcohol

Health promotion experts tell us that women should not imbibe more than 14 units of alcohol per week, while men should not exceed 21 units. One unit is *not* a pint! Nor is it a large glass of wine! In fact, a *single* pub measure of spirits, a *small* glass of wine, a *small* sherry, a *half-pint* of ordinary strength lager, beer or cider, or a *quarter-pint* of strong beer equates to *one* unit of alcohol. If you drink, keep a close tally of units of alcohol consumed per week. You should not 'save up' your weekly allowance for one or two nights a week. That's binge drinking and is bad for you. You should also have some alcohol-free days to give your liver a rest. If the thought of going into a pub or meeting others who are drinking without your having an alcoholic drink, you should consider if alcohol could be a problem for you. *Never forget that a huge proportion of people who have given up smoking, relapse while drinking alcohol.* Alcohol reduces your willpower and can unleash your addictive self. You can best complete your journey to sobriety from tobacco and other addictions by avoiding all mood-altering substances and processes in what is still your early-to-mid recovery phase.

Relaxation

Whether it's only 10 or 20 minutes, you need to take time to relax each day. Failure to make time for relaxation will set you up for a fall. Remember the tortoise and the hare. There is much to be achieved by slowing down. In this regard too, become self-aware however and whenever you travel. If you drive, do you do so furiously, exceeding the speed limit, anxious to overtake, endangering your life and that of other road-users? Is your driving (or biking, commuting by train or even walking) a metaphor for your life? Consider slowing down by 10 per cent. Plan your route better. Leave earlier. Take your time.

Physical Exercise

When you're busy, physical exercise can be the first thing to suffer. If you find yourself skipping your 20 minutes physical exercise a day, you need to ask yourself if you are abusing your body. You need to get away from your desk or away from family responsibilities for aerobic activity once a day. As you know, it will enhance your mood (naturally - without artificial stimulants) and decrease depression, while increasing vitality and heightening self-esteem. Let skipped physical exercise be a further warning to you that you are losing your work-life balance. Take immediate corrective action. Schedule a time and keep to it. When you come back from your walk, run or bike ride, you'll actually work much better!

Assertiveness

Are you expressing your real needs, especially to yourself? You'll discover your real self and needs through your journal. Do you need to develop assertiveness with others? Do you use aggression, including passive aggression, instead of assertiveness to resolve conflict? Do you listen well to others? Are you sensitive to them? Do you discuss at an appropriate time real problems that need to be solved or do you bottle things up, ignoring or denying yourself, to the detriment of the growth of your relationship?

Interdependent Relationships

Is there give and take in your relationships? Is your primary relationship one of mutual support, healing and growth or does one party play the helper while the other acts out the role of receiver? The ideal is to achieve a balance of mutual giving and receiving. Do you have a problem giving or, as is often the case, do you have a problem receiving?

Work–life Balance

Do you let your work take over? Do you prioritise work over your relationship with yourself and with significant others in your life (spouse/partner, children, parents, close friends)? No one is indispensable. When wisdom strikes, few ever regret not spending more time in the office. Many regret not spending more time with sons, daughters, a spouse, a parent, a friend. Don't wait to learn the hard way.

Finances

Are you managing your finances well or are you spending more than you're earning? Do you pay your bills? Have you a good credit rating? Do you go overdrawn? Do you know where it's all going? If you keep your money log as recommended in Week Six, you'll know exactly how you spend your money. Set aside time regularly to get on top of your finances.

Thinking

Are you getting better at identifying when it's your addictive self who's thinking? Do you find your higher self is getting more of a shout in nowadays? When you find your addictive self is doing your thinking, do you take corrective action? What do you do?

Sponsor and Supporters

Are you keeping in contact with your sponsor? Now that you've been off cigarettes some five weeks, the temptation is to think that you've 'cracked it'. With respect, nobody cracks an addiction as powerful as nicotine that fast. You still need your sponsor and other supporters. Use them. They will continue to be happy to help.

Admitting When We Are Wrong

Within Alcoholics Anonymous and Nicotine Anonymous people are taught to examine their behaviour, its consequences and to readily admit when they are wrong. The tenth of the Twelve Steps states: "Continued to take personal inventory and when we were wrong promptly admitted it." The same wisdom applies to you as a former smoker. Each time we spot we've gone off course, we correct our trajectory, as an aircraft pilot does, towards our higher aims and goals. When we fail to do so, we simply go further off course. That's why a nightly examination of awareness or *examen*, as suggested in Week Nine, is so important. Sarah Ban Breathnach in her brilliant book *Simple Abundance: A Daybook of Comfort & Joy* suggests we keep a gratitude journal, becoming grateful each night for the manifold blessings of the day. Gratitude is incompatible with depression. If you feel depressed, count your blessings, literally. Write them down. Gratitude also converts our interpretation of apparently negative things into a positive light.

Activities for Week Eleven

1. Write down three things you want in each of the following areas: health, wealth, fun, work, relationships, and personal growth.

2. Imagine your whole life has been lived to get to this present moment. What opportunity do you now have to advance your personal mission?

3. Gratitude. In a place where you will not be heard, speak aloud your thanks for specific things with which you are being blessed even as you read this. For example: 'I am thankful for my health.' 'I am thankful for my wife/husband/partner.' 'I am thankful for my children.' 'I am thankful for my car.' 'I am thankful for electricity.' 'I am thankful for the food I ate today.' 'I am thankful for my friends.' 'I am thankful for my ears and hearing.' 'I am thankful that I can read.' 'I am thankful for air.' If you feel up to it, why not sing out your thanks? (Someone once said that when we sing we pray twice.) If you prefer, whisper it! And if you cannot even whisper it, write it down! Are you keeping a gratitude journal every night, recording at least five things for which you are grateful?

4. Do you have a symbol of hope in your home or at work? It could be a phoenix, which rises from the ashes. Or a laughing Buddha. Or a cross, symbol of the triumph of hope over despair. It could

be an egg or a chrysalis, each symbols of transformation. Do you display in your home or workspace some personal achievements? Or, through mock embarrassment or a failure to recognise and respect your hard-won successes, perhaps you keep things like certificates, degrees, medals and awards filed away unseen, by you as well as other people. Take them out. Honour them and your higher self that made them possible by displaying them. They can sustain you when your light is low.

5. Continue to keep an eye on your weight. Any increase in weight should have been fairly minor (and better for you than smoking) but it shouldn't still be increasing. If you are eating a healthy diet and exercising regularly, you shouldn't at this stage be gaining weight. If you are, talk to your doctor about it, or double check that you aren't compensating for not smoking by pigging out on chocolate bars or biscuits! If weight remains an issue for you, have you read any books on blood type diets, as mentioned in Week Four? Dr Peter J. D'Adamo's *Eat Right for Your Type* suggests that eating wheat if you have blood type O will put on weight (and that eating potatoes leads to arthritis). If you are developing any substitute addiction or other unhealthy coping mechanism, write about it in your journal, discuss it with your sponsor or seek professional help.

Review of Week Eleven

1. Did you do your morning journal every day last week? Did you do a full three pages every day?

2. Did you take your congé? What did you do and did it open up any possibilities for you?

3. Did you meet or speak with your sponsor? What did you share?

4. Do you feel you're making progress towards sobriety, as distinct from maintaining abstinence?

5. What steps have you taken in the last week to move closer to fulfilling your personal mission?

12

Embrace of Life

This week you return to 'ordinary life' as you come to the end of this programme. You do so aware of the continued need to keep addictive thinking at bay. You are advised that although these 12 weeks draw to a close, your goal of sobriety from smoking and other addictions is not yet complete. And, of course, your personal mission has yet to be fulfilled. You are strongly advised to continue writing your morning journal for the next three months, to continue with your weekly congé and to monitor lifestyle balance each day. You explore the place of loss in your life and look at fear, responsibility for self and on-going attentiveness to your higher self. You are reminded to reward yourself for all your hard work and to celebrate the wonder of each day. You conclude with a new commitment to the practices and activities known to maintain and develop your sustained growth.

Your One Year Target

Acclaimed addiction authorities James O. Prochaska and Carlo C. DiClemente, mentioned in Week Eight, writing in *The Transtheoretical Approach: Crossing Traditional Boundaries of Therapy* note that "across a range of therapies nearly 80 per cent of clients resume smoking within a year of terminating treatment". They further show that "smoking relapse rates are as high as those of alcoholics and heroin addicts".

Against this 'sobering' statistical backdrop, you must appreciate that your challenge is far from over. This is why you are strongly advised to continue to use the key tools of this programme which have served you so well to this point. Sometimes clients taking this programme stop using the core tools of the morning journal and weekly congé. While they used the tools, they had become abstinent from tobacco. They became invigorated with self-belief. They might have joined a gym, improved their personal appearance, taken several steps in the direction of their life's aims and goals. Then, for some reason, they discontinue the journal, skip congés, stop visiting the gym. The twinkle leaves their eyes. Sooner or later they start smoking again. The addictive self resumes control.

Keep doing the journal

All they had to do was to continue with the journal. It is a simple as that. When you avoid the journal, you avoid yourself. For what is the journal but you expressing yourself? Reluctance to face your journal is reluctance to face yourself. Resistance to writing it is resistance to naming and claiming whatever is going on in your mind and feelings and spirit. Not making time for the journal is not making time for yourself. And, if you don't have time for someone, is it any wonder you end up abusing them? Recognise inner resistance to the journal for what it is: resistance to yourself. What do you fear might emerge if you stuck with the journal? That you might need to face that you're gay or straight? Admit to yourself that there are problems in your relationships? Recognise that you will die? Face your discontent with your life? Maybe you fear for your sanity. Perhaps you don't want to face the shadow side of your personality. You might even be afraid that were you to do the journal you'd discover you were somebody quite different than you perceive yourself to be. The journal might confront you with your personal mission as never before and you might be afraid of the responsibility of fulfilling your highest calling, your vocation, your personal mission. It is so much easier to be one of the crowd. To mark time. To wait for your pension. Not to rock the boat. Not to put your head above the parapet. But what if God really meant it when you were sent with a higher purpose? What if the dreams you have dreamt for your life could really come true? Do you shudder at the responsibility of truly becoming yourself? Would fulfilling your potential for you be a fate worse than death? What do you fear you would lose by actually believing in yourself and being willing to pay whatever price is required to fulfil your personal mission?

You *know* what that mission is. You know why you were sent. You wrote it in Week One. Are you living it today to the full? If not, why not? What are you afraid of? What blocks or obstacles do you count as blessings because they provide an excuse for not living your life to the full?

You know that smoking and any other addiction was a cul de sac. It got you stuck. You know it numbed you into a sense of indifference. You know it depleted your personal energy. You know it robbed you, for a while, of your faith in yourself. Continue to use your abstinence and sobriety from smoking and other addictions as your fuel to be who God made you to be. Let yourself emerge as a person. Create whatever it is that you were born to create.

Proceeding towards your core calling and aim in life can be as simple as picking up a pen and writing down what you are thinking. It's as simple as that. So, do recommit yourself at the end of this week to keeping your morning journal for the next 12 weeks. If that seems daunting, ask yourself why? Perhaps you should feel daunted at the prospect of really listening to yourself in the way that has been suggested throughout this programme and especially last week, when we looked at active listening. Imagine the cataclysmic effect it could have on any residual addictive thinking! Consider the prospect of your spending the next 12 weeks doing what you were born to do! What changes might that bring about? Your relationship with yourself and others would improve. Your career could suddenly take off as you work with, rather than against, your higher calling. Lady Luck could smile on you, as you make your own luck and good fortune by the quality of your preparation and application to what you were sent to do. Things start coming together. But it is still grace and gift when doors open and opportunities knock. Now that you're more attuned to your personal vocation, you realise that opportunities were always being offered to you even when you operated out of your addictive self but you were too blind and drugged up then to notice.

Using the statistic cited earlier in this chapter, your twofold target is to be one of the 20 per cent who will be smokefree a year from your recent Quit Date *and*, in that time, to live your singular calling to the full. On your first anniversary, looking back, may you thank God for the day you picked up your pen and listened to your higher self express in your journal. Likewise, the joy you felt during your favourite congés can permeate your whole life – and not only for two hours off per week. Indeed, that is their long-term goal, to awaken natural joy, pleasure and fun so that you experience every moment of every day as grace. Each moment you are bombarded with love and opportunity. Beauty surrounds you everywhere. Just as your weekly congé was central to your discovery of joy without smoking or other addictive behaviour, why would you want to discontinue such a healthy and effective instrument for happiness and balanced living?

Freedom to Live Your Life to the Full

If my father's first wife had not died, had my stepbrothers not lost their birth mother, I would not have been born. I would not exist. And yet my father at his first wife's funeral must have wondered what good could come out of this dying and sundering of his family. What seemingly meaningless deaths or losses have you experienced which later turned out to be the vehicle for a profound blessing?

Joseph Campbell in *The Hero with a Thousand Faces* says "every creature lives on the death of another". Wisdom resides in perceiving the "imperishable life that lives and dies in all". Campbell, at the conclusion of his analysis of the universal hero's journey, suggests that we should not be "anxious for the outcome" of our deeds but rather rest them and the fruits of our actions "on the knees of the Living God". In so doing, we feel free and detached. As is written in the Bhagavad Gita: "Do without attachment the work you have to do." Or, as Henry Wadsworth Longfellow wrote:

> Let us, then, be up and doing
>
> With a heart for any fate;
>
> Still achieving, still pursuing,
>
> Learn to labour and to wait.

The spiritual writers of the West taught likewise. St Ignatius of Loyola, founder of the Jesuits, wrote about the need for detachment in order to choose and act well. Modern thinkers such as Edward de Bono have made a similar appeal, urging that we think through decisions before acting on them, exploring the advantages and disadvantages of each in an objective, detached way. Your higher self is working through you as you labour to achieve your personal mission. You are being supported in your aims and goals more often than not in ways you do not even know. In Christian thought, the idea of the guardian angel meant as much: that you are not alone. You have a mission to accomplish and, with the help of on high, so long as you are humble and admit the work is God's and not ours, you shall prevail.

Campbell urges us to listen to the Imperishable in ourselves. This we do par excellence in our daily journal, through active listening to, and spontaneous expression of, our thoughts, questions, insights, understandings, judgements, feelings, desires, dreams, aspirations and loves.

Believe in Your Personal Mission

Re-read your personal mission. Do you feel any blocks, similar to the blocks you had about stopping smoking? Is there a single word or phrase in it that you feel is unrealistic, one that aims too high for you? What is it? What would it be like if you believed in your personal mission, including any phrase or word you have your doubts about fulfilling? Think what energy and confidence you would manifest if you believed in it! Faith can move mountains. The greatest obstacles can and are overcome everyday by men and women around the world carrying out their daily tasks and aiming for their life goals. Can you imagine someone else achieving that one thing you have your doubts about? Why do you think that they can succeed but you cannot?

Be willing to make mistakes and learn from them. Dr Irene C. Kassorla's superb book *Go For It! How to Win at Love, Work and Play* confirms many of the themes of *WW2SS*. She has a wonderful image for the winner's attitude to making mistakes. She paints the picture of someone who wants to get across a frozen pond, where it is known that the ice is thin in places. She compares how a loser will approach the task of getting across that pond to the mentality of the winner. The loser proceeds fearfully and slowly, concentrating on avoiding failure at all costs. If he falls in, he lambastes himself for his error and calls himself stupid and sits there analysing where he went wrong. He loses all sense of time in his preoccupation not to fall in. When he finally arrives at his destination he recounts his every mistake in detail to others. In contrast, the winner does his homework but focuses on what he wants to achieve (rather than avoiding failure). He accepts he'll probably fall in so he gets prepared (wears a wet suit) and isn't worried about making mistakes, which he learns from. Regardless of how often he falls in, he praises himself that he didn't fall more often. When he arrives he listens with genuine interest to other people's experiences and shares from his own story whatever is amusing or of mutual benefit.

As you progress towards your personal mission, you *should* make mistakes. If you do not, how can you learn anything? Don't regard mistakes as setbacks. Genuinely see them as evolutionary moments getting you closer to your goal. Never blow the whole thing just because you stumble or fall. Get up straight away and head as directly as you can for your goal. Keep at it and your persistence will win you the day.

Our Timbre

When we are free of acting out addictions and are on our authentic path, our voice, literally and metaphorically, is attuned to our higher mission. We live one day at a time. We truly are responsible for what we think, feel, say, decide and do. We accept responsibility for the consequences that resulted from our addictions. Damage we have done is redeemed. Increasingly free of addictive thinking and behaviour, we manifest our higher self in our relationship with ourselves and others. By attending to our core mission and freed from our cravings, obsessions and compulsions, we dare to believe that we were indeed put on this planet to do something wonderful, something that only we can do. We further believe that we are on course to doing it.

Conscious of our human frailty and fragility, we accept support and praise when it is offered to us. We no longer rely on nicotine, alcohol, caffeine, excessive money, compulsive sex, shopping, or gambling or any other addictive substance or process to gain our sense of self-worth. We know we are of inestimable worth. Whether we believe in a traditional view of God or simply in some generic sense of a power greater than ourselves, we have a sense of the sacred within ourselves. Divinity lives and breathes and moves in us. We are interdependent people, accepting and receiving love and practical support. We care for our mind, feelings, body, and spirit. We no longer allow ourselves to lose the plot through working too hard, eating too much, drinking more than we should or smoking even one cigarette. We are gentle with ourselves. We know life is short and precious. We take time to savour it daily.

Your Hard Work

Over the past 12 weeks you have achieved something wonderful. You have grown, healed, learned, discovered, acted. There is no more important thing that you could have done for yourself or for humanity over the past three months than what you have achieved. If you do nothing else of importance all year, you can stand proud for having accomplished, with the help of your higher power, this gracious and profound milestone in your life, turning from addictive thinking and behaviour towards recovery and self-discovery.

Always remember that you remain addicted to smoking. The addiction doesn't go away. You have *not* been cured of your addiction. If you try a cigarette in a month, a year or 10 years from now, sooner than you could imagine you would return to the slavery of your addicted self. You are *not* an exception. Nobody is.

Your responsibility now is to ensure you *maintain* your recovery from smoking. Go now to your diary or calendar and mark the date that will be your first six months free of smoking. Be sure to organise a celebration for that day. Mark the first anniversary of your abstinence. Look forward to that date. Consider ways to celebrate it. A great way of celebrating it is to achieve another milestone in your personal mission. Use the skill of visualisation which you have practised in this programme to *see* your self-realisation on the first anniversary of abstinence from addictive behaviour. Smoking and any other addictive activity impoverished your freedom, health, wealth, self-esteem and energy. Now, new challenges will present themselves. You can rise to meet them, grown strong in your self-belief .

Become who you are called to be. Create something wonderful and unprecedented with your life. That may or may not be something visible in the outer world or it may be primarily your journey of self-discovery, which can reflect in your eyes and attitudes for all to see.

If you feel lonely, don't flee from that truth since all must die and die alone. Facing your inner loneliness may in the past have been avoided through acting out addictions. Now, you dare to feel those feelings alone or with others and, if you choose to, you write about them in your journal or share them with trusted friends, your sponsor or spiritual guide.

Beware Perfectionism

Perfectionism is as insidious a vice as any other compulsion. It is insane. It is crazy. It is an illusion. It can never be achieved. And yet the tyranny of perfectionism damages lives and relationships. I stand guilty as charged. But even when I recall that life is about process rather than perfection, I need to remind myself of that time and time again. Addicts need to beware of perfectionism. It is a curse. But it can be managed, just as one learns to live well without cigarettes or other addictive products or processes. At the end of any day, all one can hope to be thankful for is further progress made – never perfection achieved. And so long as you are making progress, that's perfect!

Beware feelings on self-indulgence, feeling you 'deserve' a little something, be it drink, drugs, illicit sex, or driving up your credit card on a shopping binge. Right living is its own reward. Healthy living and sane choices bring natural joys that deeply satisfy. People who take this programme often profess to being delighted with themselves for remaining smokefree. Authentic feelings of genuine self-worth bubble up after staying abstinent and 'sober' from smoking and other addictions.

Getting Unstuck

Just because you are maintaining your abstinence from smoking and other addictions does not mean that you might not at times still feel 'stuck'. Perhaps you feel your career is at a dead-end. Or your primary relationships might seem moribund. You might feel miles away from fulfilling your personal mission. Or you might feel that you've made no progress in some other important area of your life. While you smoked, you compounded your 'stuckness' by addictive thinking and behaviour. Now that you are abstinent and well on your way to sobriety, you appreciate that addictions only make matters worse. If you feel stuck in some area of your life, resolve to spend at least 15 minutes each day working on the problem, just as you did for your Big Idea, as suggested in Week 10. Avail of counsellors or therapists who are especially skilled in helping you to resolve developmental tasks or to heal what needs healing. A few sessions with a good counsellor, therapist or a life coach could change your life for the better.

New Challenges: An Exercise

Now that you have quit smoking and remained smokefree for several weeks, have you considered what other seemingly impossible tasks you could do? Central to getting unstuck is looking at long-standing aims, goals, challenges and objectives that have seemed impossible to meet. Now that you have progressed so well towards fulfilling your objective of 'sobriety' from cigarettes, cigars or the pipe, you could start believing in other things you'd love to do or achieve.

Play with your pen in your journal for a bit. Write down dreams you once had that you've long-since buried. Include things you might like to do or adventures your partner would be interested in doing. Keep writing until you've quite a list of things that you'd love to do. Now, instead of asking how you could possibly do these things, ask yourself why not do them? Dare to dream the impossible dream. Try to pick one dream and write down intermediate steps that you need to take to fulfil it. Get your calendar again. Draw up a realistic, measurable action plan with dates and specific things that you want to have achieved along a timeline. Do you find blocks coming to your mind telling you this cannot be done? Look again at those blocks from Week One. Recall the work you did in Week One translating them into affirmations. Use those affirmations now, repeat them in your morning journal and translate any sabotage attempts by your addictive self into new affirmations.

You're Looking Good

Take a moment to consider how much better you look now that you've stopped smoking. Your complexion is better, you teeth and fingers are no longer yellow. Your eyes look healthier, more alive and vibrant. Your clothes no longer stink of stale smoke, nor does your breath. Inwardly, you feel stronger: you have successfully managed to attend to your higher self and become abstinent from addictions and are well on your way to sobriety. Be thankful for your great efforts and the power of your higher self which has made it possible, acknowledging that more needs to happen as you advance further on your unique path.

Check-up with Your Doctor

It is advisable that you consult with your doctor or pharmacist about how and when to wind down your use of nicotine replacement therapy or other medication, if you have been using any. For certain products, you may need to continue using it for another few weeks yet. For instance, if you've been using nicotine gum, your doctor might advise you to gradually cut down on it over the next while before you finally eliminate it. Likewise, if you've been using patches, your doctor or pharmacist could recommend you move from strongest patch to milder ones. You should not go on using nicotine replacement products indefinitely (see Appendix 1). Your doctor or pharmacist can advise you on how best and when to wean yourself off them.

Celebrate

By the end of this week, you will have been off cigarettes, cigars or the pipe for eight weeks. You will have completed this programme, even though you'll have lots more work to do! Celebrate your achievement in some way, perhaps at the weekend. You deserve to mark this milestone with an extra special or day-long congé. You could pamper yourself by booking into a health farm or spa. Or treat yourself to a night at the theatre, cinema or visit a place you love. Or buy yourself something special, a luxury that you wouldn't normally buy.

Take a calendar and plan a system of rewards for yourself over the next year. I know of one woman who put money aside every week with a jeweller (money she would previously have spent smoking) and, before long, she had paid for a fabulous piece of jewellery she loved. Or you might save for an extra special holiday, one which, up to this, you wouldn't have permitted yourself or been able to afford. Be sure to have some intermediate rewards too, as you work towards the more expensive pleasures.

My New Commitment

I _____ acknowledge the hard work I have done towards my growth over the past 12 weeks. I am thankful for it. I know it did not 'just happen'. I responded to the call of my higher self to quit smoking and any other addictions and took specific steps towards the fulfilment of my life mission.

I _____ re-commit myself to the pursuit of my personal mission. Conscious of my human frailty and the power of my addictive self, I commit to continuing to write my journal every morning for the next 12 weeks and to taking my weekly congé. I commit to living a balanced lifestyle and to a constant vigilance towards my health and well being. I shall carefully monitor on a daily and weekly basis my diet, physical exercise routine, sleep, and my relationship with myself and others. I shall spend time every day focusing on the different aspects of who I am: exercising my body, using and developing my mind, becoming aware of and expressing my emotions in a healthy way, and attentive and responsive to my spirit and higher self.

In order to move towards the fulfilment of my personal mission, I shall focus for the next six weeks on the following specific activity, behaviour or objective, monitoring my progress on a weekly basis:

(Here name what you will do, something within your control, that is specific, realistic and measurable) _____

I re-commit to exploring my path with my sponsor or another guide, someone who understands my journey and appreciates what has already been achieved and the goals that still lie before me. (Here name your sponsor or guide.) _____

Signed: _____

Date: _____

Activities for Week Twelve

1. Write down your hopes and fears.

2. Tweak your mission statement, making any necessary changes. Acknowledge milestones and any progress you have made towards its fulfilment. Write or update your 12-month action plan to make your dreams a reality. Incorporate ongoing monitoring of (a) your lifestyle balance and (b) your sustained abstinence and sobriety from smoking and other addictions.

3. Relax and detach from your hopes, fears, aims and goals. Place them in the hands of God. Commit to doing the work to bring them about but leave the outcome to God.

4. Assemble a group of supporters who will help you to move closer to your higher purpose.

Review of Week Twelve

1. Did you do your morning journal every day last week? What was it like for you? Have you committed to continuing with the journal for the next 12 weeks?

2. Did you take your congé? What did you do? Is your weekly congé helping you to bring more natural joy, pleasure and fun into your life? Have you renewed your commitment to it for the next three months?

3. Did you meet or speak with your sponsor? Have you scheduled regular reviews of your sustained abstinence and sobriety with your sponsor or another guide in three, six and 12 months' time? Have you thanked your sponsor for being there for you?

Epilogue

This book has taken me more than three years to research and write. A couple of years ago, my young son made me a tinfoil crown to wear for the book launch. I look forward to wearing it next January when the Minister for Health and Children, Micheál Martin, launches the book. For me, this book became a spiritual journey. I set out on the journey convinced that I had been called by my higher self to write it. From the outset, I felt that the inspiration was not mine but God's. The instrument for my inspiration was Julia Cameron's *The Artist's Way*. I was inspired to write it while taking that wonderful programme to tap into one's creativity. If her peerless book could help people get in touch with the artist child within, a somewhat similar approach could help addicts to get in touch with the higher self within himself or herself that did not need to smoke. As I creatively embarked on this work, I have lived, to the best of my ability, its message. *Express yourself each morning in your journal. Believe in yourself. Discover your voice and do what you were sent to do.* Writing this book has been like walking that labyrinth of which I wrote in Week Eight. At one point, after years of work, I seemed no closer to my destination than when I had set out.

If at the start of my journey I was blessed to be guided in my research by Norma Cronin, smoking cessation specialist with the Irish Cancer Society, much later, and at my lowest point, another angel was sent my way. Dr Prannie Rhatigan, former director of the ICGP/STAG smoking cessation programme, loved my book. She gave me such heart to continue and I did.

More recently, I have been humbled and brought to my knees in thanks as I was privileged to hear the working out of the message of this book in the lives of people who have taken the programme. Indeed, it was people who had successfully embarked on the programme who urged me to seize the hour and publish it. I believe that this book is indeed an instrument for people's liberation from addiction. In that, it is a creative work, with a creative message. I pray that it will go on releasing people from the pandemic of tobacco addiction long after its human author has passed away.

If the programme has worked for you, please pass this book on to a friend. And do please let us know how you got on with the programme. You can contact us by writing to the publishers or through our website www.writeway2stopsmoking.com And we don't only look forward to hearing of your success in stopping smoking and other additions. We ask you to let us know of your experiences of following your bliss, becoming who you were born to be and doing what you were sent to do.

Thank you and God bless you.

Joe Armstrong

December 2003

Selected Reading

Ban Breathnach, Sarah. *Simple Abundance: A Daybook of Comfort & Joy*. London: Bantam Books, 1997. A masterful book for attaining and maintaining an authentic balanced lifestyle.

Cameron, Julia. *The Artist's Way: A Course in Discovering and Recovering Your Creative Self*. London: Pan Books, 1993. The peerless guide for attending to and unearthing the inner artist and my inspiration for *Write Way to Stop Smoking*.

Campbell, Joseph. *The Hero with a Thousand Faces*. London: Paladin, 1988. First published in the USA by Princeton University Press 1949. A masterpiece by the renowned mythologist.

Carnes, Patrick. *A Gentle Path through the Twelve Steps: the Classic Guide for All People in the Process of Recovery*. Minnesota: Hazelden, 1993. A wonderfully insightful, helpful and practical book for anyone recovering from an addiction.

Collins, Sean Dr. *Tipping the Scales: How to Fight Back Against Serious Illness*. Ardagh Clinic/NICABM (Ireland), 1997. An eclectic tool-kit to help readers to take control of serious illness.

Covey, Stephen R. *The Seven Habits of Highly Effective People*. Bath, Great Britain: Simon & Schuster, 1992. A must-read for anyone seeking to fulfil their potential.

Cronin, Norma. *Smoking Cessation Training Workshop Materials*. Dublin: Irish Cancer Society, 2000. A concise, practical and authoritative resource for smoking cessation facilitators.

D'Adamo, Peter J. Dr. *Eat Right for Your Type*. London: Century, 2001. The individualised blood type diet to stay healthy, live longer and achieve one's ideal body weight.

De Mello, Anthony. *Sadhana A Way to God*. Anand, India: Gujarat Sahitya Prakash, 1978. A classic, practical do-it-yourself resource for learning relaxation, meditation and serenity.

DiClemente, C.C. *Addiction and Change: How Addictions Develop and Addicted People Recover*. New York: Guilford Press, 2003. From the renowned authority on recovery from addiction.

Feldman, Christina. *The Buddhist Path to Simplicity: Spiritual Practice for Everyday Life*. London: Thorsons, 2001. Excellent and stimulating reading on themes such as simplicity, renunciation, and awakening.

Fisher, Edwin B. *Seven Steps to a Smoke-free Life*. New York: John Wiley & Sons, Inc. 1998. A very helpful guide from the authoritative American Lung Foundation.

Gebhardt, Jack B. *The Enlightened Smoker's Guide to Quitting*. Dorset, UK: Element Books, 1998. An excellent book that focuses on the motivational force of joy.

Gordon, Thomas Dr. *Parent Effectiveness Training: The 'No-lose' Program for Raising Responsible Children*. New York: Peter H. Wyden, Inc., 1970. Recently reissued by Three Rivers Press, New York, this classic and brilliant book is not only for parents but for anyone wanting to improve the quality of personal relationships.

Gorski, Terence T. *Passages Through Recovery: An Action Plan for Preventing Relapse*. Minnesota: Hazelden, 1989. A remarkable book that takes a holistic, grounded and spiritual approach, particularly good on the distinction between abstinence and sobriety.

Jeffers, Susan. *Feel the Fear and Do It Anyway: How to Turn Your Fear and Indecision into Confidence and Action*. London: Rider, 1991. Another great book for getting unstuck, turning fear to one's advantage, and paralysis to energy and power.

Kassorla, Irene Dr. *Go For It: How to Win at Love, Work and Play*. London: Futura Publications, 1984. An international bestseller that does what it says in the title.

Litvinoff, Sarah. *The Essential Quit Guide to Stopping Smoking: Expert Advice from the world's busiest Quitline*. London: Coronet Books, 2001. A very useful guide that stands out from others for its authority and association with Quitline.

Mackay, Judith Dr., Eriksen, Michael Dr. *The Tobacco Atlas*. Geneva: World Health Organisation, 2002. Compulsory reading for anyone concerned about the global tobacco pandemic.

Miller, William R., & Rollnick, Stephen. *Motivational Interviewing: Preparing People to Change Addictive Behaviour*. New York: The Guildford Press, 1991. The undisputed authoritative guide for therapists, doctors and counsellors helping others to change addictive behaviour.

Osho. *Osho's Meditation: The First and Last Freedom*. New York: St. Martin's Press, 1996. A very interesting perspective on smoking cessation.

Prochaska, James O., & DiClemente, Carlo C. Transtheoretical Therapy: Towards a more integrative model of change. *Psychotherapy: Theory, Research, and Practice*, 19, #3, Fall, 276-288, 1982. The groundbreaking article which identified the basic stages of change.

Prochaska, James O., & DiClemente, Carlo C. *The Transtheoretical Approach: Crossing Traditional Boundaries of Therapy*. Homewood, Illinois: Dow Jones-Irwin, 1984. A heavily requested item from the British Library but well worth the wait, expanding in book form the authors' profound insights into the stages of change.

Rowe, Mark Dr. *The Management of Smoking Cessation in General Practice*. Dublin: The Irish College of General Practitioners, 2003. Essential reading for all doctors, pharmacists and smoking cessation counsellors.

Sherwood, John J., Scherer, John J. *The Dating Mating Game: How to Play Without Losing*. Indiana: Purdue University, 1974. The source for the Pinch/Crunch model for resolving conflict and growing authentic and fulfilling relationships.

Vincent, Margaret. *Love Needs Learning: A Relationships Course for Young People*. London: Geoffrey Chapman, 1994. An excellent, group-based resource introducing the lamentably underused Pinch/Crunch model of human relationships.

A New Approach to Help Smokers Quit: Doctors' Pack. Sponsored by Smoking Target Action Group, HEBE, Irish College of General Practitioners, Irish Cancer Society and the Health Promotion Unit of the Department of Health and Children, 2002. A very handy, user-friendly pack for busy doctors.

APPENDIX

Treatments

Products	Patches	Gum	Inhaler	Microtab	Lozenge	Zyban
Period	Generally a 12 week course.	Up to 3 months.	Used regularly for period of up to 3 months.	At least 12 weeks – then reduce gradually.	At least 12 weeks – then reduce gradually.	7 to 9 weeks. Start taking 8 to 14 days before quitting.
Dosage	21mg or 15mg for heavier smokers. 10mg for lighter smokers. Choose between 24 and 16-hour patches.	4mg for heavy smokers. 2mg for lighter smokers. 10-15 pieces a day.	6 to 12 cartridges per day.	16-24 per day for heavy smokers. 8-12 per day for lighter smokers.	8-12 lozenges per day up to a maximum of 25 per day.	(Day 1 to 6) 1 x 150mg tablet each morning; (day 6 onwards) 1 x 150mg tablet a.m. and p.m.

Products	Patches	Gum	Inhaler	Microtab	Lozenge	Zyban
Advantages	Very easy to use. Auto-matically gives the right dose. 24 hour patches can help with early morning cravings. Not addictive in the long term.	Easy to regulate dose. Gives extra help at difficult moments.	Helps keep hands and mouth busy. Easy to regulate dose.	Can be used discreetly. Very few side effects. Easy to adjust dose.	Discreet, easy to use and sugar-free.	Good short-term research results. Easy to use. Noticeable reduction in urges to smoke.
Dis-advantages	Not orally gratifying. Small possibility of skin reaction.	Tricky with dentures. Needs to be used correctly.	Not so good for healthy smokers. May attract attention when used in public.	Needs to be used correctly. Wasted if swallowed.	May cause initial throat irritation/ indigestion.	Possible sleep disturbance. May cause headaches and dry mouth.

© Joe Armstrong 2004 www.writeway2stopsmoking.com

© *A New Approach to Help Smokers Quit: Doctors' Pack.* Sponsored by Smoking Target Action Group, HEBE, Irish College of General Practitioners, Irish Cancer Society and the Health Promotion Unit of the Department of Health and Children, 2002.

Disclaimer: the above provides only a summary of main points and neither the author nor the publisher can accept responsibility for errors or omissions. As with all medicines, always read the instructions and follow your doctor's advice.

APPENDIX

B

12 Steps of AA

Many smokers are dependent on other substances or processes apart from nicotine. Alcohol dependence in particular often features among smokers or, where the person is not an alcoholic, alcohol is often a contributing factor in a smoker's relapse.

The Twelve Steps of Alcoholics Anonymous

1. We admitted we were powerless over alcohol – that our lives had become unmanageable.

2. Came to believe that a Power greater than ourselves could restore us to sanity.

3. Made a decision to turn our will and our lives over to the care of God as we understood Him.

4. Made a searching and fearless moral inventory of ourselves.

5. Admitted to God, to ourselves, and to another human being the exact nature of our wrongs.

6. Were entirely ready to have God remove all these defects of character.

7. Humbly asked Him to remove our shortcomings.

8. Made a list of all persons we had harmed, and became willing to make amends to them all.

9. Made direct amends to such people wherever possible, except when to do so would injure them or others.

10. Continued to take personal inventory and when we were wrong promptly admitted it.

11. Sought through prayer and meditation to improve our conscious contact with God as we understood Him, praying only for knowledge of His will for us and the power to carry that out.

12. Having had a spiritual awakening as the result of these steps, we tried to carry this message to alcoholics and to practice these principles in all our affairs.

Feedback

To help improve further editions and to encourage future smokers to stop smoking, we welcome all feedback on this programme. If it worked for you, please let us know. If it didn't, we'd like to hear of your experience too.

Please answer any or all of the following and email your responses to info@writeway2stopsmoking.com

Did *WW2SS* help you to stop smoking?
How long had you been a smoker?

Would you recommend this programme to other smokers? If so, why?

What did you find most helpful about the programme?

What did you find least helpful?

What suggestions do you have for future editions?

How long have you been smokefree?

Has *WW2SS* helped you to get unstuck in your life, as well as helping you to stop smoking? If so, how has your life changed for the better? Do you feel you are now doing what you were born to do?

Comments:

Appendix

Self-help, Group or Personal Guided Support

You can use *Write Way to Stop Smoking* alone as a self-help manual or with a group, depending on which you find most helpful. Support groups can use it as a resource or structure for meetings. Since the 12-week programme is longer than many support groups such as the excellent smoking cessation programmes run by the Irish Cancer Society or by health boards, *WW2SS* can provide added support for members during and/or after a group has ended. Personal guided support by telephone and/or email through the 12 weeks of the *WW2SS* programme is offered for a nominal fee, subject to terms, conditions, and availability. For details, check out our website:

www.writeway2stopsmoking.com

or email info@writeway2stopsmoking.com

The **Irish Department of Health and Children** has set up the National Smokers' Quitline telephone 1850 201 203. Callers to the Quitline can receive confidential advice on quitting, a free information pack, and referral to local smoking cessation services. The National Smokers' Quitline is an initiative of the Health Promotion Unit of the Department of Health and Children in partnership with the Irish Cancer Society.

The **Irish Cancer Society** has years of experience in helping people to quit smoking. It provides free night nursing and home care nursing, funds cancer research, clinical trials, educational grants and professional education courses. Check out its website: www.cancer.ie

In **Britain**, the charity QUIT offers free telephone support on 0800 00 22 00. QUIT also offers email support where counsellors personally respond to smokers' emails, a service particularly popular among women. For free one-to-one professional support, send an email to stopsmoking@quit.org.uk. QUIT also offer confidential support to groups of up to 12 teenagers in school settings as well as offering support to the corporate sector. Check out their website www.quit.org.uk.